Sorties into Hell

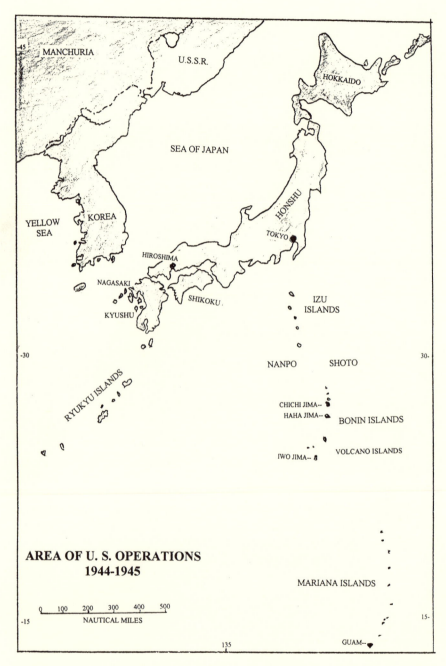

MANCHURIA

U.S.S.R.

HOKKAIDO

SEA OF JAPAN

HONSHU

KOREA

YELLOW
SEA

TOKYO

HIROSHIMA

NAGASAKI

SHIKOKU

KYUSHU

IZU
ISLANDS

-30

NANPO   SHOTO

30-

RYUKYU ISLANDS

CHICHI JIMA--
HAHA JIMA--   BONIN ISLANDS

IWO JIMA--   VOLCANO ISLANDS

**AREA OF U. S. OPERATIONS
1944-1945**

MARIANA ISLANDS

0   100   200   300   400   500
NAUTICAL MILES

-15

15-

135

GUAM--

The Nanpo Shoto includes the Bonin Islands, of which Chichi Jima is the principal island, and the Volcano Islands, of which Iwo Jima is the principal island.
They run directly south from Tokyo Bay. (Courtesy of Mary Terese Seidler)

Sorties into Hell

The Hidden War on Chichi Jima

CHESTER HEARN

PRAEGER

Westport, Connecticut
London

Library of Congress Cataloging-in-Publication Data

Hearn, Chester G.
    Sorties into hell: the hidden war on Chichi Jima / Chester Hearn.
        p.   cm.
    Includes bibliographical references and index.
    ISBN 0–275–98081–2 (alk. paper)
    1. World War, 1939–1945—Atrocities—Japan—Chichi Island.   2. World War,
1939–1945—Japan—Chichi Island.   3. World War, 1939–1945—Prisoners and prisons,
Japanese.   4. Chichi Island (Japan)—History—20th century.   5. Prisoners of war—
United States—History—20th century.   6. Prisoners of war—Japan—History—20th
century.   I. Title.
    D804.J3H43   2003
    940.54'05'09528—dc21   2003045984

British Library Cataloguing in Publication Data is available.

Library of Congress Catalog Card Number: 2003045984
ISBN: 0–275–98081–2

First published in 2003

Praeger Publishers, 88 Post Road West, Westport, CT 06881
An imprint of Greenwood Publishing Group, Inc.
www.praeger.com

Printed in the United States of America

The paper used in this book complies with the
Permanent Paper Standard issued by the National
Information Standards Organization (Z39.48–1984).

10 9 8 7 6 5 4 3 2 1

Contents

CONTENTS

Illustrations

Acknowledgments

Because of the subject matter of this book, much of the research has been classified for many years. From my own investigation into the crimes committed by the Japanese on Chichi Jima, I suspect that some information may still be classified.

Of the men who served with the 1st Battalion, 3rd Marines, few of them are still alive. Many, through their own records and through personal interviews, have contributed to reconstructing what happened on Chichi Jima during World War II in the Pacific. For good reason, perhaps, this account had been shielded from the public for fifty-five years. Nor did John R. Lewis, when he compiled 3,352 sources in *Uncertain Judgment: A Bibliography of War Crimes Trials*, discover the documents and papers covering the long investigation on Chichi Jima and the trial at Guam that followed. Perhaps Lewis missed this important chapter of World War II because the documents had been classified, and no historian to this day has opened the details of those documents to the public.

In E. Bartlett Kerr's *Surrender and Survival: The Experience of American POWs in the Pacific, 1941–1945*, a carefully researched work published in 1985, the author was apparently unaware of the documents regarding the scope of the executions on Chichi Jima. He mentioned that four men were executed, which closely patterns the Japanese side of the story rather than the truth (259).

Without the aid of Brigadier General Presley M. Rixey's papers, which were provided to me by his daughter, Ann Rixey Boyd, this book could not have been written. After World War II the U.S. Navy sent Colonel Rixey, USMC (U.S. Marine Corps), to Chichi Jima to repatriate more than 20,000 Japanese and destroy the defenses on the island. When the colonel discovered that a few American flyers might have been executed during the war, he began an investigation that lasted more than five months. He sent a copy of that investigation to his wife, who in turn passed it on to their daughter. Ann Rixey Boyd found more than 1,200 pages of testimony and exhibits in her attic and sent them to me. They now form the basis for this book.

Dr. Eugene F. Poutasse is the only surviving member of Colonel Rixey's Board of Investigation. As a young Navy lieutenant (jg [junior grade]) in the medical corps, Dr. Poutasse not only heard all the testimony; he also took 150 pages of notes, snapped more than 100 photographs, and collected statements and interviews from other participants with the intention of some day writing his own account. I am indebted to the doctor for sharing everything he collected with me.

I am also indebted to many of the surviving Marines who served under Colonel Rixey during the demilitarization of the Bonin Islands. Former Private First Class (PFC) William Monks has tried to reconstruct the human side of the Chichi story through 200 pages of personal experience. He has collected the memoirs of others and added them to his own. Monks's anecdotes are a treat to read. He kindly sent everything he had collected to me. More recently he put them together with other of his experiences into a book titled *Pearls*, published by JJ Company of New York in 2002. Bill put me in contact with other contributors, such as James W. Leary, Robert J. Gath, John H. Monaghan, and Henry Steadman. To Bill and his Marines I am much indebted. This is a book I may not have written without their insistence and without their help.

Colonel Rixey may never have begun an investigation were it not for Frederick Arthur Savory, a Japanese citizen born on Chichi Jima from American stock. I learned much about the Savory clan from John Wick, a Pennsylvania dentist who married a Savory girl. Through Dr. Wick I discovered Jimmy Savory, who owns and operates an electronics firm in California. And through Dr. Poutasse I came to know Willie Savory. The Savorys filled in many of the blanks in the twisted testimony taken from Japanese deponents on Chichi Jima.

I am also indebted to the U.S. Marine Corps Historical Branch for locating more of General Rixey's papers, especially the monograph he wrote in 1947 that explained the difficulties he encountered in getting to the truth.

Barry Zerby at the National Archives assisted me in obtaining documents from the military trial of the Japanese war criminals identified during the Chichi Jima investigation. About 400 pages were written in Japanese.

Evelyn Wesman at the Erie County Public Library provided me with dozens of primary and secondary sources through the interlibrary loan system, all of which helped to structure this book into an accurate account of the war leading up to the assault on Iwo Jima and the cause of the depredations that followed on a small, forgotten Japanese island fortress called Chichi Jima.

I am very grateful to Wendy A. Webster, who has taken dozens of Dr. Poutasse's old photographs—some stained and others blurred with age—and digitized them into clear and usable images. Dr. Ronald Pearson has taken old maps from Chichi Jima and enhanced them for this book, and Mary Terese Seidler has added touches to maps to make them clear and more precise. I also owe a word of thanks to Jeffrey Taylor, the archives technician at the National Personnel Records Center, Military Personnel Records, who searched until he found the service records of the flyers that form the basis for this book.

I am deeply indebted to the nameless many who contributed in other ways to make this book possible to write and for others to read.

Introduction

For those who have studied World War II in the Pacific, enormous concentration has been focused on Iwo Jima. Many fine histories and personal accounts have been written, but there were other Jimas involved in the conflict. They were all overshadowed by Iwo, which lay at the southern end of a small Japanese military district called the Nanpo Shoto. Another of those little island Jimas deserves more attention.

Ten-square-mile Chichi Jima in the Bonin Islands chain became one of the war's historical oversights, but in 1944 the island ranked with Iwo Jima as a possible target for a massive American amphibious expedition. When the planners working for the Allied Joint Chiefs of Staff (JCS) drew a straight line from Iwo Jima to Tokyo Bay, they noticed that Chichi Jima lay 140 miles closer to the Japanese capital. Why the JCS decided to attack Iwo, though the volcanic island was smaller and farther away, had less to do with size and location and more to do with topography. With the exception of Mount Suribachi, a tall, inactive volcanic cone on the southern end of Iwo Jima, the remainder of the island was flat and already contained two Japanese airfields, with a third under construction.

The island of Chichi Jima was everything but flat. High cliffs rose sharply along shore, leaving only one small beach suitable for landing an amphibious force. Mountains and ravines cut through the heavily wooded interior, leaving not a level surface anywhere for building an airfield. The Japanese on Chichi created their one airstrip, and a small one at that, by connecting the main island to a small offshore islet by filling in the gap with rocks. There they built Susaki, a short airfield squeezed between two bays capable of handling small twin-engine transports and a few fighters. The Japanese navy performed most of the reconnaissance with seaplanes, which they kept at a base in the island's fine harbor.

Iwo Jima, despite its diminutive size, became the strategic target when Admiral Chester W. Nimitz, commanding the Pacific Fleet, talked Admiral Ernest J. King, commander in chief of the United States Fleet, out of assaulting the heavily defended island of Formosa, which would bring B-29s and B-24s no closer to Japan than bases on Saipan, Tinian, and Guam in the Marianas. Iwo offered other advantages because the island lay on a direct route to Tokyo from Saipan and would provide a haven for damaged aircraft limping back from bombing raids on Japan.

While Admiral King and Admiral Nimitz developed plans for establishing a foothold in the Nanpo Shoto, Iwo Jima gradually became a powerful enemy air base. Chichi Jima settled for remaining what it had been for many years, a small naval base with a vast radio communications center that controlled operations to the south and monitored American transmissions. The center lacked decoding capabilities, and this troubled the officers who ran the station.

Despite staggering and unprecedented casualties from the assault on Iwo, the Joint Chiefs of Staff made the right decision when they decided to pass up Chichi. Like Rabaul and Truk, Chichi Jima contained some of the most formidable defenses in the Japanese empire, most of which were so well hidden they could not be seen from the sky or located by aerial reconnaissance photos. The island's radio towers on top of Mount Asahi and Mount Yoake could not be hidden, but the exact location of the radio control center remained unknown because the Japanese concealed it inside a cave under Mount Yoake.

During the American amphibious assaults on Saipan, Tinian, and Peleliu in 1944 and on Iwo Jima in 1945, carrier task groups and cruiser squadrons made regular visits to the Bonin Islands to bomb and shell Susaki airfield, destroy the shipping in the harbor, and knock out the communications towers. During the latter stages of the war, Chichi Jima acted as one of Japan's principal forward supply bases, shuttling troops, aircraft, munitions, and supplies to the Marianas, the Palaus, and Iwo Jima.

In early 1944 the Imperial Japanese Army (IJA) decided to put an oversized division into the Nanpo Shoto—a chain of small islands extending south in a near-straight line for 640 nautical miles from Tokyo Bay to Iwo Jima. This district stretched from the Izus in the north to the Bonin Islands in the center and finally to Iwo Jima and the tiny outcroppings of the Volcano Islands (Kazan Retto) in the south. The army assigned the larger half of the division to Chichi Jima and the smaller half to Iwo. The Japanese expected American forces to attack both islands simultaneously, and had the Imperial planners taken units from Chichi to reinforce Iwo, the bloodbath suffered by the Marines during the conquest of the latter could have become a catastrophe.

Carrier aircraft began flying bombing missions over Chichi Jima in June 1944, mainly for the purpose of preventing enemy aircraft from annoying the landings during the Marianas (Saipan/Tinian/Guam) campaign. Antiaircraft batteries on Chichi Jima began shooting down American planes and capturing flyers. Senior Japanese officers on the island became increasingly incensed by the air attacks and took their anger out on the flyers. At first, not many flyers fell into the hands of Chichi commanders, but air strikes escalated during the days prior to the assault on Iwo Jima. As soon as the American air base on Saipan became operational, B-24 Liberators began flying 800-mile missions against Chichi Jima and nearby Haha Jima. On 18 February 1945, air attacks over Chichi continued throughout the day, and more flyers parachuted or crashed among the Bonins. They disappeared without a trace. Some of them died in the cockpit. A few flyers ditched in the ocean. Some perished, and others were rescued by cruiser floatplanes or American submarines roving with caution through enemy minefields. An unlucky number became prisoners of war (POWs) on Chichi Jima.

Some of the Japanese on Chichi held peculiar views about fighting the war and reflected those beliefs in their actions. The notions of senior officers concerning the "disposal" of prisoners had no precedent in war. Their own junior officers and enlisted men did not agree with them, but those in disagreement did not represent the professional military caste that followed their own doctrine and imposed it upon the others. Young officers had no more privileges than noncommissioned officers (NCOs). They either followed orders or were faced with disgrace, life imprisonment, or according to military protocol, execution.

What happened on Chichi Jima between June 1944, when the first American bombs fell on the island, and the capture of Iwo Jima on 24 March 1945 is not a pleasant story. Efforts made by senior officers on Chichi Jima to cover up their crimes testify to the harsh reality that those in command knew their actions violated all the conventions of war and humanity and were legally and morally wrong. As the war closed around them, they began to fear the consequences.

Marines fought most of the land battles among the islands of the Pacific. Very few were ever taken prisoner. They preferred to fight to the death rather than be captured, tortured, and killed by the enemy. Flyers did not have the same option. They floated out of the sky and often dropped among the enemy, and there were few places on earth worse to land than on Chichi Jima.

From the air Chichi looked like a peaceful island—a nice place to take a vacation. But that was before Major General Yoshio Tachibana and Rear Admiral Kunizo Mori turned the island into a fortress with a band of dysfunctional Bushido warriors. Nobody told the pilots who flew sorties over Chichi Jima about the hell that awaited them on the ground. It would take a determined Marine colonel and a staff of hard-nosed investigators the better part of six months to get to the truth.

After Colonel Presley M. Rixey's Board of Investigation finally separated the truth from the untruth, it became easy to understand why the U.S. government chose to keep the matter classified for so many years. Now the story can be told.

This narrative is taken from documents of verbal testimony translated from Japanese, from records provided by eyewitnesses, from personal interviews, from family memoirs, and from published and unpublished accounts in various depositories. The dialogue is taken from what eyewitnesses said, from what they observed, and perhaps in some instances, from what they thought they saw or heard. The Japanese soldiers on Chichi Jima, and especially the enlisted men who provided hours of testimony, proved to be perceptive observers. Though they understood little English, if any, they managed to provide vivid images of the flyers they executed. What went through the thoughts of flyers about to die can be expressed only by those who were there. This is their record.

CHAPTER 1

Prelude to Iwo Jima

Until the seizure of the Marshall Islands by the U.S. Marines in early 1944, the Japanese paid little attention to Iwo Jima, an eight-square-mile volcanic island 640 miles from Tokyo Bay. At the time, all of the Japanese forces in the Nanpo Shoto were stationed at Chichi Jima, 145 miles north of Iwo, where a small naval base built in 1914 had been gradually expanded. Early in the war the Imperial Japanese Navy added a seaplane base to Chichi Jima's fine harbor, which they used for reconnaissance. From the island's elaborate state-of-the-art communications system, a large naval detachment conveyed flight and vessel instructions to airfields, squadrons in flight, and fleets across the spectrum of the Pacific. On 7 December 1941 Imperial General Headquarters had garrisoned the Nanpo Shoto with only 1,400 troops, and most of them were naval personnel on Chichi Jima.[1]

In 1941 Imperial General Headquarters had not given any thought to fortifying the tiny island of Iwo Jima but later decided to give it a single airfield, Chidori, capable of handling about twenty planes. After losing the Marshall Islands, Imperial General Headquarters took another look at the Nanpo Shoto and began to strengthen the islands as part of their main line of homeland defense, adding over time two more airfields to Iwo and expanding Susaki airfield on the west coast of Chichi.

On 23 May 1944 the Japanese First Air Fleet, consisting of land-based naval aircraft, began deploying on bases on the eastern rim of the Philippine Sea. Like Iwo and Chichi Jima, these islands provided airfields for planes being shuttled to bases on Rabaul, Truk, Guam, Tinian, Saipan, and the Palaus. At first, none of the naval aircraft went to Iwo Jima, and only four planes went to Chichi Jima's one small airfield. Admiral

Soemu Toyoda did not know where the Americans intended to strike next, so he distributed the First Air Fleet to those islands that gave the empire the best tactical defensive protection.

On 15 June 1944 the American offensive in the Central Pacific opened with Operation Forager, an amphibious assault on Saipan and the first air-land-sea strike among the islands of the Marianas. To capture and hold the island, Admiral Raymond A. Spruance brought his Fifth Fleet, two Marine divisions, and the Army's 27th Infantry Division.

Through the wireless station on Chichi Jima, Vice Admiral Jisaburo Ozawa learned that Spruance's task force consisted of two carrier groups, though he was not certain of their exact movements. For the first time since the naval battles in the Solomons during October 1942, Ozawa put together a battle fleet of five heavy carriers, four light carriers, five battleships, thirteen cruisers, and twenty-eight destroyers. Ozawa intended to use his carrier planes in cooperation with land-based aircraft in the Marianas and after American amphibious forces landed on the island, to destroy Spruance's fleet and annihilate every American that came ashore.

Cruising south of Japan on 13 June 1944 the USS *Redfin* spotted Ozawa's battle fleet heading toward the Marianas and warned the Fifth Fleet. Spruance calculated the enemy's time of arrival and felt he could afford one quick raid to the north. On 14 June he ordered Admiral Marc A. Mitscher to detach two carrier units for an independent operation: Rear Admiral Joseph J. "Jocko" Clark's Task Group 58.1 (*Hornet, Yorktown, Belleau Wood,* and *Bataan*) and Rear Admiral William K. Harrill's Task Group 58.4 (*Essex, Langley,* and *Cowpens*). Aware that Ozawa's fleet would soon be in striking distance and that Japanese aircraft were capable of flying greater ranges than his Navy planes, Spruance wanted Clark's and Harrill's carriers to make a quick air strike against the airfields on Iwo and Chichi Jima and return as quickly as possible to the Marianas. Clark, whose Cherokee blood still carried the fighting spirit of the warrior, wanted to forego attacking the Jimas and swing in behind Ozawa's fleet, but Admiral Mitscher rejected the proposal. Many years later he said the attempt should have been made. Mitscher limited the attacks to one day, 16 June, and ordered the carriers back to the Marianas no later than 18 June. The attack would be the deepest penetration into Japanese waters by American carriers since the beginning of the war.[2]

Once under way, Jocko Clark conferred with Harrill, and they jointly decided that a one-day strike would not be enough. Instead, they resolved to begin the air strikes a day earlier, beginning with a fighter sweep against Iwo at 1430 on 15 June, followed by deckload strikes against Iwo, Chichi, and Haha Jima a half hour later. American Hellcat flyers shot down ten Zekes over Iwo and destroyed seven on the ground, losing two planes and their crews during the attack. At Chichi Jima the flyers encountered no planes in the sky and destroyed most of the enemy's aircraft on the ground, but antiaircraft batteries shot down one Navy plane. Two of the flyers landed safely on Chichi Jima, Lieutenant (jg) Calvin D. Terry and Petty Officer Oscar Long Doyle. At first the Japanese on the island did not quite know what to do with their first American prisoners. But one matter became instantly clear: They did not like to be bombed. The air raid burned out most of Yosai Shireibu, known by the Japanese brigaded on Chichi Jima as Fortress Headquarters.[3]

With the weather showing signs of developing into the pattern of a typical Pacific typhoon, Clark canceled further attacks on Chichi Jima and on the afternoon of 16 June concentrated one last strike against Iwo's Chidori airfield. Because of foul weather, the Japanese sent up no patrols and lined up their aircraft neatly on the runway. At 1330 fifty-four Hellcats swooped over Iwo Jima and destroyed sixty-three planes on the ground.

Fighting force-4 winds, Clark and Harrill headed back to Saipan to rejoin Admiral Mitscher's Task Force 58 for a showdown with Ozawa. Mitscher had made it clear to Clark that the number-one priority was the capture of Saipan, not the raids on the Jimas. However, at this stage of the war in the Pacific, the strategic planners working for the Joint Chiefs of Staff in Washington were still debating whether in the months ahead to assault Chichi, Iwo, or both. Four days later the one-sided Battle of the Philippine Sea began. Mitscher's flyers destroyed the better part of Ozawa's carrier aircraft, caught up with the fleeing Japanese fleet, and in the waning hours of twilight sank or disabled several ships. Many of the flyers lost their lives because they ran out of fuel while returning to the carriers, but those who survived remembered the campaign as "The Marianas Turkey Shoot."[4]

During the battle for Saipan, Imperial General Headquarters organized the 109th Infantry Division under Lieutenant General Tadamichi Kuribayashi and designated the smaller of his two brigades for the defense of Iwo Jima, leaving the larger brigade on Chichi. Kuribayashi moved his headquarters to Iwo, vowed to make it impregnable, and began building up his force on both islands by utilizing some of the emperor's crack defense battalions. Fortifying and garrisoning Iwo posed a problem for Kuribayashi because the island had no harbor, making it necessary for the transports to disembark all the brigade's supplies and equipment off the southeastern beaches and send it ashore on landing craft and lighters.

In early June, Admiral Mitscher discovered the vast military buildup on the island and also the enemy's many logistics difficulties. Everything Kuribayashi needed in the way of supplies came through Chichi Jima, where smaller craft operating during the night ran fast convoys to Iwo. Having learned of the enemy's nocturnal activities, Mitscher detached a carrier task group with instructions to harass the operation and sink the ships. Thus began a series of what Navy pilots called heckler attacks, nightly or early morning flyovers by Hellcats and Avengers carrying 500-pound bombs.

On 24 June Admiral Clark took the *Hornet*, *Yorktown*, *Bataan*, and *Belleau Wood*, with a screen of cruisers and destroyers, north for another raid on the Jimas. A Japanese patrol plane snooped the attack and alerted the radio control center on Chichi. As Clark's carriers approached Iwo, fifty-one Hellcats flew into an unexpected battle with Admiral Sadaichi Matsunaga's 27th Air Flotilla stationed at Cordori airfield. During the two-day dogfight Matsunaga lost more than sixty aircraft, many having recently arrived from Japan for the defense of Saipan.[5]

Ten days later Jocko Clark celebrated the Fourth of July by launching another raid on the islands of the Nanpo Shoto. While his carrier fighter-bombers tore up the two airfields on Iwo (the third had not yet been built), a predawn flight of Grumman Hellcats carrying 500-pound bombs swooped over Chichi's small, congested harbor and attacked the Japanese seaplane base and the freighters, destroyers, destroyer escorts, and other shipping anchored in the bay. When the Hellcats began their strafing run, the enemy started shooting. Never had the flyers seen so much antiaircraft fire coming from so many different directions at one time. Tracers lit up the sky, one pilot recalled, "like the Fourth of July fireworks at the local park." The Japanese had not yet received their radar aiming devices, and the firing went wild. "Streams of multicolored tracer-illuminated ammunition spewed from hundreds of guns of all sizes like from so many firehoses," said Lieutenant (jg) John Dear. About the only planes the Japanese on Chichi got into the air were Nakajima A6M2-N fighters fitted with floats: a floatplane version of the Mitsubishi Zero that American flyers called Rufes. With floats attached, the Zeroes lost their maneuverability, and the first American sorties knocked most of them out of the sky. Lieutenant Dear shot down six, but his Hellcat sustained serious damage to both wings. Had he not been able to limp back to the *Yorktown*, he might well have disappeared into the vacuum of Chichi's rugged wilderness.[6]

During the Fourth of July air attacks against Iwo and Chichi, only forty-one Zekes and thirteen bombers survived, and the Japanese recalled all the aircraft and their harried crews to the homeland for defense. As Captain Samuel Eliot Morison observed, "Clark's interest in the 'Jimas' had become so marked that the aviators . . . printed a certificate of membership in the 'Jocko Jima Development Corporation offering Choice Locations of all Types in Iwo, Chichi, Haha and Muko Jima, Only 500 Miles from Downtown Tokyo.'" Every flyer received a diploma, each being signed by Admiral Clark as "President of the Corporation." The string of islands from Iwo through the Bonins became known as

"Jocko's Jimas," and the men who flew the sorties now owned a certificate to show their participation.

Whether Lieutenant (jg) Hershel C. Connell or ARM2c (Aviation Radio Man Second Class) Lloyd Richard Woellhof carried a copy of the certificate in their possession when they parachuted onto the Bonin Islands and were taken prisoner on Chichi Jima will never be known, for they faded into the island's virtual obscurity and joined the list of flyers the Navy listed as "presumed dead."[7]

The Seabees on Saipan went quickly to work to put Isley Field into working order. On 14 July the first Liberators from VB-109 flew onto the base. To prevent Japanese air interference from other operations in the Pacific, VB-109 began a series of bombing raids against Iwo, Chichi, and Haha Jima. By 21 July, D-Day on Guam—with the Tinian assault to follow three days later—the Liberators had reduced the airfields on Iwo and Chichi to piles of rubble.

Even Marine flyers got into the act. In 1943 when the U.S. Army Air Forces did not know what to do with their surplus Mitchell B-25s, the Marines took them, trained six-man crews for night sorties, and flew them to the Pacific. Using a corner of Isley Field as their base of operation, Marine pilots flew long-range missions over shipping targets at Iwo and Chichi. Three planes searched for convoys every night, one in the Iwo area, one around Haha Jima, and the third kept watch on Chichi. If any of the three planes spotted a convoy, their radioman contacted Saipan, and three more B-25s on standby and loaded with bombs would take to the air to destroy the convoy. During July 1944 Japanese troop ships carrying the 1st and 2nd Battalions of the 17th Mixed Infantry Regiment were sunk while en route to Iwo. Survivors taken into Chichi never joined the 3rd Battalion on Iwo. Another American air attack on 14 July sank the Japanese transport *Nisshu Maru* off Chichi Jima and sent twenty-eight tanks destined for Iwo to the bottom. Had General Kuribayashi received all the men and equipment destined for his brigade but lost in the Bonins, the cost in American blood on Iwo would have been much higher.[8]

On 4–5 August 1944, Admirals Mitscher and John S. McCain paid another visit to Chichi Jima. This time carrier air strikes were supplemented with a light cruiser and destroyer bombardment. Since 15 June the Japanese on Chichi Jima had been rebuilding their headquarters, Yosai Shireibu, and the American shelling wiped out all the buildings and burned the remainder of Fortress Headquarters to the ground. "I was obliged to move," said Captain Isoda, the military police chief, and the furious headquarters staff began relocating across the bay to a less conspicuous site at Ogiura.[9]

After the assaults on Guam and Tinian, heavy carrier attacks against the Jimas subsided for a spell, though the heckler raids continued. General Douglas MacArthur secured New Guinea, and the Marines invaded Peleliu in an effort to protect the Army's flank when the general began operations to recapture the Philippines.

The last concentrated carrier attack against the Jimas during the summer of 1944 occurred between 31 August and 2 September when Mitscher sent Rear Admiral Ralph E. Davison's Task Group 38.4 to hammer the islands with a three-day air and naval bombardment. The Japanese peered seaward, expecting to see waves of Marines approaching their beaches, but Davison's mission merely served as a diversion to the Peleliu assault. Marine B-25s continued to make their nightly visits, and if finding no shipping to attack, they dropped their bombs to heckle one of the Jimas before returning to Saipan.[10]

With naval forces committed to MacArthur's invasion of Leyte on 20 October 1944, operations elsewhere in the Pacific took a breather, enabling the Japanese on Iwo and Chichi to rebuild their defenses. MacArthur's Philippine campaign took four months, and during the interregnum Admiral Chester Nimitz, commanding the Pacific Fleet, and the Joint Chiefs of Staff began to plan the invasion of Iwo Jima. Chichi would have given Nimitz a base closer to Japan, but the heavily fortified and mountainous island had only a small airstrip along the west coast that could not be lengthened, and no level ground existed on the island for building another. To work "up the ladder" to mainland Japan, Iwo Jima presented the first rung; the Bonin Islands, which contained Chichi and Haha Jima, constituted the second and third rungs; and the Ryukyu Islands with Okinawa provided the fourth and last rung. Nimitz decided to bypass the Bonins, but because they stood in the way of operations against Iwo Jima and Okinawa, the island chain, and in particular Chichi Jima, had to be bombed, cut off from Japan, and rendered unable to reinforce, supply, or communicate with Iwo Jima.

Nimitz set 19 February 1945 as D-Day for Iwo Jima. He needed the island's airfield to support the Army's air force bombing offensive against Japan, but first every inch of Iwo's eight square miles had to be captured and secured. Lieutenant General Tadamichi Kuribayashi's 21,000 troops would not hand over the island without a determined fight. Nimitz knew that it would take time to expand the airfield on Iwo Jima to one capable of supporting B-29s, which at the end of November 1944 began flying their first missions against Japan from Isley Field on Saipan. Nimitz readily observed that for damaged aircraft limping home from Japan, either of Iwo's two existing airfields would provide a place for emergency landings and refueling.

In an almost direct line to Tokyo and 145 miles to the north of Iwo Jima lay the Bonin Islands, where Chichi Jima acted as a strategic military center for enemy operations in the Pacific. B-29 bombers, which had to fly close to their maximum range with heavy payloads, did not have the fuel to give the Bonins a very wide margin during bombing runs to Tokyo—and even less margin if crippled. Capturing Iwo Jima would lessen that problem, and the small island looked much easier to assault than Chichi. Chichi had no suitable landing beaches, and the Japanese had covered the few small beaches on the western side of the island with a virtually impregnable crossfire from the cliffs that surrounded the harbor. The Imperial Japanese Army still believed that the next American attack would strike Chichi and retained many units there that might otherwise have been sent to Kuribayashi's hard-pressed brigade on Iwo. But Chichi still had an airfield that Nimitz believed capable of supporting fighter aircraft, a good deep harbor for holding warships, and one of Japan's most important and technologically advanced communications centers. He wanted all of them bombed out of commission, which was not an easy task because of the island's well-concealed and numerous antiaircraft batteries.

As more air bases became available in the Marianas, Major General Willis H. Hale began subjecting Iwo Jima to one of the longest sustained and concentrated air attacks of the war. Though most of the early raids were aimed at cratering Iwo's two airfields, occasional sorties flew to the Bonins to bomb the shipping in Chichi's harbor. Hale soon discovered that his B-24 pilots were not particularly adept at flying antishipping attacks, and for a brief period of time, except for nightly visits from B-25s piloted by Marines, Chichi and Haha Jima enjoyed a holiday from air attacks but not from the sea.

Beginning in early January 1945 Rear Admiral Allan E. "Hoke" Smith's Cruiser Division 5, composed of the heavy cruisers *Chester*, *Pensacola*, and *Salt Lake City* and six destroyers, began making regular visits to all the Jimas. Smith's division prowled the Bonin Islands looking for convoys transporting men and supplies to Chichi and Haha Jima. These deliveries were often offloaded onto small craft in Chichi's harbor and transferred to Iwo on an overcast night. The occasional air strikes and shelling of Chichi never did a great deal of damage, but they destabilized the forces on the ground and shut off the flow of supplies from the homeland. By the end of January 1945, air attacks by B-24s and Superfortresses buttressed by naval shelling began pounding Iwo night and day, and the bombardment increased steadily each day until 16 February, when the more intensive preinvasion bombardment began.

Rear Admiral William H.P. Blandy led the prelanding activities on Iwo Jima, and part of his plan called for heavy air strikes on Chichi and Haha. Rear Admiral Arthur W. Radford's carriers from Task Group 58.4 passed through the Bonin Islands on 16 February and launched fighter-bomber sweeps that destroyed several ships in Chichi's harbor, disabled the airfield, and shattered ground installations along the northern shore of the harbor. Two days later two more carrier groups took positions off Chichi and Haha Jima, one under Rear Admiral Ralph E. Davison and the other under Rear Admiral Frederick C. Sherman. The joint strike force compelled the defenders of Chichi Jima to spend the better part of twenty-four hours in air raid shelters. By then the Japanese had captured a few American flyers and tied them outside the shelter rather than inside.

In the meantime Emperor Hirohito's Imperial Guard, a specially trained unit with new radar-aiming antiaircraft batteries, arrived on Chichi Jima. They were recognized across the empire for their unsurpassed marksmanship. On 18 February, when Davison and Sherman sent in fighter sweeps of twelve planes each, the emperor's antiaircraft batteries were ready. They knocked down five American planes and one torpedo bomber. Four flyers disappeared into the nether of the island: James Wesley Dye, Jr., Floyd Ewing Hall, Marvie William Mershon, and Grady Alvan York. Many others disappeared without a trace, including ARM2c Carroll Curtis Hall, Ensign Rudolph F. Rolfing, and Joseph Edward Notony. As the carriers moved on to Iwo, the Navy listed all the men dead, presumably shot down and lost at sea. Not all of the flyers died as the Navy reported. Some of them landed on Chichi Jima. What to do with prisoners became an issue debated between Major General Yoshio Tachibana, the army commander on the island, and Rear Admiral Kunizo Mori, the ranking officer and commander of naval forces on the island. The general's and the admiral's decisions regarding the disposition of captured flyers provide the basis for this book.

On D-Day at Iwo, 19 February 1945, Chichi Jima got another respite. A heavy overcast covered the Bonins, so most of the carrier aircraft flew cover over Iwo's eastern assault beaches. The 4th Marine Division, commanded by Major General Clifton B. Cates, and the 5th Marine Division, commanded by Major General Keller E. Rickey, rode amphtracs (amphibious tractors) and dukws (amphibious trucks) ashore and formed a lodgment in the black sands under the frowning volcanic brow of Mount Suribachi.

On 20 February, with the Marines safely ashore, Mitscher sent a detachment of carriers and escort carriers from Task Force 58 to pound once more the defenses on Chichi and Haha Jima. For three days carrier aircraft flew 545 sorties in 27 missions. They dropped more than 116 tons of bombs and fired 1,331 rockets in the heaviest attack on the two islands since operations in the area began. Second Lieutenant Warren Earl Vaughn, a Marine Corps pilot flying his first mission over Chichi, did not return. Nor did AOM2c (Aviation Ordnance Man Second Class) Glenn J. Frazier. The Navy reported both men dead.

Air attacks on Chichi continued without abatement until 24 March, when conditions on Iwo no longer required air support. By then, 5,951 American soldiers lay dead and another 19,920 wounded while fighting for a piece of pockmarked landscape that looked like a pork chop and resembled the surface of the moon. The fight took the greatest number of casualties ever suffered by the Marine Corps in a single campaign. Americans howled at the toll, but before the war ended, no less than 2,251 Army Air Force B-29s, carrying 24,761 crewmen, made emergency landings on the island's reconstructed airfields.[11]

The Navy paid another toll in manpower. Though flyers were not expendable, aircraft could be replaced, and there were always other pilots who could fly them. Submarines cruised the Jimas, skirting minefields and answering calls from observation and fighter planes to pick up downed flyers. The subs looked for survivors in small yellow rubber lifeboats or for a head bobbing in the waves that belonged to a man in a life jacket. A few were found. They were the lucky ones.

For a month air raids continued over Chichi Jima, gradually diminishing in intensity. On 16 March the mopping up process began on Iwo Jima. Five days later General Kuribayashi radioed Major Yoshitaka Horie, his chief of staff on Chichi Jima, "We have not eaten or drunk for five days. But our fighting spirit is still high. We are going to fight bravely until the last." The general's message served as a morale-building pep talk to General Tachibana's brigade on Chichi Jima. Marines had squeezed the remnants of Kuribayashi's force into an area of less than 2,000 square yards, and the general could see the end in sight. He never intended to surrender. The last words out of Iwo Jima came from him. On 24 March he sent his final message to Major Horie: "All officers and men of Chichi, goodbye." When Tachibana received a copy of Kuribayashi's last message, he took immediate action to prepare his mixed brigade for the next American invasion.[12]

According to accounts made by Japanese on the island, Tachibana and Mori steeled themselves for an assault, expecting at any moment to see waves of American Marines heading toward the area of Bull Beach in the bay of Futami Ko, or at Miyano Hama, the base of the 308th Battalion near Ani Jima Strait. Admiral Mori's picket vessels roamed twenty miles offshore. Seaplanes made long-range reconnaissance sorties, expecting any hour to fall upon an approaching American task force. Sentinels posted above Miyano Hama and atop Yoake Yama and Nakayama Toge searched the horizon for ribbons of smoke. Japanese antiaircraft crews concealed in emplacements above the bay fixed their weapons on beach positions. General Tachibana ordered his battalion commanders to strengthen the resolve of the soldiers for the fight ahead. Admiral Mori did the same, perhaps with a little less emphasis. But there would be no fight. Except for a few bombs dropped by heckler attacks, mostly after dark, no American ships appeared off the coast. The Joint Chiefs of Staff in Washington wisely decided to leave Chichi Jima alone and concentrate the next invasion on Okinawa. Like the great Japanese naval bases at

Rabaul in the Solomons and Truk in the Carolines, the powerful brigade on Chichi Jima escaped the balance of the fighting war but not the agony of waiting.

The only Americans seen by the Japanese on Chichi Jima were the flyers shot down by antiaircraft fire. Most of them died in the cockpit or when they crashed in the mountains. A few survived and became prisoners of war. Tachibana and Mori decided to build the morale of their men by using captured flyers as Bushido examples. What the two senior officers on Chichi Jima did with their prisoners is not a nice story.

Books have been written about Japanese torture, enslavement, execution, and other horrors of war, but a flyer captured on Chichi Jima after 4 July 1944 faced an unspeakable hell. The crimes committed by the drunken officers commanding the forces on the island never faced the consequences of their acts until the war suddenly ended and the prospect of discovery became a worrisome threat. Had Stephen King been on the island to write a script for his next horror story, he would not have found it necessary to resort to fiction to cast his plot. The charade hatched by General Tachibana and his confederates to cover up their crimes provides a lucid example of Japanese craftiness.

After 4 July no flyer captured on or near Chichi Jima had the slimmest chance of escaping and living out the war. There were three exceptions. In early August a flyer bailed out of a burning plane and landed over Chichi Jima's harbor. A wingman dropped him a raft, but he could not get out of the harbor and was caught in heavy crossfire from the surrounding cliffs. A cruiser floatplane had no chance of swooping into the harbor and rescuing him. With the task force scheduled to depart within the hour, Mitscher brooded on the transom. Rear Admiral Arleigh Burke broke the silence and said, "Well, what about it, Admiral?" Mitscher looked up and said, "Jesus Christ, I can't leave that fellow in there. Keep the fighters circling until dark, and then get a submarine to come in close to the reef and send their rubber boat after him." The unnamed flyer owed his rescue and his life to Mitscher and a few brave men from a submarine.[13]

In early September 1944 another flyer parachuted onto Chichi Jima and landed in the hills near the remote home of a man named Takahata. The flyer went into Takahata's home, remained overnight, and when Japanese military police searched for him in the morning, he shot one and chased the others away. He stole a canoe, paddled into Ani Jima Strait at night, and was rescued by a submarine. The identity of this flyer has never been discovered because Takahata could not remember his name.[14]

The third flyer to escape from the clutches of this isle of death became the forty-first president of the United States, Lieutenant (jg) George Herbert Walker Bush. On 2 September 1944 Bush flew off the USS *San Jacinto* in an Avenger loaded with four 500-pound bombs. His target—Radio

Station #6 on Mount Asahi, located a thousand feet north of the Yoake Wireless Station, one of Japan's most important communications centers. Number 6 provided Yoake's high-frequency long-range radio transmissions that electronically guided Japanese naval aircraft from the mainland to island air bases in the Pacific. Commander Shizuo Yoshii, who had four weeks earlier arrived on the island to take charge of the station, did not appreciate his buildings being bombed and vowed revenge.

At 8,000 feet Bush formed with the squadron to begin the standard glide bomb run, during which the descent of the aircraft reached speeds of 350 miles per hour. In the early morning sun Bush easily spotted the long shadow of the 200-foot tower at Radio Station #6. As he began his descent, the nearby power plant and transmitter station came into view. As soon as Bush kicked into a dive, bullets from Emperor Hirohito's crack antiaircraft batteries began tearing into the Avenger's engine. Flames shot out the cowlings and smoke poured into the cockpit. Bush stayed with the dive, dropped his four 500-pounders on the target, and headed for sea. When he splashed down off the northeast coast of Chichi Jima, both of his crewmen were dead from enemy fire. Japanese boats pushed off from shore to capture Bush but were driven away by two of the squadron's hovering Avengers, whose pilots had radioed for help. Sailors on the submarine *Finback* spotted a tiny yellow raft bobbing in the chop. After crawling carefully through a minefield, the *Finback* pulled alongside Bush and snatched him from the water. Bush eventually received the Distinguished Flying Cross and gave many more years of service to the country.[15]

Had Bush parachuted to the island, the future president's life may have ended with all the others who mysteriously disappeared without a trace after seeking refuge on Chichi Jima.

This book is not about George Bush. It is about the other flyers whose names first appeared on the list of those missing in action among the Bonin Islands and presumed dead. Bush is mentioned for one reason: What happened to the others could as easily have happened to him. It would have changed the future history of the United States and eliminated two presidents and two governors named Bush.

When Colonel Presley M. Rixey (USMC), commanding the U.S. occupation forces, faced the Japanese delegation from Chichi Jima to discuss the demilitarization of the island, he expected to find a strong but humiliated garrison of men anxious to get back to Japan and renew relationships with their families. He did not expect to accidentally discover a cover-up that involved the execution and cannibalization of American flyers. The Board of Investigation he established spent more than five months trying to untangle a web spun to hide the truth. War in the Pacific bred hate and promoted atrocities, but the Japanese on Chichi

Jima added a new page to the sordid side of war when they decided to become cannibals.

Rear Admiral John D. Murphy, director of war crimes on Guam, once affirmed that while the Tokyo trials made headlines, the Guam trials involving the cannibals on Chichi Jima made law.

It is also essential that public attention be focused on this unusual and efficacious proceeding for the sole purpose, if nothing more, to demonstrate that international atrocities, be they large or small, can be rooted out of cleverly camouflaged acts against humanity and impartially investigated, and the perpetrators brought to justice.

CHAPTER 2

War Comes to Chichi Jima

During World War II American military planners looked often at Chichi Jima because it lay only 640 miles directly south of the Japanese capital. The island's physical features—a fine protected harbor, a temperate climate, and a fertile soil—had attracted Americans and Europeans for more than a hundred years. But in 1944, U.S. Navy photoreconnaissance revealed terrain features that took Chichi Jima off the list of possible airfield sites. The Japanese were already hard at work building Susaki airfield, which they created by filling in the channel between the cliffs along the western shore and Goat Island Head. Because the airfield lay across a short, narrow neck of peninsula, it could not be lengthened to accommodate long-range American bombers without creating months of work for heavy construction equipment. Admiral Nimitz did not have that kind of time. The hilly topography of Haha Jima, located 40 miles to the south, was even less suitable for airfields. So the Joint Chiefs of Staff discarded the idea of occupying the Bonins and decided instead to land an amphibious force on Iwo Jima, 145 miles to the south.

During early 1945 the Japanese on Chichi Jima held strong views about the war. They believed their force should be employed in the decisive battle for the home islands, but after losing three naval battles during the opening days of the Philippines campaign, the Imperial Japanese Navy began running out of ships, and the lack of transportation prevented Chichi Jima's First Mixed Brigade from being returned to Japan. General Tachibana's army brigade and Admiral Mori's naval units had no choice but to spend the balance of the war on Chichi Jima. So more than 22,000 men, who never stopped work on building fortifications,

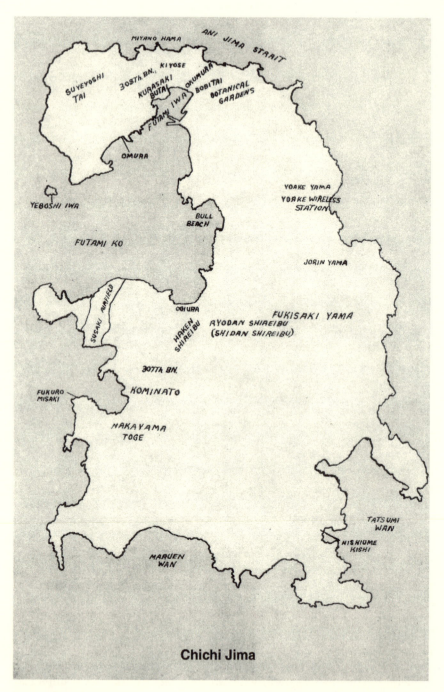

Chichi Jima

Map of Chichi Jima exactly as drawn by the occupation forces on the island in 1945–1946 and as it appears in the documents of the *Investigation*. With the exception of the Yoake Wireless Station on the east coast, most of the activity on Chichi Jima centered around Futami Ko (Futami Bay). (Image enhanced by Dr. Ronald Pearson) settled into their barracks and air raid shelters to await the outcome of the war.

Tachibana and Mori suspected that American forces would never invade Chichi Jima because of the island's mountainous terrain and the absence of good beaches for amphibious landings, and they were right. They were wrong, however, in their conception of American intentions. Tachibana warned his senior officers that the Americans would bypass Chichi Jima, conquer Japan, and at some later time use the military forces stranded on the island as slave labor, which is exactly what the Japanese army had done with Allied prisoners captured in Burma and the Philippines. The propaganda machine emanating out of Imperial General Headquarters also warned the forces on Chichi to prepare for American air attacks using chemical and biological weapons. The Japanese understood that "the most painful blow to Americans is the loss of personnel," so they vowed to "kill as many of the enemy as possible" and developed their own special methods for doing it.

In an effort to harden their forces for battle, and to a lesser degree for bondage, Tachibana's commanders tried to convince their units that Americans were *kichiku*, meaning bestial, or the equivalent of the devil. On other fields of battle thousands of Japanese soldiers, sailors, and flyers became victims of this propaganda and made foolish suicide attacks. When faced with defeat, instead of surrendering with a hope of returning to their homes, they planted a live grenade against their bodies and blew themselves to pieces to escape the indignity of American *kichiku*. On Chichi Jima, however, instead of being the victims of *kichiku*, General Tachibana encouraged his officers to harden their men by practicing it.[1]

When war finally came to Chichi Jima, it was not at all like the battles fought by Marines on Guadalcanal, Tarawa, Iwo Jima, or Okinawa. It was, as Colonel Presley M. Rixey recalled, acts of brutality in response to the bombing raids. It was this brutality that led Tachibana and his samurai warriors to concoct, for self-preservation, a vast deception. Rixey more gratuitously described what he discovered about the enemy as "Japanese Camouflage" and referred to the incidents of his investigation as "not a pretty story but one that will reveal the true character of the Japanese military mind." To understand the Japanese attitude toward outsiders is to understand, to some degree, the history of Chichi Jima before World War II.[2]

In 1543 a Spanish explorer by the name of Villalobos discovered and charted the islands, but the Imperial Japanese Empire arranged history to support their own claim. According to legend, in 1593 a mythical warrior prince, Sadayori Ogasawara, landed on the island chain and claimed it for Japan. Ogasawara found the islands uninhabited and named them *bunin*—which meant "empty of men" or "land of no men."

Westerners corrupted the name and cartographers adopted the corruption, calling the tiny specks in the Pacific the Bonins. For more than two centuries the principal islands in each of the three main clusters became known as Chichi Jima, Haha Jima, Muko Jima, and they remained exactly the way Ogasawara found them—empty of men.

In 1823 Captain Reuben Coffin, a shipmaster from Nantucket, anchored the whaler *Transit* off Haha Jima and claimed the Bonins for the United States. Since no delegation came out in boats to receive him and the islands appeared to be deserted, the captain proudly named them after himself—Coffin Islands—and then sailed away to harpoon whales in the waters around Japan.

Four years later Frederick W. Beechey of the Royal Navy arrived in the HMS *Blossom*. Having never heard of the legendary Ogasawara or of Captain Coffin, he gave Chichi a good British name—Peel Island. Beechey attempted to make the island a British colony, and soon a shipload of English settlers arrived with ten Sandwich Island (Hawaiian) concubines to keep them company. The British promptly ignored their colonists and then forgot about Peel Island.

In 1853 Commodore Matthew Calbraith Perry, after his celebrated expedition to the Far East and the signing of the treaty of friendship with Japan, tried once again to claim the island chain for the United States. On 14 June he brought the USS *Susquehanna* and the USS *Saratoga* into a marvelously deep harbor and sent a party ashore on Chichi Jima, a lush green island surrounded by palisades of cliffs. From the air, the outline of the island resembled a running short-legged dwarf in a tasseled stocking cap. Much to his surprise, Perry found the mountainous island occupied not by Japanese but by British, Italians, Sandwich Islanders, Danes, and the American family of Nathaniel Savory, a Yankee adventurer and trader from Bradford, Massachusetts. In 1832 Savory had bought a schooner in Honolulu and transported the first settlers to Chichi. Savory spent the rest of his long life vainly trying to make the Bonins a possession of the United States and demanded the same of his clan.[3]

Savory and the commodore became fast friends. Perry believed that the United States should take an energetic role in shaping the destiny of the Pacific. He advocated occupying the Bonins and Iwo Jima, using the principal island of Chichi as a coaling station. Writing in 1855, he said: "In no part of the earth can be found a more prolific soil than in those parts of the Bonins that have been brought into thorough cultivation." Perry also stopped at Iwo Jima and found nothing but rocks and dry volcanic sand, very little vegetation, few signs of life, no natural barriers for cover, and an extinct volcano at the southwestern tip of the island.

The commodore became enthralled by Chichi's magnificent natural harbor, its abundance of food and water, and its close proximity to the Japanese whaling grounds. He became so impressed with the beauty and fertility of the island that he paid Nathaniel Savory—who held no special rights to the island—$50 to acquire a section of land close to his anchorage at Ten Fathom Hole, which was located at the north end of the harbor. When he returned to the United States, he proposed a joint stock company to create an American settlement by encouraging young married couples to migrate to the Bonins and plant crops. No one seemed interested.

To protect his investment, Perry appointed Savory resident U.S. agent at Port Lloyd, drew up a document entitled "Articles of Agreement of Settlers of Peel Island," and made Savory chief magistrate. Had Perry gotten his way, war between the United States and Japan may have occurred at a much earlier date. The islands lay in what a few decades later became Japan's sphere of influence, and foreign interlopers were not at all welcome.[4]

Nobody in the nation's capital could follow the reasoning of men like Savory, Perry, or Captain Coffin. If they paused to look at a map of the North Pacific, they would see an inaccurate depiction of the island of Japan, a scattering of islands in Micronesia to the south, and in between a few improperly placed dots the size of pinpricks that represented the Bonin Islands. Even whalers had little good to say about the islands, though they occasionally stopped for water or to make repairs to their vessels.

On 17 January 1862, while Americans were at war with themselves, the Japanese warship *Kanrin Maru* sailed into Port Lloyd. A detachment went ashore and planted the Japanese flag on a thousand-foot hill and named the peak Asahi Yama—"Mountain of the Rising Sun." Eighty years later Asahi Yama would hold the towers for Japan's most sophisticated radio equipment. But there were no radios in 1862 when Mizuno Chikugo, dressed in purple ceremonial robes, came ashore wearing double samurai swords and asked Savory whether any other nation had claimed the island. Savory wisely refrained from claiming the islands for the United States, so Mizuno invoked the story of Sadayori Ogasawara, politely repudiated rights of any foreign nation to the chain, and claimed the Bonin Islands for Japan, thereby scotching Perry's plans. Mizuno persuaded Savory and the islanders to accept Japan's control, and once more Peel Island became Chichi Jima, and Port Lloyd became a small village on Futami Ko that settlers called Yankeetown.

Before the year ended the first shipload of Japanese colonists arrived in Futami bay and established the town of Omura. When Japan discovered that the island could not grow rice, an Imperial ship arrived to take the colonists back to Japan. Before embarking, Governor Obana Sakunosuke took Savory aside and sternly told him that the abrupt departure did not mean that Japan intended to relinquish its claim to the Bonins.

During the passage of many years, renegades, deserters, shipwrecked

sailors, and disabled seamen came ashore. Few stayed long because doing so involved work, and unlike the picturesque islands of the South
Pacific, Chichi provided no charming bare-breasted women. Among the
scamps who stayed was Matteo Mozarro, a Genoese black-bearded rascal
who claimed to be British with full rights to the control of the island and
especially its fine harbor. The only person standing in his way was Nathaniel Savory. While Mozarro plotted, an Englishman took Savory aside
and handed him a remarkable document that told of how Mozarro
planned to kill him. Savory wasted no time preparing to meet the threat.[5]

Because Mozarro failed in his scheme of murder, Savory lived to produce descendants that ninety years later would have an impact on the
sordid wartime history of Chichi Jima. By the strangest of all coinci-
dences—if such could be credited to coincidence and not foul play—
Mozarro unexpectedly died. Having lost two common-law Polynesian
wives, Savory in 1850 married a Guamanian (Spanish-Chamarro) belle
by the name of Maria Dilessanto, who happened to be the widow of
Mozarro. He took her out beyond the three-mile limit on a Yankee
whaler and paid the captain to perform the marriage ceremony. At the
age of fifty-six Savory settled into a quieter life and through Maria con-
ceived a small brood of legitimate sons.[6]

Nathaniel Savory died in 1874 at the age of eighty, but his descendants
stayed on the island and raised their families. The boys respected their
father's wishes and remained loyal to the United States—a country they
had never seen. Except for an occasional murder, the islands became a
paradise shielded from the greater world. The Savorys never seriously
considered returning to America, but each year on Washington's Birth-
day and the Fourth of July they raised the Stars and Stripes and held
private celebrations in their homes.[7]

Horace Perry Savory (named for Commodore Perry) and Benjamin,
sons of the family patriarch by way of the Guamanian belle, found wives
and started their own families. When old Nathaniel lay on his deathbed,
he called Horace to his room and told him to always fly the American
flag whenever a ship entered the harbor. Horace made the mistake of
flying the Stars and Stripes in November 1875 when an official party
from Japan arrived on the *Meiji Maru* and spotted the American banner
streaming from the Yankeetown flagpole. As a consequence, Horace became targeted by Japan's emissaries as a nonconformist and performed
the dubious honor of being the first to sign away the independence of
the settlers. Perry once had warned that unless the island shed its unproductive, primitive way of life, it would be "swallowed up" by a more
efficient race. The "more efficient race" had come, not from the West but
from Japan.[8]

The year 1875 marked the beginning of Japan's expansion in the Far
East. They occupied the Kuriles in the north as well as the Nanpo Shoto

in the south. Japan then shipped a thousand unwilling settlers from the Izus to the Bonins, renamed the island group Ogasawara Gunto, and reestablished the seat of government at Omura. By 1882 all the Western-ers, including the Savorys, became naturalized citizens of the Imperial Japanese Empire, and Yankeetown at Ten Fathom Hole became a village with a new name—Okumura.[9]

Japan continued to expand, occupying the Ryukyus in 1879 and For-mosa and the Pescadores in 1895, and at the end of World War I it obtained mandates over the Marianas, the Marshalls, and the Carolines. While viewing his new island possessions the divine emperor began thinking in terms of his own Asian Monroe Doctrine. There were no military activities in the Nanpo Shoto area until 1914, when the Japanese General Staff began building fortifications on Chichi Jima. During the next three years they added a few pieces of heavy artillery and a naval radio station to monitor the weather.[10]

After the Great War, delegates from the nation of the Rising Sun went to an arms control conference at Washington to make a strong bid for annexing the Bonins, which they already occupied. Such approval by the Washington Conference would enable them to fortify Futami Ko and build a naval base without restriction. The Japanese lost their case but disobeyed the agreement. A few years later Emperor Hirohito visited Chichi Jima to watch his expanding navy exercise at war games. A new road, stretching from Okumura to Omura, bore his name. In 1935 the military placed the entire Nanpo Shoto under martial law, making it off limits to foreigners and posting "no trespassing" signs written in both Japanese and English.

Nathaniel's youngest son, Benjamin, grew up during the years when the Japanese began closing off the islands to foreigners. He went to Japan and received his education at an American mission school. After return-ing to Chichi Jima he married and passed the legacy of the family to his son Daniel. Daniel wanted to see America and signed on a sealing ship for the Aleutians. He finally reached Seattle, but his papers described him as Japanese. Frustrated by social segregation, Daniel returned to Chichi, married, and soon became the proud father of a son, Frederick Arthur Savory. At an early age the lad learned the first inviolable tra-dition of the Savory clan. "I had to speak English to my father or he would beat me," and the English Fred learned had the flavor of cockney with a touch of "Harvard."

Daniel wanted a better life for eight-year-old Fred and sent him to St. Joseph's College in Yokohama. Twelve years later—on the eve of the 1940 American boycott on Japanese goods—Fred opened a mercantile business in Japan. The boycott ended Fred's business career, and he re-turned to Chichi Jima. He did not know at the time that his most important asset, and one that would affect the lives of Americans and Japanese alike, was his ability to speak fluent English and Japanese.[11]

Everywhere on Chichi Jima, Fred observed signs of Japanese preparations for war. During his long absence the Imperial Japanese Navy (IJN) began filling in the shoreline near Commodore Perry's Ten Fathom Hole and converting it into a strong, deep-water naval base. Yet by 7 December 1941—to Americans, Pearl Harbor Day—there were only 1,400 troops stationed on the Nanpo Shoto, and all of them were garrisoned on Chichi Jima. Two years passed before the Japanese decided to increase troop strength on Chichi to 3,800 men and to build Chidori, their first tactical airfield for twenty planes on Iwo Jima instead of on Chichi.[12]

The Japanese discriminated against Bonin islanders with Caucasian features. As soon as the authorities spotted Fred on the island, they conscripted him for the local labor corps and made him a *gunzoku* (conscripted laborer). While pouring concrete for a secret, underground radio station, he made a mental note that if war came, he would have valuable information to share with Americans. A tenacious fidelity to the United States somehow managed to trickle through four generations from Nathaniel to Fred.

The extensive underground radio stations remained secret until 1944, even though Navy code-breakers at Pearl Harbor began picking up messages in November 1941 from the Chichi Jima communications center. Chief Radioman Homer Kisner, operating a radio listening post on Heeia, Hawaii, became aware that Japanese warships, air units, and transports were moving south and east toward Guam, Wake, Midway, Hawaii, and the Philippines. The purpose of the movements remained unclear because the United States and Japan were at peace, even though Kisner warned that the actions of the Imperial Navy looked warlike. Although the U.S. Navy learned of the powerful wireless station at Chichi Jima in 1941, they could not locate it until mid-1944 when photoreconnaissance spotted radio towers on Mount Yoake and Mount Asahi near the island's east coast. One of those installations eventually became the target for a young Navy flyer and future American president, Lieutenant (jg) George H.W. Bush, who would remember his brush with death for the rest of his life.[13]

When war came in late 1941, Chichi Jima stood near the top of a long string of island fortresses stretching south from the Izus through the Bonins to Iwo Jima, and from there to strategic military centers at Saipan and Tinian in the Marianas, and to Rabaul in the northern Solomons. Along the shores of Futami bay Fred watched work parties composed of Korean *gunzokus* dredge anchorages to accommodate freighters and midsized warships. They built a seaplane base, wharves, and a long pier that jutted into old Ten Fathom Hole. He also observed men blasting and boring deep into the hills behind the harbor and inserting air-

This picture of George Bush was taken on 2 November 1944, exactly two months after he was shot down over Chichi Jima. Flanking Bush is radioman Joe Reichert (right) and turret gunner Leo Nadeau. (U.S. Navy Photo, National Archives)

Aerial view from 2,000 feet of Chichi Jima's harbor at Futami Iwa. Naval Defense Headquarters and Admiral Mori's command post is in the center of the photograph. (Courtesy of National Archives)

conditioned bombproof caves for storing ammunition and supplies. Fred became more than a keen observer. He became a self-appointed displaced American observer—one who had never seen his motherland but loved her just the same.

Thirty months passed before the war reached Chichi Jima. During those months Fred maintained a good relationship with the Japanese, though they never completely trusted him or any of his many relatives. During the first six months of 1942 the Japanese went about their activities with great energy because for them the Imperial war machine had conquered the Philippines, Singapore, the vast oil empire of the Netherlands East Indies, and more recently the Solomons. According to propaganda sources, Japan would soon take possession of New Guinea and invade Australia.

Chichi Jima served as one of Japan's forward bases for shuttling supplies to the south. News of the Imperial Japanese Navy's defeat in the Coral Sea and at Midway never became known on the island, nor did Jimmy Doolittle's raid on Tokyo or the Marine invasion of Guadalcanal. The Japanese fortifying the Bonins went about their work oblivious to the Allied invasion of the Solomon Islands. Without such information, they could not envision these events as the first of many stepping-stones that would eventually lead American forces to their strategically located island fortress.

Late in 1943 the Allies built their plans around the concept of a Pacific triangle with Tokyo at the apex. As the Allied island-hopping war progressed, the base of the triangle shortened upwards through the South Pacific islands and New Guinea, coming ever closer to the Nanpo Shoto and Japan. The Joint Chiefs of Staff planned advanced bomber bases, with routes to Tokyo that cut through Okinawa to the west and the Bonins to the east. In the final analysis they decided not to invade Chichi. Iwo was smaller and more difficult for Japan to defend, and its flatter topography made it ideal for building airfields. But first came the Marianas and a bitter fight for Saipan and Guam.

Japanese strategists considered the Nanpo Shoto part of an 1,800-mile collection of islands that comprised the "home defense arc." The arc stretched down to western New Guinea, and as early as the 1930s the Japanese had begun fortifying the Micronesian islands to provide the final protective shield for the empire. If American forces broke through the arc, the Japanese mainland would become vulnerable to air attacks and eventual invasion. Beginning in May 1944, this arc became the battleground for American air and amphibious attacks. Two carrier armadas roamed inside the arc: Task Force 38 under Admiral William F. Halsey and Task Force 58 under Admiral Raymond Spruance, each consisting of about eight carriers of the *Essex* and *Independence* class supported by battleships, escort carriers, cruisers, and destroyers.

During the first phase of the Marianas campaign, two carrier task groups under Vice Admiral Marc Mitscher sailed north and on 15–16 June 1944 launched fighter sweeps and bombing missions against Chichi Jima, Haha Jima, and Iwo Jima. On Chichi the attacks came as a shock because the average Japanese soldier had not heard that the war was beginning to threaten the home islands. Despite unfavorable flying conditions, Hellcats and Avengers from the carriers *Essex*, *Hornet*, and *Yorktown* reduced the ability of the Japanese to resist and temporarily rendered the Bonins unable to reinforce the Marianas with aircraft and supplies. Weeks would pass before the enlisted men of Chichi's battalions began to receive word of the American invasion of the Marianas and of the Imperial Japanese Army's bitter monthlong failure to defend Saipan.[14]

During the mid-June attack, carrier planes destroyed a third of Chichi Jima's above-ground fortifications. The sorties burned out half of Okumura, Perry's old Yankeetown tract where the Savorys lived. A bomb blast blew Fred off a bridge within a stone's throw of where the original home of his great-grandfather once stood. Fred had been attempting in vain to make contact with the U.S. Navy, but his time on the island was about to run out. Orders came from Imperial Japanese Headquarters to evacuate all civilians to Tokyo and Yokohama. The Savory clan packed a few personal belongings, boarded a Japanese freighter, and on 23 July 1944 said good-bye to their homes. As the Savorys departed for Japan, thousands of Japanese troops originally earmarked for Micronesia began flowing into Iwo and Chichi Jima. For the next seventeen months Fred worked on the Japanese mainland as a painter.[15]

During the latter phase of the Allied battle for the Marianas, Japan sent aircraft through the Bonins to Iwo Jima and from Iwo to Saipan. Admiral Chester A. Nimitz issued orders for Admiral Spruance to stop the flow of reinforcements. Rearmed and refueled, two carrier task groups under Rear Admiral Jocko Clark set a northward course on the morning of 1 July and on Independence Day launched heavy air attacks against the Jimas. After that, enemy air opposition all but ceased, and on 9 July organized resistance on Saipan ended, paving the way for an attack on Guam. On Chichi Jima, Lieutenant General Tadamichi Kuribayashi looked at the rubble that had once been Susaski airfield and issued orders to repair it.[16]

To support the Guam assault scheduled for 21 July and the Tinian assault on 24 July, carrier raids on Chichi and Haha continued through the balance of the summer, the first respite for the Bonins coming in mid-September. The U.S. Air Force, operating long-range B-24s and B-29s out of Saipan, began bombing missions against targets on the Japanese mainland. By then the 1,800-mile "home defense arc" had been reduced to 680 miles and stretched from Tokyo Bay south to Iwo Jima, drawing ever closer to Chichi.

On 30 June 1944 Imperial Japanese Headquarters formed the 109th Infantry Division and sent half of it to Iwo Jima and the other half to Chichi Jima. The division consisted of two reinforced brigades, both under the command of General Kuribayashi, who with the Second Mixed Brigade established his forward headquarters on Iwo Jima. Major General Tachibana commanded the First Mixed Brigade from Fortress Headquarters on Chichi Jima. Major General Koto Osuga, the former commander of Fortress Headquarters, went to Iwo Jima with General Kuribayashi to command the Second Mixed Brigade.

After his move to Iwo, Kuribayashi placed staff officer Major Yoshitaka Horie on Chichi Jima and put him in charge of the 109th Division Detached Headquarters. Horie's small staff acted as intelligence, communication, and supply liaisons tying the Imperial Japanese Army headquarters on the mainland with Kuribayashi's headquarters on Iwo Jima. Rear Admiral Mori, though senior officer on Chichi, concerned himself with the protection of the Bonins at sea and did not directly involve himself with Tachibana's army brigade or with Horie. This command structure remained unchanged until the U.S. Marines captured Iwo Jima.[17]

Horie knew that General Kuribayashi had served as a deputy military attaché for several years in Canada and made frequent visits to the United States. He was aware that the general had traveled throughout the United States and understood the American mind and their way of life. During a more serious moment in 1931 Kuribayashi once said to his wife, "The United States is the last country in the world Japan should fight. Its industrial potential is huge and fabulous, and the people are energetic and versatile. One must never underestimate the Americans' fighting ability."[18]

Once during dinner, when rum and sake flowed freely, the portly general asked Major Horie's opinion about the defense of Iwo. Horie replied that the island was as vulnerable as "a pile of eggs," and the best thing to do with the island "would be to sink it to the bottom of the sea. It could be done," Horie added, "with enough explosives." Kuribayashi disliked the idea of defending this desolate heap of volcanic ash and would have much preferred to concentrate his force on Chichi Jima. Kuribayashi probably agreed with Horie that it would be better if Iwo did not exist: in American hands "it would be a dagger aimed straight at the heart of the homeland."[19]

By mid-1944 the military and defensive buildup on Chichi Jima and Haha Jima became frenetic. The Imperial high command shoved more than 22,000 army and navy personnel onto the Bonins, many of the men being reservists who had already served a tour of duty in China, Burma, or the Netherlands East Indies. They said they were tired of war, and their apathy concerned Tachibana and his battalion commanders. Some of the reservists were reluctant to leave their families again, but they had no choice because General Kuribayashi believed that American forces intended to assault Iwo, Chichi, and Haha Jima simultaneously. Though Tachibana doubted whether American forces would attack the Bonins, though in many respects he hoped they would, Chichi Jima became a pivotal point in the defense of the mainland and among the last strongholds of the Nipponese Island Empire. To bolster morale, Emperor Hirohito sent his own palace guard of antiaircraft gunners to the island because, in the opinions of his advisers, they were the best antiaircraft units in the empire. The crews set up their 25mm and 75mm gross-batteries in clusters around the island but mainly on the thousand-foot mountains near the Yoake Wireless Station and on the cliffs overlooking Futami Ko.

Military personnel on Chichi Jima made grandiose projections on the number of casualties American forces would suffer if they invaded the island. They had emplaced 100 big guns in concrete abutments and spread another 15,000 guns in revetments around the island. They also operated 166 torpedo and suicide boats, with which they planned to attack American transports and Navy escort vessels. Off the harbor navy crews planted hundreds of mines at a depth of ten feet. Tucked into the mountains of Chichi, almost every heavy gun emplacement and fortified position connected to a network of galleries, and every gun on the cliffs overlooking the harbor had been bracketed on either the airfield or the small beaches that could be assaulted during an amphibious landing. Antiaircraft units repositioned their guns so they could be used as artillery. Major Horie estimated that an assault on the island would cost the Americans 150,000 men. Though his calculations could be challenged as grossly exaggerated, the Allied Joint Chiefs of Staff made the right decision in bypassing Chichi Jima.[20]

During the Japanese buildup, Fred Savory continued to work with Koreans as a *gunzoku* on Chichi's fortifications, but he knew nothing about the advance of Allied forces through the islands of the Pacific. His first indication of the approach of fighting came on 15 June 1944 when a swarm of American fighter-bombers from Jocko Clark and William Harrill's task groups struck the airfield and the naval base. Japanese antiaircraft fire shot down the first American plane. Two American aviators parachuted into the water off Chichi Jima from an SBC2 Helldiver. A Japanese submarine chaser rescued the flyers and brought them to the Bobitai naval base near Fred's home. The military police incarcerated Lieutenant (jg) Calvin D. Terry and Petty Officer Oscar Long Doyle at the Omura radio station and a few days later shipped them to the Yokosuka Navy Base in Japan. Terry and Doyle became the first airmen captured on Chichi Jima. They were the lucky ones. Aircraft could still land on Susaki airfield, and ships were still able to get into Chichi's harbor with supplies and return to Japan.[21]

At 10:00 A.M. on 4 July Jocko Clark's carriers returned and sank or disabled most of the shipping in Chichi's harbor. A pilot believed to be twenty-year-old Lieutenant (jg) Hershel C. Connell parachuted from his aircraft and landed in the hills behind the Japanese naval base. Sailors from Bobitai captured Connell, blindfolded him, and brought him to navy headquarters. Fred picked up the news that evening while working in the Kiyose air raid tunnel and went to see the flyer. He found the pilot sitting on a stone with his wrists bound around a tree and six strands of rope lashed tightly around his chest. Connell escaped the usual treatment of being tied to a post with his hands bound so high behind him that he could neither sit nor stand, leaving the upper body nearly parallel to the ground and in an excruciatingly painful position. An ordinary Japanese sailor stood guard with fixed bayonet, while two navy officers, an ensign and a lieutenant, tried to interrogate Connell using bad English and hand signals. Fred volunteered to translate and for ten minutes did so. He learned that the pilot had been in the Marianas campaign and came from the new USS *Hornet*. After the flyer asked Fred, "Tell me, friend, is there anyone like [you] left on this island?" a lieutenant commander from the naval base stepped into the conversation, glared at Fred, and hit the aviator over the head with the scabbard of his sword. Fred departed in a hurry and returned to the tunnel. Though he never learned the pilot's name, he noticed that the man had brown hair, weighed about 180 pounds, and had broad shoulders and three gold teeth. Without this description, later efforts to identify flyers shot down on Chichi may never have connected the name Connell to this pilot.[22]

A few days later Fred's uncle attempted to see Connell, who had been moved from Bobitai to Omura. Samuel Savory did not get close to the flyer but from the distance could see that the man had been beaten. He asked the Japanese carpenter who wielded the club why he struck the pilot. The carpenter replied, "I got revenge on him." Samuel learned later that the carpenter had lost his only son in a recent air raid. For about three days Connell remained accessible to anyone who cared to come to Fortress Headquarters and throw a few punches. Major Horie, chief of staff for the 109th Division Detached Headquarters, interrogated Connell for about ten days, in the interim leaving him tied to a tree outside his office. On 15 July Horie sent him back to the naval base, and Connell embarked on a seaplane bound for Japan. At the time, Connell did not know that he would be the last American flyer to leave the island alive.[23]

Heavy American carrier attacks on 4 July put the Japanese on alert. They prepared for an assault that did not come, but the partial destruction of Fortress Headquarters at Omura and the uncertainty of attack left the Japanese agitated and retaliatory. Their attitude toward rescued flyers changed after American bombs began shattering every installation that pilots could see from the air. Flyers like Terry, Doyle, and Connell got off easy, though they spent the next thirteen months in Japanese prison camps on the home islands. Others unlucky enough to parachute among the Bonins later would face an unspeakable hell.

On 4 July the Japanese on Ani Jima captured another flyer from Clark's carrier command, an American radioman whose name they could not understand, so they called him Wolf. The flyer had received a bullet wound in the shoulder and another wound in the leg, though both, with proper medical care, did not appear to be serious. After learning little from Wolf, they shipped him over to the naval base at Bobitai. The navy had agreed to let the army perform the interrogations, and a car transported the wounded flyer to Haken Shireibu, where Major Horie and Captain Kimitomi Nishiyotsutsuji interrogated him. Wolf received a modest amount of medical attention, but Nishiyotsutsuji stuffed him into a garage to die of starvation and thirst. Wolf, as Horie called him, survived and began to heal.[24]

On the night of 4 August Admirals Marc Mitscher and John S. McCain launched attacks on Chichi Jima and Haha Jima. From bases in Saipan, B-24s joined in the attacks. Japanese antiaircraft shot down a B-24 over Futami Ko, and the aircraft crashed into the water near the Bobitai naval base. Two of the crew survived the crash. One was alive and unhurt, a corporal, but the second man died of his injuries in the enemy sickbay. A detail buried three bodies from the crash in the island's former Botanical Garden and turned the corporal over to the 307th Infantry Battalion. The Japanese made no effort to determine the names of the dead when they buried other members of the crew at sea. To the Japanese, American bodies were simply trash.[25]

Lieutenant Commander Minoru Yonehara and a junior officer interrogated the uninjured corporal. The following day, on orders from Admiral Mori's headquarters, they tied him to a tree during Mitscher and McCain's 5 August air attack and cruiser bombardment of the naval base. Having survived the attack, the unknown corporal and Wolf were transported by truck to Haken Shireibu, Major Horie's headquarters. Shortly thereafter, Major Horie departed for Iwo Jima, leaving the two prisoners with Captain Nishiyotsutsuji.

Air raids prior to the invasion of Iwo Jima became frequent and severe, and hatred toward Americans increased after each wave of bombers dropped their payloads on the island. General Tachibana became livid, behaving like a man who never expected such treatment from the enemy. He demanded that during air raids prisoners not be taken to a shelter but left outside where they could suffer through the bombings. With Commander Shizuo Yoshii of the Imperial Japanese Navy and Major Sueo Matoba of the 308th Battalion, the general found agreement that extreme measures were justified, though not every soldier and sailor on the island felt the same way. If any of the officers on Chichi Jima had ever heard of the Geneva Convention and the articles concerning the treatment of prisoners, they made no effort to follow them.[26]

By then, Fred Savory, along with hundreds of civilians evacuated from Iwo Jima, had been put on a boat and deported to Japan. He heard no more about American prisoners until some months later. He listened to the scuttlebutt trickling through the screen of secrecy draping the island. He still had a stake in Chichi Jima. It was his place of birth. He wanted to go back and, if possible, to make his home a part of America, thereby restoring the hopes and dreams of his great-grandfather 113 years before. Chichi Jima had not seen the last of Fred Savory.[27]

CHAPTER 3

The Question

In July 1944, after the Savorys departed from Chichi, no Western eyes penetrated the screen of activity blanketing the island but for the few unfortunate American flyers unlucky enough to be taken prisoner. For the next seven months sorties flown from Saipan and from carriers continued to pummel the island, but the flyers overhead could see little of the activity on the ground, only dense foliage, a few scattered buildings, and here and there a serpentine road zigzagging along the coast and winding upwards into the hills.

A year passed and the war ended. On 3 September 1945 Commander John H. Macgruder, commanding the heavy cruiser USS *Dunlap*, stopped at Chichi Jima and secured the surrender of the island from Lieutenant General Tachibana. Major Horie and the headquarters staff watched in silence as Cadet Oyama interpreted the terms for the general. Admiral Mori did not attend the surrender ceremony, leaving the embarrassing task to the general who had usurped command of the island. Macgruder asked no searching questions and sailed away without going ashore. Six weeks later the threat to pierce the veil of Chichi Jima's sordid secrets magnified as the first U.S. Marines and naval personnel approached the island—but not if the cabal of high-ranking Japanese officers on Chichi Jima could prevent it.

General Tachibana, a short, squat man with a bulging stomach, ascended to the command of the 109th Infantry Division on Chichi Jima after General Kuribayashi lost the battle for Iwo Jima. Like many honorable officers of the Imperial Japanese Army, Kuribayashi took his own life by enjoying a marvelous supper and then carving out his bowels with his ceremonial sword. Tachibana did not pursue the same honorable death, and until Americans came to take physical possession of the island, he had no reason to consider suicide. He enjoyed power, drank heavily, ate well, and became excessively fat while his brigade struggled through the latter months of the war on half rations, whatever fish they could catch in the ocean, and what vegetables they could raise. Most of the wild pigs on the island had long ago been hunted and shot. Tachibana's men remained hungry, subsisting off soup containing whatever the cooks could find to throw into the huge simmering pots. No armed force had invaded Tachibana's stronghold, and the few flyers taken prisoner he dispatched in his own way.[1]

Though Tachibana exercised overall command of the district, until May 1945 the senior officer in tactical command had been Admiral Mori. The admiral limited the scope of his duty to repulsing an American invasion from the sea and paid only a small amount of attention to Tachibana's inland deployments. Mori commanded his own battalions, but those units operating in districts under the army's purview came under the influence and more often the control of Tachibana's battalion commanders.

Early in 1944 Mori acceded to Tachibana's demand that all prisoners captured on the Bonins be turned over to the army. A somber individual, Mori enjoyed the beauty of life more than the bloodshed of war. He wrote poetry and looked upon the world as a vast wonder of creation. Though he swore to do his duty to the emperor, Mori still wondered how war fit into the equation of life's many gifts. He did not object to abrogating some measure of his authority to Tachibana, who seemed to be much better fitted to the brutality of war.

After the invasion of Iwo Jima on 19 February 1944, the heavy air attacks on Chichi became less frequent. After 23 February 1945 the Japanese captured no more flyers, and only a sporadic raid by B-24s, B-25s, or B-29s interrupted the nightly revelry enjoyed by the officers and men under Tachibana and Mori. They waited for an invasion that never came, not realizing until six weeks after the war ended that their problems were just beginning. Many of the officers close to Tachibana wondered what the world would say if someone broke through their code of silence and uncovered their hidden secrets.

From the perspective of Tachibana, Mori, and their chief subordinates, they had survived the war and fought it honorably, though in their own way. So let the record show the world outside Chichi Jima that they had performed their duties with an honor equal to their kinsmen who had died in the swamps of Bougainville or shed their blood on the coarse black sands of Iwo Jima. More important, those on Chichi Jima represented the few in the Pacific islands who survived, and having survived, they no longer wanted to die for a cause now lost. The great imperial quest for expansion had ended in bitter and permanent defeat.

Officers and enlisted men alike looked forward to becoming civilians again, but before that day of resurrection came, they must once more apply their oriental ingenuity and design a fully scripted, finely tuned sideshow with every soldier, sailor, and *gunzoku* on Chichi Jima playing a supporting actor's role—no easy task for the 20,656 Japanese army and navy personnel manning the Bonins and the 2,285 civilian laborers and prostitutes who had been transported unwillingly to the Bonins by Imperial General Headquarters.

From command headquarters on Chichi Jima, Tachibana, Mori, and their key officers met for more than a month to rehearse a script written by Major Horie. Battalion commanders questioned their officers and enlisted men, those who had been in direct contact with the flyers, and those who had never been involved with the prisoners but served in units where flyers had been taken for execution. The senior officers thought they had identified their areas of vulnerability—the foreign laborers who disliked their oppressive Japanese masters and had been forcibly brought to the island—so Tachibana sent his officers to shut their mouths by using persuasion through intimidation. Of more concern were the drunken officers' parties. The participants could not remember who was there, what they said, who might have seen them, what the guards might have heard, or the nature of the scuttlebutt passed from the officers' mess by cooks to the sentries posted outside. The officers understood the damage that could be caused by the circulation of rumors and strove to silence the tongues of the conscripts. Everyone must read from the transcript. There can be only one story: the one created by Major Horie, the general's clever chief of staff.

As September 1945 came to a close, Horie believed he had pinpointed every officer and enlisted man who needed to be drawn into the cabal. He designed what statements they should make to American inquiries, and he made certain that those statements created credible and consistent testimony. He gave the unwritten script its final touches and rehearsed it one more time. Horie understood the consequences if the truth began filtering through the wall of deception, but he could do no more. What details he may have missed gave him constant worry, but he assured Tachibana and Mori that the Americans would never discover the truth. So the two commanders and dozens of their subordinates tried to relax while waiting for the Americans to come.

After the formal signing of the surrender in Tokyo Bay, the U.S. Navy initiated a program designed to demolish Japanese defenses and repatriate the defeated survivors to the home islands as quickly as possible. With so many fortified islands bypassed during the war in the Pacific, the chore would take months. For an American force involved in the work of peaceful occupation, there could also be danger. Because of the unpredictable nature of the Japanese military mind, entry into the former

Among the first to leave Chichi Jima are repatriated prostitutes and their families, most of which were Koreans or Chinese sent to the island by Imperial General Headquarters. (Courtesy of Dr. Eugene F. Poutasse. Digitally enhanced by Wendy A. Webster)

enemy's zone of control required a force strong enough to get the·work done without a resumption of fighting or an unnecessary loss of life because of samurai mischief or booby traps.

Chichi Jima presented a potentially explosive situation for the Navy, so the command center at Guam sent a hard-nosed Marine colonel by the name of Presley M. Rixey to deal with Tachibana and Mori. To clean up the island, the Navy also sent the 1st Battalion of the 3rd Marine Regiment. Their mission: to keep the Japanese in line and demilitarize the island. Rixey evidently had the talent for putting the fear of the Almighty into some of his Marines. When young PFC William J. Monks of Brooklyn, who was then a proficient Browning Automatic Rifle (BAR) man, was asked to describe Rixey many years later, Monks said, "I can't. I never looked at him. I don't know if any enlisted men really looked at him. It was like looking at God, and I don't think he liked people staring at him." Aviation Ordnance Man Third Class (AOM3c) Robert J. Gath, on temporary duty from the Navy, characterized Rixey as "tall, handsome, intelligent, and a 'Poster Marine,' " which agreed with the general consensus of others.[2]

On a heavily overcast afternoon on 6 October 1945 the destroyer USS

During the search for clues into the identities of missing flyers, Marines sort through the belongings of Japanese during the repatriation process. (Courtesy of Dr. Eugene F. Poutasse. Digitally enhanced by Wendy A. Webster)

Trippe, flying the Stars and Stripes, steamed slowly into the bay of Futami Ko. On deck stood Colonel Rixey, orienting himself with the rocky heights surrounding the island as *Trippe* entered the bay. Through a thin haze he could see to the north the battered town of Omura, once the location of Fortress Headquarters, and deeper into the harbor the remains of Admiral Mori's seaplane base. Beyond lay the harbor of Futami Iwa—old Ten Fathom Hole—and the Japanese naval station at Bobitai. To the south he spotted the sand-colored runway of Susaki airfield, built a few meters above sea level where waves from the ocean once coursed their way between two rocky outcroppings. He raised a pair of binoculars and scanned the lush, green island with its high cliffs. The setting looked peaceful, except for some of the fortifications his trained eye spotted hidden among the hills. A veteran of Tarawa and Saipan, Rixey had seen defenses like that before. There he commanded the 1st Artillery Battalion, 10th Marines, 2nd Marine Division, and used his pack howitzers to smash enemy defensive positions much like those he observed on Chichi Jima. In the days to come, he would learn that his pack howitzers would have barely made a dimple on some of Chichi's gun emplacements.[3]

Colonel Presley M. Rixey (USMC), commanding the occupation forces in the Bonin Islands, sits with his dog on the island's Marine memorial. (Courtesy of Dr. Eugene F. Poutasse. Digitally enhanced by Wendy A. Webster)

A Japanese flag flew from the radio tower above Special Navy Base Headquarters at Bobitai, where Admiral Mori could look out his office window and watch as the American destroyer stood off Omura. Soon a pair of diahatsus (armed power boats) shoved off from shore and moved across the harbor toward the destroyer.

Rixey waited on deck as the launches came abeam and the first Japanese delegates began climbing the ladder to come on board. "It was then," said Rixey, "that I first came face to face with the members of the Japanese liaison mission."[4]

The two keys players in the charade—General Tachibana and Admiral Mori—remained ashore, sending Major Horie and a few trustworthy delegates to cooperate with the American staff in fulfilling the surrender terms. Even though he avoided the meeting, Tachibana wanted to make a good impression. He understood what would follow: the complete demilitarization of the island, the destruction of weapons, and the repatriation of some 22,000 men, including 8,000 on Haha Jima and a few hundred more posted on Ani Jima and Muko Jima. Tachibana wanted the same thing—nothing more or nothing less than personal repatriation—and the sooner he and his officers got off the island, the better.

Before sending Horie to the meeting, Tachibana took the major aside and spelled out the limitations of the conversation. He told Horie to be cautious but courteous, dignified and cooperative, and to not let anyone else do the talking but the interpreter. He also made it clear what the interpreter should say to deflect unwanted statements by any of the mission members. Though Horie could speak a little English, Tachibana told him to speak only Japanese. He must say nothing about prisoners of war and offer no information on any matter unless directly asked. He must also let the Americans think he can speak only Japanese so that he might overhear and understand conversations that the Americans might discuss among themselves. If the Marine colonel asked about captured flyers, Horie and his mission were to respond according to the script. As a group they must act cooperatively, remain quiet, and let Horie do the talking. Tachibana expected that the Americans would bring their own interpreter, but he rather hoped they would not.[5]

When Tachibana's delegates gathered in *Trippe's* wardroom for the opening conference, each stood, announced his name, made a polite bow, and settled into his seat. They presented a mixed group. Major Horie, a pleasant and well-dressed young man about thirty, wore a welcome though disingenuous smile. The others seemed nervous, and Rixey did not care whether they relaxed or not. He observed that Horie wanted to be agreeable and sized him up as a man well practiced in the art of gracious behavior when in the presence of superiors. Other delegates included Lieutenant Commander Ichiro Shinoda of the Imperial Navy. In an effort to establish common ground with the colonel, Shinoda mentioned that he had once visited Annapolis in a Japanese man-of-war. The colonel nodded, perhaps wondering whether Shinoda might also have visited Pearl Harbor on 7 December 1941. Captain Kimitomi Nishiyot-sutsuji, a member of Horie's staff, explained that he had once been a viscount of Japan's nobility. Rixey was no more impressed with Nishi-yotsutsuji's credentials than the Imperial high command who made their distinguished viscount a mere army captain. Most of the Japanese envoys understood a little English, but none appeared to be fluent. The delegation also included a supply officer from each of the two services and Cadet Sergeant Shigeyasu Oyama, who had lived in Hawaii as a young boy, spoke fluent English, and acted as Horie's interpreter.[6]

The meeting went swiftly. Rixey's team consisted of Captain John H. Kusiak, operations officer, First Lieutenant John F. Alspaugh, adjutant, and Lieutenant (jg) A.H. Jones, U.S. Navy (USN), interpreter and recorder. After discussing arrangements for evacuating the island and repatriating military personnel, Rixey turned to Major Horie and blandly asked a leading question, "And what became of the American flyers you captured on these islands?"

The colonel expected a denial, but Horie surprised him, answering without so much as blinking an eye,

Yes, we captured six. All Navy, I think. They received very kind treatment. Two were sent to Japan by submarine. The last four were unfortunately killed by your own bombs in an air raid against these islands during the capture of Iwo Jima in 1945. They were blown up by a direct hit. I was very beloved of them and wished them no harm. We buried what remained of the bodies after cremation. This is Japanese custom.

Horie later produced a certified document, dated 13 October 1945, explaining the incident. His document contained a masterful combination of half-truths, partial truths, complete truths, and massive lies. As Rixey would eventually discover, the document served as the centerpiece for the Japanese cover-up. Horie wrote it and Tachibana approved it. The pitfall, however, emanated from a combination of conscience and self-preservation on the part of its author, the wily major.[7]

At first the plausibility of Horie's response seemed credible—too credible, in fact, for Rixey to accept without additional proof. He knew of the raids against Chichi, the tactical reasons for neutralizing Susaki airfield, and the importance of silencing the radio stations when Marines assaulted the islands of the central Pacific. But Horie's admission that flyers had been captured came as a surprise. During the past month in Japan no such information had been given to the U.S. Navy—the assumption being that flyers lost during sorties against the Bonins had ditched at sea and not survived. The Navy listed the flyers as missing in action and presumed dead. Rixey wondered why Horie would *admit* that prisoners had been taken unless he "suspected that we knew more than we did. Somehow this story did not ring true," Rixey recalled, "yet we nodded our heads in belief."[8]

During the meeting the colonel fastened his eyes on Oyama's face and noticed how the interpreter frequently blinked and became uneasy every time someone mentioned missing American flyers. It occurred to him that Oyama, who had lived in Honolulu, might not have developed the true Japanese warrior's Bushido spirit, having learned in Hawaii the occidental values of American fair play.

Rixey decided not to press the issue at the conference table. He needed to know more about three flyers named by Horie—Hall, Dye, and Vaughn—and especially a fourth, whose name the major could not remember. He became intensely curious by the reaction of the major's delegation to his question, but he decided it would be best to let them believe that he accepted Horie's story. Yet from a single leading question had sprung a number of new concerns. Where were the flyers' personal belongings, and why were the flyers left in the open when air raid shelters were available? Why did the authorities in Japan not have their names, and what were the full identities of the four men Horie spoke of cremating and burying on the island? More important, were there only four flyers and not more? Because of Oyama's discomfort every time someone mentioned flyers, Rixey changed the subject for fear that "Oyama would spoil our little game."[9]

At the end of the conference Rixey asked Horie, "What is the name of the Japanese officer in whose custody the four prisoners had been kept?"

Horie replied, though with obvious hesitation, and said, "Major Sueo Matoba, commander of the 308th Battalion. It was his men who detained the flyers."

"Then Major Matoba must appear on the destroyer tomorrow."

Horie looked a little startled but agreed, bowed, and departed. Though he had personally tutored Matoba, Horie knew that the major did not like Americans and could not predict his behavior. As he disembarked from the *Trippe*, Horie worried that he would have to speak with and perhaps coach Matoba again, a chore he considered personally distasteful.

Rixey later learned that after the meeting ended and the Japanese mission embarked for shore, Oyama turned to Horie and said, "Do not be too sure. Maybe you have not fooled the Americans. They are thorough and you will hear more of this from them. I have lived among them."

"It is done," Horie curtly replied. "We must stick to our words. I believe our prepared story will deceive them. They will find no evidence. Bones and belongings have been thrown into the sea by [order of] General Tachibana."[10]

Between the departure of Horie's mission and the appearance of Major Matoba the following day, Rixey attempted to learn through Navy channels the names of flyers missing in action among the Bonins. The colonel did not expect an immediate answer, nor did he get one.

Matoba's arrival on board the *Trippe* the following day gave the Americans their first look at the body language of a Nipponese "Bushido" samurai warrior. For centuries every Japanese boy from the time he became old enough to toddle was taught the code of Bushido. It meant "the way of the warrior," stressing loyalty above all else to superiors and loyalty without question to the emperor. It was ignominious to surrender to the enemy—much better to kill him or to kill one's self. Under Bushido the little fellow pays, and when practicing the Bushido code, deceit, treachery, and murder become acceptable traits when used to achieve the warrior's objective. Because Bushido, though prevalent in the home islands, ran contrary to the published Japanese code of military conduct, the government never ratified the 1929 Geneva Convention's Prisoner of War articles. Prime Minister Hideki Tojo admitted that when he gave instructions to his commanders, he told them: "In Japan we have our own ideology concerning prisoners of war which should naturally make their treatment more or less different from that in Europe and America." Rixey did not need a lesson in Bushido to understand its meaning. "What we think is decent and count on when dealing with other people, means nothing to the Japanese. His notions of honor are entirely different from ours."[11]

Rixey instantly disliked everything about Matoba, especially his attitude. The major stood five feet ten inches tall, wore a perpetually insolent smile, and was, as Rixey observed,

a picture of the cruel type of Jap military man. He was larger in stature than the average Japanese. He held himself very erect and as he took his seat he folded his hands on the table in an arrogant manner. He had bowed only half as low as the others. His white shirt collar, open at the neck, showed a bull throat. The hair on his head was very short, cropped in true Army fashion, and his face showed not the least emotion. The most cold-blooded eyes I had ever looked into were half-closed. One would gather he was completely bored with the whole proceedings.[12]

In many respects, though much younger in age, Matoba resembled General Kuribayashi, who had committed suicide during the last days of fighting on Iwo Jima. The two men were the same size. Both weighed about 200 pounds, all of it hard muscle. Like Kuribayashi, Matoba had received similar training, became a harsh disciplinarian, grew up as a samurai warrior, and had pledged devotion to duty and to the emperor. As a military man who someday hoped to become a general, Matoba fashioned his life after Kuribayashi. During the war he intended to save Japan from invasion, but unlike Kuribayashi, he never got the chance. Now that the war had ended, he became determined to save Japan and himself from additional disgrace. He did not expect Americans to understand his ways, and he really did not care—not until he faced the probing questions from this American colonel.

Rixey looked into Matoba's black eyes and asked, "Major, why did you not protect these flyers like you protected yourself and your men in air-raid shelters?"

The colonel's abrupt question, coming without the social formalities exchanged with Horie's mission, jarred Matoba. He changed his expression to one of surprise and stiffly replied, "Sir, I regret the neglect of my troops. My adjutant was given strict instructions to properly care for the Americans. I believe your raid came upon us so quickly that my men had little time to act."

Rixey decided the war had not ended for Major Matoba. "You were responsible as Commanding Officer for their safe-keeping," Rixey scolded. "You should have quartered them in a well-protected shelter. Your neglect has violated the rules of International law. I shall hold you personally responsible. There will be further investigations. Tomorrow you will produce the enlisted men who were actually on watch over the prisoners."

The colonel watched as Oyama translated, noticing Matoba's suppressed paroxysms of irritation as the demand struck home. He rubbed his neck vigorously and glowered at Oyama, as if the words were the interpreter's and not the colonel's. The atmosphere turned hostile. Matoba's anger began to fester. He glanced at Horie, who nodded as if to say, "You must do as the colonel orders," so Matoba rose, saluted, grunted, and hastened from the destroyer.

Rixey listened intently when his operations officer, Captain Kusiak, asked Horie, "Were the ashes of these Americans buried as prescribed by the rules of war, and did you or Major Matoba erect a cross over the site of the graves as is usually done in the Christian religion?"

"Yes, sir," replied the affable major. "A large cross was placed over the American grave." He remained thoughtful for a minute and then quickly added, "We rendered military honors."

After two days of talking with Horie's mission, capped by a day of questioning Matoba, Rixey now smelled the proverbial rat. He understood the Japanese military mind well enough to know that downed pilots would not be buried with honors. Repatriated Allied prisoners from camps on the Philippines and Burma related nothing but horror stories of forced labor, harsh treatment, starvation, and executions. Marines captured on every island from Wake to Okinawa met with torture and death, never burial with military honors or with crosses to mark

While waiting for the Marine battalion to arrive, the USS *Wilson* (DD-406) remains on guard in Chichi's harbor. The two white buildings in the background
on the left mark the site of the battalion's campsite. (Courtesy of Dr. Eugene F.
Poutasse. Digitally enhanced by Wendy A. Webster)

their graves. Perhaps the Japanese handled prisoners differently on Chichi Jima, but after questioning Matoba, Rixey thought otherwise. Before
Horie disembarked from the destroyer the colonel looked the impish
major straight in the eye and said, "We want to come ashore tomorrow
to view the grave, and to have a photographer take a picture for my
official report to the Commander of the Marianas at Guam."[13]
    On the morning of 10 October Rixey, his staff, and twenty military
policemen from the Fleet Marine Force landed at the naval base—the
first Americans to set foot on Chichi Jima since the surrender. He cau-
tioned his men to observe and not ask questions. Horie met the party at
the pier and welcomed them to the island. He pointed to waiting staff
cars whose sides and tops contained multiple punctures from bomb fragments. Noticing that General Tachibana and Admiral Mori were not
among the group, Rixey sent for them to report at the dock, and several
minutes they arrived in battered staff cars. After a few ceremonial
exchanges, Rixey explained his purpose. The Japanese commanders nodded and followed in their cars. The others separated according to pecking order. Rixey decided he did not like Tachibana or Mori any better
than he liked Matoba.

Spewing a cloud of exhaust and dust, the cranky vehicles jerked and bucked along the coastal road to Omura. From there the cars rumbled partway up a wooded hill to the Daikonzaki Army Cemetery overlooking the harbor. There among the tombs and markers the Americans saw a neat grave covered with small rocks. Placed upright in the plot stood a three-foot cross. At first sight everything seemed properly placed and in meticulous order, but Rixey stood silent and aghast. The cross, made of new wood, showed no sign of being exposed to the elements for more than a single night. Rixey would not learn for another four months that Matoba, after returning to the island, asked his adjutant how to construct a cross and what dimensions to use. As Rixey suspected, the freshly implanted cross, without so much as a rusty nail, had not been in the ground twenty-four hours.[14]

During the afternoon the Japanese enlisted men who allegedly stood guard over the flyers came aboard the destroyer. Rixey peeled them away from Horie's mission and turned them over to Lieutenant Jones, the Navy language officer. They represented a six-man machine-gun squad from Matoba's 308th Battalion, and they came aboard the destroyer dressed in their very best uniforms. Judging by the fits, Jones suspected they had to borrow some of the clothes from their fellow comrades.

Jones understood exactly what Rixey wanted and questioned each man separately. Every soldier told exactly the same story and used the same words when describing the fate of the four airmen. According to Matoba's and Horie's own statements, the deaths had occurred "about" eight months previously, but each enlisted man recalled the exact spot and the precise time of death *to the minute*, the direction of flight of the American bombers, and the number of bombs dropped. But to questions concerning what the flyers wore—the color of their uniforms and insignia on their flight jackets—all but one man drew a complete blank, became visibly disturbed, and did not know how to answer the question.

Sergeant Bunsuke Sugawara, the NCO of the Machine Gun Section, claimed to be eating in a cave used as an air raid shelter when the flyers were killed. The prisoners, he said, were also eating. They were kept in an unlocked house sixty yards from the cave and could have come into the shelter for protection but chose not to because they were also hungry and eating. A bomb fell on the house, leaving nothing but a hole, and killed them all. Sugawara was the only witness who attempted to describe what the flyers wore—"jumpers," an obvious answer—but not all of the same style or color, though he thought they were "green." His answers to most questions were either yes or no, and he became visibly confused when asked to expand on something he said. After questioning the sergeant, Lieutenant Jones remarked, "Sugawara is a bright man, but he is hiding something." Rixey made a mental note to learn more about

The burial site the Japanese hurriedly constructed to substantiate their cover-up. The freshly cut cross and the green bamboo surrounding the grave fooled no one. (Courtesy of Dr. Eugene F. Poutasse. Digitally enhanced by Wendy A. Webster)

this man Sugawara, who evidently saw something the others did not, and if that were true, then it might be possible that every other man in the machine-gun squad may have seen nothing at all.

Major Matoba missed a point when he forgot to describe the flyers' clothing to the enlisted men. When they departed for shore they all looked worried. Jones wondered whether the men's apprehensions emanated from being unable to answer the questions or because Matoba, after hearing of the problem, would beat them.[15]

For the next two months Rixey met almost daily with General Tachibana's mission, always probing in subtle ways for more information about the flyers. He found it strange that not a single record had been kept. No one seemed able to describe an article of any flyer's clothing. There were no identification tags, no rings, no watches, or weapons, not a solitary personal belonging or even an American penny. It began to look as if the Japanese had fabricated the whole story and that no flyer had ever ditched on Chichi. The reason would not become clear until several months later.

In September 1945, after Tachibana and nine of his officers went on board the destroyer *Dunlap* to sign the surrender agreement, the general returned to island headquarters and ordered all articles belonging to the Americans thrown into the sea from the cliffs overlooking Ani Jima Strait. As Rixey recalled, "Old Tachy" (as he sometimes called the general) "tried hard to cover his footprints." The colonel made no new discoveries into the missing flyers and decided to postpone an investigation until his Marine battalion arrived. He needed evidence and a more persuasive way of getting it. He had seen the work of Japanese executioners on the islands of the central Pacific, and he trusted no one. "Our task . . . appeared hopeless," Rixey lamented some years later, "yet we never gave up."[16]

While marking time on the destroyer, Rixey put the Japanese to work clearing up the wreckage around the harbor and repatriating the first 3,000 soldiers to their homeland. At first he did not realize that Tachibana and Horie were carefully inserting into the repatriation list many of the officers and enlisted men who witnessed the fates of the flyers. Both tasks, however, proceeded at a snail's pace. The Japanese military demonstrated little interest in tidying up the island and left the work mainly to Korean *gunzokus*. The former Japanese navy lost so many ships during the war that only a decrepit destroyer stopped infrequently at the island to pick up the next batch of processed military personnel. The delays worked to the colonel's advantage by keeping more key personnel on the island, some of whom would later become helpful in shedding light on the deaths of American flyers. The delays also made more men available for job assignments, and the colonel's staff put idle hands to work building a camp for the Marine battalion on the way from Guam.

During the fine weather of autumn, Rixey traveled about the island with an interpreter, never straying too far from the harbor. The Japanese became accustomed to seeing him, as did the Koreans. The colonel remained aloof, taking in the marvelous scenery of the island while inspecting the harbor fortifications he had been sent to destroy. After a few days he realized that the Joint Chiefs of Staff made the right decision when they decided to invade Iwo Jima instead of Chichi. He had witnessed the defenses on Tarawa and Iwo and wrote:

Nothing previously seen can compare with the coast and artillery defenses surrounding Chichi harbor. Concrete emplacements high in the mountains with steel door openings are too numerous to count. Artillery and machine gun fire which could have been placed on the airfield would have prevented *any* . . . attempt at a landing there. With camouflage as practiced by the Japs in place, [naval gunfire] spotters would have had a very difficult time locating these cleverly placed positions. . . . The emplacements have to be seen to be appreciated. The Jap plan was to permit an entrance into the harbor or onto the airfield, then to give us the "works." Most of these positions are inaccessible and many could not have been reached by [naval gunfire] as they are situated on narrow slopes facing east.[17]

As daylight broke on the morning of 13 December 1945, three LSTs (landing ships, tank) chugged across the bay of Futami Ko and disembarked a reduced battalion of 500 Marines. For Colonel Rixey, the long-awaited day had come. His staff hustled the battalion into their newly arranged campsite with orders to clean themselves up and report to headquarters for the official flag-raising ceremony.

At ten o'clock the Japanese garrison, led by Lieutenant General Tachibana and Vice Admiral Mori, began collecting at the naval base. High-ranking army and navy officers, wearing their finest uniforms, fell into line on one side of the base radio tower. Above, on a stubby flagstaff, flew the Japanese flag. Every officer carried for the last time his samurai sword. Then came 800 Japanese enlisted men, a small number picked from the 20,000 men still on the island. Some of them perhaps wondered if the ceremony was merely a ploy to get them before a firing squad. They came to attention and stared pensively at their national emblem drooping atop the tower.

Every Marine from the 1st Battalion filed into place across from Tachibana's 109th Infantry detachment. "It was an eerie sensation," Bill Monks recalled. "There just a few yards from us were those God damn sons of bitches, out in the open at last. . . . They appeared so small and harmless, yet we knew what a horrible fate we would have faced if the situation had been reversed." Every Marine among them had heard of Wake Island, Singapore, and the Bataan Death March. "These bastards,"

The Marine battalion stands at attention as the flag-raising ceremony is about to begin. In the background is the LST that landed the battalion during the morning. (Courtesy of Dr. Eugene F. Poutasse. Digitally enhanced by Wendy A. Webster)

Monks added, "had never shown any mercy to their captives. Yet here they were; docile, compliant, and behaving like they had come to participate in a grand and festive event."[18]

At 10:15 A.M. all watched as the emblem of the Rising Sun tumbled down the flagstaff. A Japanese color guard composed of two soldiers folded the flag, carried it to the American side, and presented it to Colonel Rixey. The colonel strode over to where the Japanese staff stood at attention and handed it to Tachibana. The fat little general saluted and tucked the flag under his arm.

At 10:25 the Marine drum and bugle section sounded colors and everyone present, American and Japanese alike, raised their hands in salute as Old Glory winged its way up the staff. As the Stars and Stripes touched the peak, Captain John Kuziak stepped forward and read the proclamation of occupation, directing that all powers of the government of the Japanese empire be suspended. It probably came as some relief to Japanese enlisted men when Major Horie came forward and read the same address, confirming that all existing customs, religious beliefs, and property rights would be respected. No Marine could deny that the occasion climaxed a bloodless invasion of the Bonins and the beginning of

During the surrender ceremony on Chichi Jima, the Japanese come forward to lay their swords on a table. (Courtesy of Dr. Eugene F. Poutasse. Digitally enhanced by Wendy A. Webster)

a peaceful occupation of Chichi Jima. On that day, such were their thoughts. Even the colonel observed: "The Japs loved a ceremony even if they were on the losing end." One newly arrived Marine wrote proudly: "On December 13, 1945, the American flag returned to Chichi Jima after 117 years." Some of the Marines had been at Iwo; some had fought on Guam. The moment became unforgettable, and a few tears flowed down the cheeks of even the toughest old Leathernecks.[19]

Veteran Japanese officers, especially those who had fought on other battlefields, reacted without enthusiasm. General Tachibana stared blankly into space throughout the ceremony. Admiral Mori fumbled with buttons on his uniform. Major Horie smiled respectfully. Major Matoba squinted, his jaw set hard against his teeth, his black eyes cold and inscrutable. Pensive frowns furrowed the faces of other officers, men such as Commander Shizuo Yoshii, Captain Noburo Nakajima, Lieutenant Colonel Kikuji Ito, and Captain Kesakichi Sato. They harbored hidden concerns, deeply rooted in the recent past. Their careers had ended ignominiously. They must have wondered, Was the worse yet to come?

Others smiled, radiating cautious glances of deliverance. The military had pulled them out of the reserves and sent them to Chichi, and now

During the surrender ceremony, Colonel Rixey receives the sword of Vice Admiral Kunizo Mori. (Courtesy of Dr. Eugene F. Poutasse. Digitally enhanced by Wendy A. Webster)

they were going home. Their cities and homes had been bombed, their families put under great stress, and they felt a driving compulsion to get back to loved ones and help rebuild what four years of war against the Americans had destroyed. They hated the island for what it had done to them, and they hated the ruthless officers who had ruled it.

Everyone watched as Tachibana and Mori stepped forward to lay their swords on a table. Then came the officers, all in single file and arranged by rank, each surrendering his sword until it seemed that the table could hold no more. With the surrender of the last sword, Colonel Rixey declared:

I accept these swords in the name of the United States of America. The raising of the American flag and surrender of all officers' swords signifies the actual termination of Japanese rule over all islands of the Ogasawara group. The establishment of United States occupation of Muko Jima Retto, Chichi Jima Retto, and Haha Jima Retto, is hereby proclaimed at ten minutes to eleven on 13 December 1945. We shall demilitarize these islands for all time. We shall destroy all evidence of war. I hope these islands will be rebuilt into a peaceful land.

As the colonel concluded his acceptance of surrender, Lieutenant James T. Sanders, a Navy chaplain, delivered a prayer in memory of

At the end of the surrender ceremony, a Marine MP (Military Police) stands guard over more than a hundred swords that will later be distributed to the Marines. (Courtesy of Dr. Eugene F. Poutasse. Digitally enhanced by Wendy A. Webster)

those who gave their lives on the battlefield and at sea. Following the prayer everyone uncovered and bowed their heads as a Marine bugler sounded taps. Then it ended, but not for everyone. Unknown to all but those who formed the inner sanctum of Colonel Rixey's staff, the hard work was yet to come.[20]

For most of the 500 Marines who attended the ceremony the short tour on Chichi would be the last of their military career. They wanted it to be over. Rixey rewarded them with a bonus: a much-prized samurai sword from the pile collected the preceding day, two Japanese Nambu pistols, and a pair of binoculars. All soldiers liked souvenirs, especially when they did not have to remove them from dead bodies rotting in some sweltering jungle. The Marines packed away their trophies and went to work demolishing the fortifications.[21]

Something about the "brown-skinned devils" irritated the men of Company C. "They were continuously smiling and bowing to us, polite and cooperative," Monks recalled.

All our knowledge of the Japanese added up to a fearless enemy who showed no mercy. We rejected them as if they were not human. We wanted payback for

Even the Japanese love a ceremony. As their flag descends from the flagstaff on the radio tower, they salute as the Stars and Stripes are raised to the peak. (Courtesy of Dr. Eugene F. Poutasse. Digitally enhanced by Wendy A. Webster)

the utter misery they had caused us. The atom bomb was not personal enough. I would not have been surprised when we landed on Chichi if some guy had yelled out "GET A ROPE."[22]

Had there been such a guy, his call for a rope would eventually be heard—but not for another twenty-two months. Nor did all the Japanese who surrendered that day deserve to get the rope. Hidden among the pack were more than a hundred men who could fit together pieces of a puzzle that would write a new chapter of diabolical warfare committed against helpless prisoners of war.

CHAPTER 4

Return of the Natives

On 16 December 1945 a bright winter sun bathed the island in warmth as an old beat-up Japanese coast guard cutter pushed through the chop and pulled up to the navy pier at Bobitai. Rixey watched as "[a] most interesting and presentable group of civilians debarked." Making inquiries, he learned the company consisted of twenty-five-year-old Fred Savory and his three uncles, Samuel, Roger, and Willie, and a cousin, Richard B. Washington, all former inhabitants of the island. To the colonel they seemed a curious lot, being neither Japanese in appearance nor behavior, though they had apparently come from Japan.[1]

As soon as Fred stepped off the cutter, he asked to speak to the American officer in command of the island. He spoke of journeying with his uncles and cousin more than a hundred miles across war-torn Japan to hitch a ride on a ship headed for Chichi Jima. Fred came because he had a goal: to get back home to see the Stars and Stripes raised on the island of his birth.[2]

The Savorys arrived too late to witness the flag-raising ceremony, but Fred had a more perplexing mission on his mind and went directly to the colonel's office at the "White House," a stately building near the navy base that had somehow escaped serious damage during the 1944–1945 air attacks. Rixey shook hands with the unexpected visitor, a tall young man of five feet ten inches, deeply tanned, and physically fit. He had thick black hair and a trimmed mustache, and his brown eyes looked you straight in the face. He spoke perfect English and perfect Japanese. At first Rixey did not realize the importance of this articulate young man, for Fred Savory was about to become the agent for cracking open an investigation into the puzzling disappearance of American flyers. The

This view of Chichi Jima's harbor shows a view of the "White House" in the foreground, Marine barracks near the pier, and the rugged surrounding landscape of the island. (Courtesy of Dr. Eugene F. Poutasse. Digitally enhanced by Wendy A. Webster)

colonel called in his staff, and together they listened, taking notes as Fred related his experiences:[3]

Sir, in Japan, I heard certain rumors talked about by soldiers whom you have shipped from Chichi. These stories are not nice ones. I must tell you what I have heard and believe.

They are saying that their officers on Chichi executed perhaps 15 American flyers. Some had witnessed these executions. I have heard that two men were tied to stakes and bayoneted after having been speared by bamboo sticks. And, sir—there is a rumor most prevalent that in the area of the [308th] battalion, a Major Matoba ordered his medical officer to removed the aviator's liver after execution and to deliver it to his orderly. A member of this battalion believes that Matoba and a few of his officers ate this liver at a sake party the next day. From my knowledge of the Japanese military caste, I too believe this is true.

I am here to assist the Americans in bringing punishment to these officers. They have been cruel to my family and other Bonin natives of white blood. I will remain here on Chichi, my native land, as long as I can be of help. I am familiar with all areas and at one time served in the Japanese Army here when I was conscripted as a gunzoku. I interviewed an American naval flyer here but never learned his name. When the flyer refused to answer a question asked by a Japanese officer regarding the number of planes on his carrier, the officer struck the American in the face with the scabbard of his sword.[4]

Rixey digested Fred's account, recalling: "We were flabbergasted at first. We expected beheadings . . . but never cannibalism. What manner of men were these? Polite and cooperative, obedient soldiers, brave and fearless—but beneath this veneer, barbarians and worse." When Fred mentioned Matoba, Rixey expressed no surprise, for he had met the samurai warrior and knew that Matoba must be closely watched.[5]

Out of curiosity, or perhaps to test Fred's memory if not his veracity, Rixey asked, "What can you tell me about the air raids on Chichi before you were sent to Japan?"

Fred thought a moment and replied, "I recall them quite well. The first raid occurred on June 15, 1944, the second on the 4th of July, the third on the 18th, the fourth on the 19th, the fifth on the 20th, and on the 23rd of July I left the island."[6]

"Can you tell us the name of the officer who struck the pilot with his scabbard?"

"I am not certain, but I believe it may have been Lieutenant Sumiyoshi."

Captain Kusiak rifled through a pile of papers and said, "We repatriated him. He's back in Japan."

Rixey told Kusiak to contact Supreme Commander Allied Powers (SCAP) at headquarters in Tokyo and tell them to apprehend Sumiyoshi and ship him back to Chichi. Sumiyoshi would never return to the island. Knowing the reason for the summons, he committed suicide in Japan.

Fred had an excellent memory for detail, but he never asked the flyer's name. The Japanese had taken the prisoner's jacket, leaving him with only his boots and green flight fatigues. When asked about the flyer's dog tag, Fred replied, "I did not know what a dog-tag was, but he was wearing a chain around his neck."

After asking Fred a few more questions, the colonel thanked him and dismissed him, but he kept the young man in mind. Five days later he hired Fred as an interpreter.

"We now renewed our efforts with added zest," the colonel recalled. "It became a 'must' to uncover the full facts. The world would know—must know—what bestial principles lay hidden under the guise of 'bushido.' "[7]

Rixey deliberated over the problem of how to break through the silence and persuade at least one Japanese officer in authority to talk. That person must be someone who other officers and enlisted men respect and whose lead they would follow; yet that person must also be someone the colonel could trust. Only one person came to mind, Tachibana's clever chief of staff, the cooperative and pliable Major Horie. But the

Colonel Rixey might never have probed into the identities of missing flyers had Frederick Savory (pictured above) not returned to Chichi Jima with his uncles and reported what he had heard in Japan. (Courtesy of Dr. Eugene F. Poutasse. Digitally enhanced by Wendy A. Webster)

fellow appeared to be a slippery devil, and Rixey knew he would have to be patient and ply Horie with overtures of friendship.

Two incidents occurring within forty-eight hours gave Rixey a good reason to create a Board of Investigation: Fred Savory's unexpected disclosures and a curious complaint from Major Horie about problems with the Korean *gunzokus*. Horie approached Rixey with a single motive: to shed the problem of supervising a large number of squabbling Koreans by turning them over to the Marines. He did so during one of the colonel's daily liaison meetings by grumbling,

We are having trouble with Koreans in our forces. They object to working on repairing of roads and the airfield as you require. They say your President Roosevelt before he died proclaimed that Korea should be free and all Koreans would be liberated. Their group [is] headed by one bad trouble-maker [Pyungehi] Ahn [who] asks that you allow them to present their case.[8]

Rixey agreed to speak with Ahn's committee, and forty Koreans, accompanied by Horie, filed into the conference room at the White House. Charged with emotion and obviously nervous, they all tried to speak at once, demanding to be sent home. After they winded themselves the colonel explained that he intended to ship them to Japan as soon as transportation could be arranged. There they would be separated from the Japanese army, and until then they were technically still soldiers and as such must continue their labors.

Rixey noticed that his reply did not curry favor among the complainants, but his mind began to work. He wondered how many of these unfortunate conscripts hated the Japanese, what they might know, and what they might be willing to tell. With Horie and his mission present, the colonel could not be too obvious, so he carefully offered a concession. He turned to Ahn, the ringleader of the group, and said, "You must continue to work for the benefit of all. However, I shall move those Koreans who so wish into the limits of the American occupation zone. You shall work under your own leaders on projects directed by me."

The arrangement pleased the Korean delegation, and on 21 December Ahn and his forty *gunzokus* crossed the line and moved into the American sector. The Marines found room for them near the stables, provided them with tents and cots, gave them clean clothes, treated them with respect, and employed them as orderlies to watch over eighteen superbly trained riding horses confiscated from "Old Tachy's" army staff. Ahn proved to be a willing volunteer and good company for a platoon of idle Marines who needed a diversion from guard duty. PFC James W. Leary chatted with Ahn one day and learned he had been a Methodist divinity student studying in Seoul when conscripted from Korea and assigned to a forced labor brigade. At first, Ahn did not entirely trust the Americans any more than he did the Japanese, having been led to believe by the latter that the Americans intended to continue his enslavement.[9]

Not many days passed before the Koreans shed their suspicions and over the Ping-Pong table made quick friends with the Marines. The *gunzokus* began to put on weight, mixing food from the Marine's mess with their own diet of rice and fish. On occasion they attended the nightly movie, taking special interest in westerns and war films. As PFC John Monaghan learned, two of the conscripts—named Kim and Pak—did not want to return to Korea. Monaghan asked why, and they replied, "Communism." Kim and Pak asked for the names and addresses of American universities, and Monaghan got them. Such considerate treatment of the Koreans did not sit well with the Japanese, but they could do nothing about it.[10]

Rixey watched with interest the blending of the Koreans with his own Marines. Ahn and his consortium began to feel liberated when the colonel granted them candy and cigarette privileges. "I even looked the other way," Rixey recalled, "when it was reported to me that Ahn was selling 'home-made' hara-kiri knives to visiting Navy personnel." In appreciation for the colonel's kindness, Ahn decided to return the favor in an unexpected way.

The establishment of a Board of Investigation, though confidential in nature, sparked a number of rumors in the Marine encampment about what was being investigated. Whether Ahn heard the scuttlebutt is debatable, but he had been sharing his thoughts with Lieutenant Oliver, the colonel's intelligence officer. Late one night, and a few days before Christmas, Oliver slipped Ahn into Rixey's sleeping quarters at the weather station. Though visibly nervous, Ahn opened the conversation and in surprisingly good English said, "I have been very anxious to speak to you. I created a situation in the Japanese forces hoping I could contact you with information of value."

Rixey noticed Ahn's sudden ability to speak clear English when not in the presence of his former employers. The colonel also observed that many Japanese, as well as Koreans, did not wish to expose their knowledge of English. The Japanese preferred having an interpreter speak for them, enabling them to buy time to formulate answers when questioned.

Ahn continued, more calmly now, and said, "Among the Koreans now under American control are six of us who are loyal to the United States. The others I cannot trust. Many are true Japanese with relatives living on the mainland. A few would be loyal but they fear retaliation from the Japanese here and in Japan."

Rixey understood Ahn's concerns but assured him that no harm would come to any Korean on the island, and he doubted that there would ever again be reprisals in Japan.

While Ahn paused to collect his thoughts, the colonel offered him a cigarette. Ahn took it, sucked in the smoke, and blew it to the side. When he opened his mouth to speak, he almost shouted, as if the long years of suppression could no longer be contained. "I . . . heard of an execution of an American flyer near Okumura in July of 1944." Ahn paused between puffs, and the nicotine seemed to settle his nerves. "It is said that Colonel Ito supervised the beheading and that there were about 100 Japanese troops at the scene. The American was very brave. He refused a blind-fold. He was smoking a cigarette when they tied his feet. I believe he was an officer but I never heard his name."

Ahn paused again, reflecting on the past. "Other Koreans have heard of executions. One at the [Yoake] wireless station high in the mountains, supervised by Commander Yoshii, who was sent to Japan seriously wounded in 1945, and another killed by the Torpedo Boat Squadron near the navy base."

Ahn did not have his facts quite straight, but a year had passed. He admitted being uncertain of the exact dates, but he emphasized that most of his information came from conversations he held with trustworthy *gunzokus*. Much of what Ahn related sounded credible and increased Rixey's suspicion that the number of American flyers captured by the Japanese on Chichi Jima far exceeded those mentioned in the innocuous report provided by Horie. There were also many unanswered questions about the treatment of flyers, so the colonel plied Ahn again by asking, "What else have you heard?"

Ahn nodded as if he expected the question and said: "I have heard that Major Matoba ordered his doctor to cut out the liver of an American aviator after the beheading. This liver was cut into small pieces after drying. Matoba's adjutant placed the pieces in the soup eaten by the enlisted men. I am sure that Matoba has eaten human flesh. He made Navy officers eat some flesh taken from the thigh of the body. Many of the Navy officers vomited when told its true character. I have heard that the major bragged about this trick on the Navy. His men hate him. He kicks and hits them with his fist. They are afraid and will not talk."

"How certain are you that all this is true?" Rixey asked.

"I would not tell you this unless I felt certain. There are many men who could tell you the same."

"Who are they?"

"Private [Itsuichi] Suzuki was in charge of the supply department of the Ryodan Shireibu (Brigade Headquarters) and knows all about the rationing of human flesh. Superior Private Wakabayashi told me that the men in his company received flesh in the soup and ate it. I heard that in the 308th Battalion a Japanese doctor cut open the stomach of an American flyer, and that Lieutenant [Yasuo] Kurasaki ate human flesh, too. He had it cooked and ate it as a side dish while drinking sake."

"There is still something that seems to be bothering you," the colonel said.

Ahn hesitated, then replied. "Yes," he said. "I saw human flesh in the soup served to us, and the men said it was very tasty because it did not have any fat on it, but no one enjoyed it."

Rixey shook his head solemnly and asked, "Do you know anything more about the flyers?"

"I think the flyer who was taken to the [Yoake] wireless station was named Jimmy. My friend, who was standing guard, heard the name mentioned, but I can only remember Jimmy. Corporal Hajime Hiroishi should remember all the names because he interpreted for the flyers."

Rixey thought for a moment. Horie had given him the names of three flyers, Vaughn, Dye, and Hall. Could Jimmy be the first name for one of them?

"Who executed the flyers?" Rixey asked.

"I can't say, but I know that men from my company were once involved."

"Did the orders come from General Tachibana?"

"I believe they all came from someone in the general's office to either Warrant Officer [Yanagizawa] Matsuyoshi or the third company commander, Captain Mariyama."

Rixey paused, because he needed names, especially the names of those directly involved. "Did the men ordered to execute the flyer also bury him?"

"Yes," Ahn replied. "Three bodies are buried at Nagatani. I can show you the exact location. One man, Tsuguo Obdora, took the identification tag off the body. It is possible that he took it with him to Japan."

Rixey thanked Ahn and bid him a good night.

As Ahn departed he turned and said, "I will listen to the talk of my Koreans each night, and I will report everything I hear to Lieutenant Oliver."

After the door closed, Rixey turned to Oliver and asked, "What is your assessment?"

"I think Ahn is telling the truth, at least as he believes it. He did not see any of those crimes committed; he only heard about them. But I believe most of what he said is true."

"What about the names he gave us?"

"I have already checked them out with SCAP. All the enlisted men have been repatriated to Japan, but some of the officers are still here."

"Good. We will eventually want their testimony, so tell Captain Kusiak to keep them here."[11]

When on 21 December 1945 Colonel Rixey formed the Board of Investigation, he designated Major Robert D. Shaffer as officer in charge. He

Pictured from left to right are Lieutenant (jg) Daniel N. Williams, Frederick Savory, and Shigeyaso Oyama, all of whom served as interpreters. (Courtesy of Dr. Eugene F. Poutasse. Digitally enhanced by Wendy A. Webster)

assigned Fred Savory to the board as interpreter, but he also knew that Fred could provide valuable insight into the quirky statements he expected to hear from the Japanese summoned for questioning. Other members of the board included First Lieutenant Wilburn Caskey, U.S. Marine Corps Reserve (USMCR); Lieutenant (jg) Eugene F. Poutasse, U.S. Naval Reserve (USNR) Medical Corps; and Lieutenant (jg) Robert E. Parcell, USNR, an attorney who Rixey asked to lead the questioning. As time passed and the investigation progressed, Rixey added other members to lighten the board's load. Lieutenant (jg) Daniel N. Williams, USNR, shared interpretive responsibilities with Fred Savory, and PFC Donald K. Buth, USMCR, acted as reporter.[12]

Shaffer had more on his hands than the investigation. He came to Chichi with the principal task of directing the destruction of the island's military fortifications and facilitating the repatriation of the Japanese military force. The Marines had barely begun their work of demolition when Rixey wrote ComMarianas and asked for a delay in the timetable to allow his board to finish its investigation. Shaffer jockeyed his time between the laborious tasks of listening to Fred Savory translate testimony, which occurred almost every other day, and the demolition work performed by Marines and navy personnel who had come from Guam.[13]

The Marine battalion wanted to finish the job and go home. They were mostly a fun-loving, restless lot of late-war enlistees who preferred civilian life to the womanless islands of the Bonins. At Guam, many of them felt cheated as some of their buddies shipped home while they remained behind as the loose ends of war. Three months later they filed on board LSTs bound for Chichi Jima for a few weeks of occupation duty, a little demolition work, and then freedom—or so they thought. No one anticipated the scope of the colonel's investigation or the enormous number of concrete fortifications buried in the hills. They had witnessed the comings and goings of Major Horie's committee, never suspecting that those daily discussions were about to be overshadowed by months of investigation. None of the brass explained the reasons for the delays, and the silence made the enlisted men irritable.

The men of Company C, 1st Battalion, 3rd Marines, got their first look at the island on 13 December as they entered Futami Ko. They gaped at the string of fortifications ringing the heights as they approached the bomb-scarred ramps of the seaplane base near Bobitai. Someone remarked, "Those carrier planes sure knocked the hell out of this place." Then they scanned the sharp, up-thrust rocky heights rising steeply along shore and changed their minds. "We were literally struck dumb by the Jap defenses," Bill Monks recalled.

Nothing previously seen in the Pacific could compare with the coast and artillery defenses surrounding Chichi harbor . . . the only suitable landing area for an invasion. We all agreed that the whole Corps would have bought it on Chichi. Iwo was hell, Chichi impossible. Sailing into that bay we should have been kneeling on the deck thanking God that we passed this one up.[14]

The gun emplacements the Marines observed as they entered the harbor represented only a small part of the island's network of defenses. During the next several days detachments of Marines hiked high into the hills and discovered concrete bunkers with thick steel doors, some so well hidden they could not be seen until the work party stumbled upon them. As the men roamed the hills overlooking Futami Ko, they uncovered shielded artillery emplacements so huge and numerous that only a massive effort by thousands of construction workers could have built them over the course of the war. To the demolition teams from Company C, it became obvious that the enemy intended to lure an amphibious force into the harbor and then open fire on the waves of Marines as they struggled ashore. After wandering over the island, Monks declared,

The cliffs surrounding the harbor are filled with antiaircraft, though none can be seen through photographic lenses. With few exceptions, cliffs surrounded Chichi Jima, making it almost impossible to assault. (Courtesy of Dr. Eugene F. Poutasse. Digitally enhanced by Wendy A. Webster)

The emplacements dug into the sides of the mountains were so plentiful that it gave the island the appearance of a block of Swiss cheese. They must have worked on the fortifications for at least 30 years. It was no doubt the Gibraltar of the Pacific. . . . The surface damage on the island was quite extensive, but . . . we hadn't scratched their defenses, which were expertly concealed underground and in the sides of the mountains.[15]

Demolition teams spreading across the island found stairs leading to gun emplacements buried in the hills. Some structures concealed huge naval guns, and how the enemy hoisted such heavy pieces into the nooks and crannies of the rocky heights mystified the teams charged with destroying them. An elaborate network of tunnels, some large enough to hold two-and-a-half-ton trucks, led to fuel and ammo dumps embedded deep in the hillsides. Marines found generators the size of boxcars installed underground and surrounded by concrete walls three feet thick.

On Kiyose, above Okumura, Marines discovered a huge air-conditioned vault dug into the side of the mountain. They found it by entering an unpretentious cave thirty feet long and being stopped in front of a thick copper-lined bank-vault door. Breaking through the door,

How the Japanese emplaced a six-inch naval gun into a concrete revetment carved into the side of a mountain amazed the Marines sent to demilitarize the island. Demolition crews found twelve such guns on the island. (Courtesy of Dr. Eugene F. Poutasse. Digitally enhanced by Wendy A. Webster)

they entered a massive vault 144 feet deep and 16 feet wide lined with copper sheathing. Ninety feet away they ran across two more vaults, one 90 feet deep and the other 50 feet deep, connected together by a 60-foot tunnel. Puzzled by the copper lining and an elaborate exhaust system, those who inspected the vaults speculated on their purpose. Rumor spread that the caves had been built to store the Imperial archives if the Allies attacked the Japanese mainland. Another rumor called it a holding vault for the emperor's treasure. Others suggested the Japanese had built a bunker system for hiding the Imperial family. Major Horie said the vaults were meant to be "the final stronghold of the Nipponese Island Empire," whatever that entailed. The Japanese on the island added to the guesswork, some believing that the vaults were meant to store Adolf Hitler's heavy-water A-bombs. The actual purpose of the caves remains a small mystery. The Americans put them to use a few years later, using them to hold atomic bombs during the Korean War because the Japanese would not allow such weapons on the mainland.[16]

The work of demolition progressed at a snail's pace. Most of the Marines had nothing to do, so a few of them formed a salvage crew, lugged jackhammers into one of the copper-lined vaults, and went to work cutting out rivets that held the copper sheets together. A few hours later the men began falling off scaffolds. "We didn't know what the hell was going on," one Marine recalled, "till it dawned on us. The gas generators at the mouth of the cave driving our jackhammers were pumping in carbon monoxide. We carried the guys outside and shut down the operation."[17]

Time passed slowly for the enlisted men. They began to notice that Colonel Rixey spent an inordinate amount of time entertaining Japanese officers. His stern composure had softened. He smiled and laughed, and so did Major Horie and the rest of his band. It seemed unnatural for the colonel to treat the enemy with so much congeniality. Questions began circulating through the ranks, questions like, "What's the colonel doing with those damned Japs all the time?" Others replied, "The colonel knows his business. He's just doing his job." Then someone else said, "But he's getting too cozy with those bastards." Another voice piped in, "Shut your damned trap. The old man just wants to get us off the island." "Yeah," another said, "and it can't be too soon for me. I got a gal back home, and if I don't get there pretty damned quick, she'll probably up and marry some guy who got a ticket home."

So the chatter continued, day after day. Few Marines ever saw the colonel in the campsite. He spent all of his time at the White House. The battalion had too few demolition men and too many grunts to get the work done swiftly. While the hills rumbled and shook from explosions, the bulk of the Marines idled through each day looking for something to do. From their perspective, Rixey did not seem very interested in putting them to work or getting them back to the States. He ordered no inspections, no drills, no calisthenics, and not much guard duty for the brigade because the Japanese behaved well and remained inside their sector. Company officers and NCOs let the men roam the American sector without restraint. Neither the company commanders nor the platoon leaders knew that the colonel had selectively slowed the repatriation process. If destroying fortifications took a little longer, so much the better for the investigation. Rixey was far too busy courting the Japanese to schedule activities for the enlisted men, so the boys devised ways to amuse themselves.

One day Company C woke up and spied a large supply ship in the bay. Word circulated that she carried refrigerated stores, so men from the company volunteered to unload her. They stacked cartons of fresh turkey and steak on the beach, piled up crates of oranges and grapefruit, and built a mountain out of the beer, Coke, and Chocolate Cow. The battalion had no way of keeping articles such as turkey and steak fresh. There was not an ice cube on Chichi, so Company C lugged the entire load up to the caves. Bill Monks, whose memoirs captured the company's shenanigans, wrote:

We had about 200 men in the unit and enough fresh food off that ship to keep a regiment of 5,000 supplied for more than two or three months. I don't know what the opposite of scurvy is, but it looked like we were about to die from it. There was only one thing we could do, and that was to set a new record for gluttony. Never did so few eat so much. We gorged ourselves day and night. In the evening we built fires on the beach and had beer and steak parties. We ate steak for breakfast, turkey for lunch, and steak again for supper.

Finally we noticed the steak and turkey were turning blue, and the oranges and grapefruit were putting on fur coats. We just couldn't eat anymore and had hardly put a dent in the food mountain. All the meat and fruit in the caves suddenly turned rotten. WHEW! We dumped nine-tenths of it into the bay. By morning it was all over the beaches, and we ended up burying it. We finally went back to basics: powdered eggs and dehydrated potatoes, etc., but we still had plenty of beer, Coke, and Chocolate Cow.[18]

During the days of idleness, PFC Jerry Candelaria discovered an off-limits warehouse behind the noncom's quarters. It contained a cache of enemy artifacts—everything from samurai swords to machine guns. The company commander never bothered to post guards, so one day Jerry and his buddies walked by and noticed that the roofing material sagged about every twelve inches: a tip-off that the Japanese had never bothered to lay wood over the roof's trusses. One Marine suggested that by cutting three sides of the roofing paper a small man could be lifted onto the roof and dropped between the beams. Once inside, he could scoop up enough treasure for two men to carry and, when leaving, could roll the roofing paper back into place and stick it fast with thumbtacks. One dark night at 2200 hours two volunteers made the attempt and lugged the loot back to their tents under ponchos. A pipe-smoking NCO sitting on a porch spied the pair returning but said nothing. Others took advantage of the loosened roofing until there was nothing left inside but heavy weapons. By the time the officer in charge discovered the theft, nobody much cared.[19]

The colonel paid little heed to the stories he heard about his mischievous Marines, but AOM3c Bob Gath, a Navy demolitions expert, finally got his attention. Gath had taken an English-speaking Japanese prisoner with him to help blow up a gun emplacement. Along the way they came upon an elaborate thick-walled concrete building tucked inside the mountain. It had double doors with a spoke wheel. Gath thought the doors might be booby-trapped and sent the prisoner to open them. "You can imagine my bulging eyes," declared Gath, "for there before me lay the colonel's stash of booze; cases and cases of neatly stacked Kinsey, more than enough for the company." Gath never confessed how much he drank. Every Marine on the island knew that the colonel liked his whiskey. He eventually discovered the theft but not the thieves.[20]

The colonel began to run out of patience because of his pestiferous

Officers from all over the Pacific stopped at Chichi Jima for souvenirs. In the wardroom of a Japanese freighter, Captain John H. Kusiak, Rixey's chief of staff (second from left), and Lieutenant Eugene F. Poutasse (third from left) acted partly as liaison and partly as the entertainment committee for visitors. (Courtesy of Dr. Eugene F. Poutasse. Digitally enhanced by Wendy A. Webster)

Marines. One day he noticed a ragged man dressed in filthy mustard-colored fatigues drawing C1 and C2 charges at the ammo dump. He turned to Captain Kusiak, pointed, and said, "Is that a damned Jap drawing explosives over there?" Kusiak leaped from the jeep and came face to face with PFC James Leary, who had turned almost as yellow as his fatigues and looked more Asiatic than the Japs. Because he held packs of charges in his arms, Leary could not salute, so he waited stiffly for Kusiak to speak.

"What the hell happened to you, private?" the captain hollered.

"Well, sir," Leary replied, "I ran out of explosives up in the hills and found some picric acid. I knew the stuff would blow, and it worked just fine, but I didn't know it would turn me yellow."

Shaffer shook his head and chuckled. "Carry on, private, but you better change your fatigues before an MP picks you up and shuffles you over to the Jap sector."[21]

When Kusiak explained the situation to the colonel, Rixey said, "You know, John, I think we've got too damn many Marines on this island.

When you get time, radio ComMarianas and see if we can't shed some of these men."[22]

The board spent the first seven days of its investigation talking to members of the Savory clan. Shaffer needed a starting point before calling the first Japanese witness. He found the testimony of Fred and his uncles consistent, credible, and provocative. Their eyewitness accounts, though spiced with rumor and hearsay regarding claims of executions and acts of cannibalism, varied only slightly in detail and tended to corroborate Ahn's meeting with Rixey. After digesting the Savorys' statements, Rixey told Shaffer to get on with the investigation.[23]

On the afternoon of 28 December the Savorys completed their testimony, and they said enough for Rixey to begin "piecing together each bit of information hoping to draw the net tighter around those Japanese who had violated all human ethics and principles of treating captured prisoners. However," he added, "we were stumped at every turn."[24]

Shaffer had now gathered a list of many names, all potential eyewitnesses to the allegations made by the Savory family. As for irrefutable proof, he had none, only what others had heard through a grapevine that stretched from Chichi Jima to Japan. Rixey blamed Tachibana and Mori for the outrages, but he could not build a criminal case against either officer with only Ahn's statement and the testimony of the Savory clan.

Richard Washington, Fred Savory's cousin, told the board that the Japanese had "chopped a flyer's head off down near the present Memorial for the Japanese War Dead, and [another] flyer was executed near the [Yoake] Wireless Station. After they executed them," said Washington, "they cut them up and gave out the pieces to the different battalions."

"You understand that both of the flyers were eaten?" asked Lieutenant Parcell.

"Yes, sir," Washington replied. But when asked if he had actually seen the executions, Washington said, "A Korean told me."[25]

Faced with a schedule for "buttoning up" Chichi, Rixey asked Kusiak whether any word had been received from ComMarianas regarding an extension.

"Not a word," Kusiak replied.

"Well, something has to be done and done quickly," the colonel replied. "It's time to play our ace in the hole. We have to pull Horie in from the Japanese liaison mission and pick his brains."

"Horie's a slippery little devil."

"But he's also intelligent and a regular Army officer. He has an eye for grasping an advantage. He probably knows as much about what happened on this island as 'Old Tachy' himself. He's probably also involved in this mess and wants an easy way out. I will have to drop my official air and gain his friendship and confidence."

"You're taking chances, colonel," Kusiak warned. "There are some tough old Marines on this island, sir, and they will misinterpret your intentions."

"I have no choice. Either I befriend Horie or drop the investigation. Without Horie's cooperation we may as well wrap this job up and let the damned cannibals go free. You know me, John. I can't let this happen."

"It's your call, colonel," Kusiak replied. "I'm with you all the way."[26]

And then it began, the campaign to win the confidence of Major Horie, because, as Rixey said, "[t]here was a higher prize to be gained. We will have to endure the stares of our associates to get to the root of the evil that hangs like a diabolical stench over this island."[27]

CHAPTER 5

The Entrapment of Major Horie

The colonel's courtship of Major Horie began the very next morning. In addition to Captain Kusiak, Rixey drew two other members of his staff into the scheme, Chief Warrant Officer Cox and Lieutenant Alspaugh. All three men had participated in the daily conferences with Horie and his Japanese mission. During the discussions, Cox and Alspaugh had sharpened their instincts about the major and provided the window dressing Rixey needed to give the façade authenticity. The Marines and the Koreans working at the stable looked twice when they observed Rixey and his staff cantering about the island on horseback with Horie, who always wore a happy smile. The colonel appeared to be enjoying his rides with Old Tachy's crafty chief of staff, and the Marines began to grumble among themselves. One night when Rixey brought Horie and his friends into the movie theater—a former garage—the Marines walked out. The colonel became furious and threatened to "hang the instigators from the yardarm," as if some form of mutiny had been perpetrated. Regarding allusions to the yardarm, Bill Monks observed: "There was a little Navy in every Marine." Rixey did not want his plans corrupted by a bunch of pestiferous malcontents, but he never caught the instigators of the walkout or asked the Navy for a yardarm.[1]

On New Year's Eve 1945, the colonel decided to literally "uncap the bottle" to see what pearls of information might spill from Horie's lips. He invited the major to go riding and brought along Alspaugh, orderly PFC David W. Mahaffey, and two Army officers from Iwo Jima who had stopped for souvenirs on their way to Japan. He told the Army officers nothing of his plans and asked Alspaugh to keep them amused.

At the termination point of the cross-island ride, officers of the battal-

One of the windfalls on Chichi Jima were the fine horses owned by Japanese officers. Colonel Rixey frequently rode through the area on horseback, followed by other members of his staff. (Courtesy of Dr. Eugene F. Poutasse. Digitally enhanced by Wendy A. Webster)

ion had established a beach house as a sort of riding club "19th hole." Rixey arranged for the bungalow to be empty and set the stage for Mahaffey to produce from his saddlebags, the moment the men dismounted, a fifth of fine bourbon from his private stock that had previously been stored in a no-longer-secret cave.

With everyone chilled from the morning ride, they tied their steaming horses outside a small Japanese shack near Miyano Hama beach and entered a bare, unfurnished room. As they sat on straw mats in cross-legged Japanese fashion, Mahaffey passed around glasses, ginger ale, and the bottle. "We all drank with relish after our stiff cool ride," Rixey recalled, "and I watched [as] Horie's face reddened."

The major soon relaxed and dropped his semiofficial composure, bantering back and forth with his newfound friends. He humorously referred to himself as B.T.O. (Big Time Operator), a title given to him by Lieutenant Alspaugh. He bragged about hanging a sign on the main harbor road near his new command post that read, "This way to office of B.T.O.—Major Yoshitaka Horie." The colonel encouraged the bragging, and Mahaffey kept Horie's glass filled.[2]

Major Yoshitaka Horie also enjoyed horses, and those rides through the country with the colonel eventually led to revelations about the systematic executions of American prisoners. (Courtesy of Dr. Eugene F. Poutasse. Digitally enhanced by Wendy A. Webster)

Rixey flashed Alspaugh a prearranged signal, and the lieutenant got to his feet, stretched and yawned, said he wanted to inspect some nearby caves, and urged Mahaffey and the two Army officers to join him. After the four men departed, Rixey reached for the bottle and poured Horie a "real super-slug of bourbon," which the major tried to refuse. But Rixey, who could hold his liquor, poured one for himself, clinked his glass against Horie's, and both of them drank. Horie understood English much better than he spoke it, and when the rosy glow that an excessive amount of bourbon can produce tinted his features, Rixey poured him another drink and said: "I consider you the only true soldier among the Japanese I have seen on Chichi."

Major Horie appreciated the compliment and from his sitting position smiled and politely bowed.

"You probably are the only officer who knows anything about international law and the Rules of Land Warfare as set forth in the Geneva Convention."

Horie acknowledged the truth of Rixey's comment with another bow.

"I have seen and admired your defenses," the colonel said. "As a military man I appreciate what you did for your Emperor and your country. I consider you my friend and I need your aid."

The words touched off a faint alarm. The major straightened a bit and asked, "Yes?"

Rixey knew he had tripped the spring but not quite caught the rat. He would never get another chance. All his cards had to be tossed faceup on the table.

"You may not know it, major, but I have much information about what occurred on these islands before the Americans arrived. I know of executions and other acts that followed these killings. I know also that you were not involved."

Rixey had no way of being certain whether Horie played a part in the executions or could have used his influence to prevent them. The investigation had neither implicated nor vindicated Horie, but from informal inquiries made by his staff he suspected that the wily major might never have committed a war crime. Rixey chose his words and made his proposition carefully because he suspected that if Horie agreed to talk, he would want some guarantee of immunity from prosecution. Fixing his eyes on Horie's, Rixey probed and, to give the major something to think about, said, "My investigations have convinced me that you apparently tried to befriend captured American aviators. You warned General Tachibana and Major Matoba that they were violating the rules and they paid no heed, and you advised them to send all captured prisoners to Tokyo for interrogation as the Japanese Army general staff ordered."[3]

Horie sat motionless, his head lowered and his eyes fixed on the glass of unfinished bourbon. Rixey waited for a sign, a gesture, a comment, but none came. But he knew he had Horie's attention and continued the pursuit.

"Major, I view this investigation as a crusade. I must have the facts, and I shall not rest until I know the full truth. Those guilty must be punished." Horie looked more interested when Rixey added, "I will protect you because I know you are not guilty of any wrongdoing. You lied to me on the *Trippe*, but I forgive that. You were acting under orders of your senior officers . . . it is understandable that you attempted to protect them. But I now appeal to your friendship and your honor as a true brave soldier. I give you the opportunity, here and now, to correct your misrepresentation by telling me the whole truth of what transpired."[4]

Horie now knew that the colonel had arranged everything: the ride to the beach, the bottle of bourbon, the departure of the others, and finally, the private conference to find the truth. At first he must have felt deceived and entrapped, but those feelings quickly passed. He reassessed the colonel's forthright and unexpected expression of protection. The ride in the brisk winter air, the disarming bourbon to loosen his tongue, and the expression of friendship during the past several days all coalesced into a final moment of decision. The major remained silent. Seconds passed as he mentally studied his options, perhaps pondering his honor or maybe his disappointment, but Rixey's appeal offered a rare opportunity—self-respect and a life without shame. On the other hand there were certain of his fellow officers, men who still wielded power within the ranks. What would they think? More important, what would they do? Brand him a traitor? Murder him? He knew them as executioners. They killed for revenge and killed without compunction. Killing a traitor would give them pleasure. They were, after all, Bushido warriors who never liked him. Such thoughts, and many others, must have flowed through Horie's mind.

Horie raised his head and fastened his eyes on the colonel. He studied those eyes for a long time, searching for assurance but uttering not a sound. The major's face reddened, and Rixey must have wondered: Was it rage or embarrassment? Then Horie began to shake his head from side to side, as if something that had confused him suddenly became clear, and then he grunted, as if the irony of his entrapment deserved special recognition for such dexterous duplicity.

Rixey sensed the conflicts brewing in Horie's thoughts. He reached for the bottle and poured the major another drink, but Horie only smiled, as if to say: "I need no more."

Having read Horie's mind, Rixey said softly, "You are now under American protection and thus you can speak freely."

Horie nodded, for he believed that this American colonel *would* protect him. Slowly and deliberately he said, "Yes, colonel, I have known that you must know all these things soon. Cadet Oyama warned me. The Savorys and the Koreans must have told you something." And to affirm Rixey's pledge of protection, Horie fastened a hook into the colonel by adding, "Now you are my friend, and I believe as you do. I am not a war criminal."

Horie sighed, and for a few moments he quietly reflected in silence. He probably remembered the time he spent with the American flyers. He tried to keep them nearby so they could teach him to speak better English. He could not question them with effect because the flyers had trouble understanding him. He was curious about America and asked one aviator, "How many street cars are there in St. Louis?" probably because he had heard Judy Garland sing about them in a movie.[5]

"The principle that I believed was that my country was fighting America and not fighting one or two prisoners of war," Horie said, shaking his head sadly, "and I firmly believe in this principle. I was beloved to your aviators. They were brave men. I tried to save them but the devil was in my general. He ordered all executions in retaliation for Japanese troops killed by your bombings. There were 11 total. Now give me a pencil and paper," he said firmly, for the remorse had vanished, "and I

Major Yoshitaka Horie became the star witness for the investigation and the trial at Guam. Some members of the Board of Investigation never completely trusted his testimony, but without the cooperation of the major, they may never have found the answers to any of their questions. (Courtesy of Dr. Eugene F. Poutasse. Digitally enhanced by Wendy A. Webster)

shall write for you all the names of those guilty of crimes on these is-lands. I shall go with you to arrest them tonight."[6]

Rixey needed the records of the flyers—those kept by the Japanese after the capture. Then the investigation could move swiftly. All the loose ends would come to the surface. In two or three weeks he could begin to close down operations on Chichi and send most of the men home. He produced a pencil and notebook from his pocket and handed it to Horie. Then he asked, "Who kept the records on the flyers?"

"I did," Horie replied, "but towards the end of the Iwo Jima campaign I burned them."

Rixey gasped. "By whose orders?"

"On my own initiative."

"Was there a copy made?"

"Yes. I sent it to Captain Kanji Harashima, the intelligence officer at Brigade headquarters."

"Does that copy still exist?"

"I know for a fact that it does not. Captain Harashima destroyed it on General Tachibana's orders, along with all the personal belongings of the flyers."

"So what is left?"

"Nothing. Absolutely nothing."[7]

The colonel tried to conceal his disappointment. He had Horie on the hook and did not want to lose him, but he had to ask, "Then the report you gave me when we first met on the *Trippe* was false?"

"Yes. I am now ashamed of the fact that I was chief of staff to General Tachibana."

"Did he instruct you to falsify the report?"

"No. I falsified the report and issued the order. I brought the question before General Tachibana and he approved it, but General Tachibana issued a general order that no one was to say a word about the American flyers."[8]

While Horie scribbled the names of the officers involved in the exe-cutions, Rixey asked, "Are there men in the 308th Battalion who will talk openly about these executions?"

"If you question men in front of Major Matoba and General Tachibana, they will not tell the truth, but if you question them privately, I believe they will talk. Major Matoba would beat such a person. Major Matoba and General Tachibana are friends, and it is very dangerous to be in their presence when they are together. They are both heavy drinkers, and they keep no one's company but their own."[9]

Horie finished writing and handed the notebook back to the colonel. At the top, written in clear English, was the name of General Tachibana, commanding general of the 109th Division, followed by the name of

Admiral Mori. Next came division staff officers, battalion line officers, and finally Tachibana's adjutant, Captain Seiji Higashigi.

Major Horie reached for his drink and finished it. He wore the look of a man relieved but humiliated. The colonel assured him of the solidarity of their friendship and said, "We will start the year right. The men on your list will be arrested and confined tomorrow, New Year's Day. You will come to my quarters and stay with me, as I intend to protect you."

"I will stay with you tonight," Horie replied, "but I have no fear for my life once General Tachibana and Major Matoba are in the stockade."[10]

Rixey called a late afternoon meeting at headquarters and gave Horie's list of names to Major Shaffer. "They are to be arrested in the morning," the colonel declared.

Shaffer anticipated no resistance, the possible exception being Major Matoba, commanding the 308th Battalion. He dispatched 1st Lieutenant Joe England to Company C with orders to recruit six men for a special mission. The lieutenant stepped into the first tent where he heard voices and said, "How about six volunteers?" The tent contained Bill Monks and his buddies.

"Nobody in the Marine Corps volunteers for anything," Monks recalled, "but we were all bored stiff. We were tired of playing baseball, tired of swimming, and tired of watching whales. One of our bazooka men considered getting his weapon and shooting one, just for the experience of chewing on fresh blubber, but he restrained himself. So when the lieutenant came bursting into our tent clamoring for volunteers, we looked at each other, said 'what the hell,' and volunteered. That's when we learned that the lieutenant wanted us to arrest Major Matoba, the 'Tiger of Chichi.' "

Lieutenant England worried that apprehending Matoba could turn violent. The Japanese, though they were supposed to stay in their sector, always kept an eye on what transpired in the American camp, so as a precaution the patrol concealed their weapons, extra ammo, and steel helmets in two seabags.

"Early in the morning New Year's Day we placed our seabags in the bottom of our boat," Monks recalled, "which had a load of garbage on board. We crossed the bay to Omura disguised as an unarmed working party. We looked harmless, wearing only our helmet liners, dungarees, and boondockers."

After slipping into the bay, the volunteers crouched behind the bulkheads, assembled their weapons, and jammed home a clip. "We wanted to get in and out fast," Monks said. "Our orders were to rush Matoba's house and drag him back to the boat . . . before any action could be taken to defend him, or before he committed Hari-Kari [sic]."[11]

Matoba stood out in a crowd. He towered over men like Horie and

View of the 1st Battalion Marine encampment at the Japanese seaplane base. Two sunken hulks can be seen offshore. (Courtesy of Dr. Eugene F. Poutasse. Digitally enhanced by Wendy A. Webster)

Tachibana. Every man in the Japanese 308th Battalion feared him. A bear of a man with the temper of a demon, Matoba knocked men about as if they were made of tinsel. His reputation as an excellent swordsman, a martial arts expert, and a sadistic bully made him an unpredictable foe. In order to succeed, the patrol's mission had to be performed rapidly so as not to attract attention or cause a riot.

"We hit the beach," Monks recalled, "and had one hell of a hill to run up. Japs stood on the side of the road wondering where the hell we were going. We hit Matoba's house and the lieutenant goes through the door. I remember absolutely nothing about what happened there, but I learned later that we fetched Matoba while he stood in a pink bathrobe beside his phonograph. I can faintly remember holding a BAR in my hands as I came down the hill, grateful that nobody fired upon us."[12]

While the patrol transported Matoba back to the base stockade, another detachment sent by Major Shaffer arrested Tachibana and several of his staff officers as they were preparing breakfast. A third detachment arrested Admiral Mori and six naval officers. Others came when summoned by Major Horie, who now had the dubious distinction of commanding the division. By the time Tachibana and his consorts entered the hastily built stockade, on which Ahn and the Koreans had labored with unabashed delight, they all knew the reason for their arrest. They scowled at Horie, whom they knew had broken their bond of secrecy.

The imprisonment of Tachibana and his officers quickly began to pay dividends. Later in the afternoon a Japanese soldier approached one of the outposts that separated the boundary between the American and the Japanese sectors and handed the sentry a letter. The note did not reach headquarters until 4:00 P.M. and, because it was written in Japanese, required translation. The Officer of the Day sent the letter to Shaffer, who promptly summoned Lieutenant Williams to come to headquarters for a translation. When Shaffer read the translated note, he noticed that it had been addressed to Colonel Rixey from "Personnel of the 308th Battalion in charge of POW[s]." Dated the previous day, the letter read, in part:

The facts concerning prisoners of war related to you up to the present are false, and even when recently summoned aboard a United States vessel and questioned, lies were reported as ordered by superior officers. At present, a large number of those ordered to stay behind at Chichi Jima as responsible parties are not responsible parties. The truth of this will be definitely established if you summon and question severely 1st Lieutenant [Bunji] Enomoto, the deviser of the above scheme. . . . The authorities have been extremely cautious, fearing the truth may leak out, even to their own subordinates. If they know that we have secretly informed the American authorities, it is impossible to know what oppressive measures they will adopt [against us]. We beg that the American authorities devise their best plans in this regard. Moreover, we request an examination at the earliest possible instant.[13]

The letter came unsigned, but having originated in the 308th Battalion, Rixey suspected from his conversation with Horie that the authors belonged to Matoba's machine-gun squad—the same group of men who had lied to him on the *Trippe*. He asked Horie for confirmation. The major knew the men of the machine-gun squad and suggested that Rixey speak first with Sergeant Sugawara, whom he believed had written the letter.

Late on New Year's Day, Shaffer summoned Sugawara and his machine-gun squad and ordered them to come to headquarters for a conference. The men were quartered a half mile north of the White House and arrived about thirty minutes later. "My staff and I waited at the long table in our conference room," Rixey recalled. "This appeared to be the 'pay-off' and we were jubilant. Soon the Japanese marched in. All bowed and [took] seats along the opposite wall."

Colonel Rixey wanted no chances taken with an unpredictable bunch of ex-machine gunners who served under the oppressive tutelage of Major Matoba. The enlisted men became disturbed when they noticed two

Superior Private Pyungchi Ahn (seated) with three of his Korean *gunzokus*, all of whom testified during the investigation at Chichi Jima. PFC John Monaghan remembered searching all over the island for enough materials so Ahn's men could build a stockade. (Courtesy of Dr. Eugene F. Poutasse. Digitally enhanced by Wendy A. Webster)

of their officers, Lieutenant Bunji Enomoto and Captain Noboru Nakajima, seated about ten paces away. Warrant Officer Cox sat benignly at
the table with a .32 caliber pistol hidden in the pocket of his shirt. Two
guards armed with Thompson submachine guns stood across from each
other near the back of the room.

Using Fred Savory as interpreter, Rixey pulled the letter from his
pocket, held it up high for everyone to see, and said, "Who present
knows about this letter?"

No one moved. No one made a sound. As if pasted to their seats, the
members of the machine-gun squad sat transfixed, heads half bowed,
uttering not a word.

"Mr. Savory," the colonel said, turning to his interpreter, "please read
the letter."

Fred complied, but the men of the 308th remained mute. Shaffer noticed movement. Enomoto and Nakajima, seated off to the side, shifted
nervously and glanced in the direction of the enlisted men. The sudden
movement disturbed the two guards, and they brought their guns to the
carry. The unexpected motion alarmed everyone.

Rixey's expectations of crashing through another barrier in the cover-
up had failed to produce any results. He considered removing the Japanese officers, but he wanted them present to observe their reactions
when the enlisted men betrayed them. He had to find a way to break
the impasse. He could not talk to them directly, only through Fred, so
he chose his words carefully.

"Do not be afraid to talk," the colonel said, hoping that one or two of
the Japanese might understand what he said in English without involving Fred Savory's translation. "You are free and your lives will be protected by American arms. Now tell me which of you wrote this letter."

The Japanese once again proved themselves unpredictable. To Rixey's
astonishment the entire group of enlisted men rose in unison, leaving
their amazed officers fast to their seats. Sergeant Sugawara paid no deference to his former superiors and replied, "Yes, we wrote the letter. We
wish to return to Japan and our families. We regret our falsehoods to
the Americans and because of your fair treatment, we will now tell the
truth. We were told we would be slaves," Sugawara said, casting a quick
glance at Captain Nakajima. "Now we know this is wrong. We believe
in Democracy and wish to be free civilians. We will each give full facts
. . . concerning the deaths of American flyers."[14]

The notion that Americans intended to enslave the Japanese population should have come as no surprise to Colonel Rixey. The Imperial
Empire had first conquered and then enslaved the Koreans. American
prisoners of war who were fortunate enough to be sent to Japan labored
for months and some for years in Japanese coal mines. Corporal Andrew
D. Carson, who had been captured on the Philippines in May 1942, spent

a year working in the Yonoroshi coal mine. "The mine was like no other experience on earth," Carson recalled, "and the darkness enveloped me. I could actually feel its presence. I wanted to flail against it with my hands to drive it away. Darkness and silence, darkness and silence. Is this what it's like to be dead?" Carson lived to tell his story, but those who landed on Chichi Jima were not so lucky.[15]

Sugawara's statement gave the board a sudden burst of elation, but they constrained their feelings. Lieutenant Enomoto started from his chair as if to run, and a guard shoved him unceremoniously back into his seat. Captain Nakajima slumped in his chair and stared morosely at the floor. Whatever their thoughts, the two officers knew the consequences. From now on it would be every man for himself.

Rixey bound the officers over to the Military Police and sent all the men out of the room but Sergeant Sugawara. The board being present, Lieutenant Williams put the sergeant under oath, and Lieutenant Parcell proceeded with the first question. Sugawara probably did not understand the oath or feel any obligation to honor it, and nothing in the testimony of the trial suggests that Sugawara or those who testified later clearly understood the meaning of perjury. Nonetheless, no deponent ever appeared before the board without first swearing to tell the truth, though many of them lied. Shaffer was going to run the investigation by the book, even though the swearing-in ceremony meant nothing to the deponents.

Late on New Year's Day 1946, the board questioned the first Japanese soldier. For Rixey the long road to full disclosure finally began, or so the colonel hoped. He had cracked the icy silence by stubborn yet patient determination. Now it became the task of Major Shaffer and his board to uncover the truth. Shaffer would soon discover many twists and turns along the way and here and there a stumbling block. His quest for facts would not come easily, not only because the Japanese had hidden the truth but because they had thrown it into the sea.

On 15 October 1945 Sergeant Sugawara had been questioned on the USS *Trippe* along with members of his machine-gun section. None of the American officers who questioned Sugawara on the *Trippe* were members of Rixey's Board of Investigation, but the board produced a copy of Sugawara's prior statement. He admitted giving false testimony under orders from Lieutenant Enomoto. Every member of his squad received the same orders. "The whole testimony about the four flyers is false," said Sugawara, "and the story . . . was just made up. I did not have custody of these flyers, and I have never seen any American flyers on Chichi Jima. Lieutenant Enomoto instructed me exactly what to say. . . . I heard of two flyers brought from the 308th Battalion to Ryodan Shireibu (Brigade Headquarters) [but] I have no idea what day or the time."[16]

The board had hoped to learn much more from Sugawara than the

sergeant was able to recall. He admitted hearing of beheadings committed by the battalion, but he did not see them. He understood that Captain
Nakajima had given the orders, though he could not vouch for it. He
also recalled hearing that a third flyer had been beheaded near the naval
base and that at least one of the flyers may have been eaten. He did not
know their names, but he believed that Matoba and Nakajima had "eaten
the flesh of American flyers."

The board reminded Sugawara that testimony taken on board the
Trippe indicated that four flyers had been turned over to his squadron
"for safe keeping."

"The whole statement is false," Sugawara candidly replied. "My squad
had nothing to do with any American flyers. The story that four flyers
were killed at the seaplane base . . . by American bombs is an utter lie.
Also, the grave of the four flyers is the grave of only three flyers."[17]

The board excused Sugawara and called in Sergeant Major Tsutomu
Kurimoto, who had also given testimony on the *Trippe*. Kurimoto admitted collaborating with Sugawara in composing the letter because he
was "afraid that . . . along with other members of my squad, I would be
held responsible for doings of my superior officer [and] for giving false
testimony dictated to me and my companions by [Lieutenant Enomoto]."
On orders from Captain Nakajima, Kurimoto admitted digging up the
bodies of three Americans, cremating the bones, and taking the ashes up
to the Daikonzaki Army Cemetery sometime during August 1945. Kurimoto recalled a trace of decayed flesh on two of the bodies but none
at all on the third. "I took every piece of the remains I saw in the hole.
These bones were all in a heap and . . . not in the normal position of a
human body's bone structure. They were not laid out as a cadaver would
be." What Kurimoto said implied that the complete bodies of two flyers
may have been deboned and their flesh removed.

Kurimoto corroborated Sugawara's testimony but could not identify
the names of the flyers. All he saw were bones. Stones had been piled
on the common gravesite but nothing added to identify the names of the
flyers. Acts of cannibalism remained an unconfirmed rumor supported
only by hearsay. At 1:30 A.M. the board retired quite perplexed because
many of the enlisted men who had witnessed the beheadings and participated in the burial details—right down to the cooks who may have
spiced the battalion's soup with human flesh—were back in Japan.[18]

Before the questioning resumed on 2 January, the board discussed the
importance of identifying the pilots. Somebody on the island besides
Horie must have spoken to the flyers, learned their names, and witnessed
their deaths. Physical evidence could be hurled into the sea, bodies could
be cremated beyond recognition, but the Japanese soldiers on Chichi Jima
had already demonstrated good memories for detail. Despite differences
in language and pronunciation, one of the first questions to be asked of

a downed flyer would be his name and unit. The logical person to ask the question would be an interpreter. Sergeant Oyama had returned to Japan, so the board summoned Corporal Hajime Hiroishi, a signal corpsman with the brigade who had been attached to Fortress Headquarters temporarily as an interpreter. When asked about the flyers, Hiroishi replied, "I do not remember these names . . . because when the flyers were captured, they were taken to Haken Shireibu, and there they were interviewed by Major Horie and interpreter Oyama. When the liaison officer finished interviewing the flyers, they were brought together with their documents to . . . Ogiura [Ryodan Shireibu] and placed in the charge of Captain [Kanji] Harashima."

"Where is Captain Harashima now?" Lieutenant Parcell asked.

"In Japan."

The questioning continued, but the board learned only what they already knew. Hiroishi exhibited numerous lapses of memory, muddled his testimony, but specifically remembered the prisoners being sent to brigade headquarters. Halfway through the questioning he suddenly remembered that one was named Connell and the other Wolf, but he had no recollection of the third. "Two of the flyers," he said, "came from the *Hornet*."

Rixey recalled Horie mentioning four pilots whom he identified as Hall, Dye, Vaughn, and an "unknown," but Hiroishi mentioned two more, Connell and Wolf. The board already knew that Connell had been sent to Japan, so Wolf might be the "unknown." For the time being, in the absence of any better information, the board decided to accept Wolf as the unknown flyer, but the nagging question resonating through the testimony was whether there were more than four flyers involved in the Chichi cover-up. Horie had said eleven. So who were they?

Shaffer reached for Fred Savory's testimony taken on 26 December and on page 8 found both names—one spelled Connel (*sic*) and the other Wolff (*sic*) and a third unnamed pilot who parachuted onto Ani Jima. But Fred had never heard of men named Hall, Dye, or Vaughn. Perhaps, Shaffer surmised, the Savorys were no longer on the island when Hall, Dye, Vaughn, and the unknown flyer came down. The major went back to Horie's testimony and concluded that the unknown flyer must have parachuted onto the island in February 1945 and therefore could not be Wolf. If so, the unknown could not be one of the four known flyers but a fifth.[19]

Parcell turned to Hiroishi and asked, "Who is the senior noncommissioned officer in your organization who can shed more light on the names of the flyers?"

"Sergeant Major Ota."

"Where is he now?"

"In Japan."[20]

The board wore a look of exasperation. Shaffer turned to Lieutenant Caskey and said, "Try to bring Captain Harashima and Sergeant Ota back to Chichi. We need to talk to them."

Hiroishi could remember little more, only that General Tachibana issued orders for the three flyers to be interrogated and tied to trees in the garden in front of the adjutant's office. "The general's orders stated that they would not be allowed inside the building or be given shelter in case of miserable weather or bombings. Then we had an air raid," Hiroishi said, "and after that the prisoners were gone." He believed that two of them went to the 308th Battalion to be executed on orders from the general and that the other was turned over to the navy to be killed.

"Did Major Matoba kill the two flyers sent to the 308th Battalion?"

"Yes, I heard that," Hiroishi replied.

"What happened to the bodies of the two flyers?"

"I have heard . . . the bodies of these two flyers were eaten, but personally I do not believe that such a thing could happen."

Shaffer began to question whether Rixey could trust Horie and told the board to review the Japanese major's written statement. Hiroishi must have understood English better than the board realized because he said, in Japanese, "I believe that Major Horie acted on orders from General Tachibana, who said that all souvenirs from the flyers, such as dog tags, bracelets, rings, wrist watches or anything else must be burned along with all personal diaries kept by Japanese soldiers. I do not believe that any soldier disobeyed any part of this order. I also have heard that Major Horie said to every battalion, 'Don't kill the war prisoners.' "[21]

To the question whether the flyers were beaten, Hiroishi replied, "I believe that Captain Harashima beat [them] . . . with his hands. I did not see this, but I have heard of it. I took food to the flyers after dark, and after that I heard that Captain Harashima beat them once or twice. They were tied to trees for two or three days before men from the battalion killed them with bamboo spears."

"Did Major Matoba execute any of these men?"

"Yes, Major Matoba speared two of them."

"Then those flyers may have been Dye and Hall?"

"Yes. Perhaps. The other flyer, I think his name was Wolf, had been wounded in the leg and was in pain. Captain Harashima interrogated him later."

"Did a doctor attend to Wolf's wound?"

"Captain Koyama Ryo (surgeon) gave the flyer medical attention."

Believing the doctor may have learned something more about Wolf, Shaffer asked, "Is the surgeon still on the island?"

"He is in Japan."

"Then what happened to Wolf?"

"I heard rumors that he was taken to the 308th Battalion and executed with the others."[22]

There were those words—"heard rumors"—again, and after another exhausting day of testimony the board suspended the investigation at 1:00 A.M. and retired to their quarters. They felt they had gained some momentum and a little more insight into the atrocities on Chichi Jima, but the hard evidence they sought continued to elude them. But who were these men: Dye, Wolf, Hall, and Vaughn? Was there a fifth, an unknown? Were those their names or awkward phonetic translations by Japanese corruptions of the English language?

Perhaps the time had come for Colonel Rixey to get out another bottle of bourbon and speak once more with Major Horie. First there were four flyers, then three. Now there might be five and possibly as many as eleven. Was it possible the count would continue to grow? Shaffer could not get the question off his mind, and he went to sleep very late that night wondering how to unearth the truth.

CHAPTER 6

The Search Begins

Colonel Rixey did not need another bottle of bourbon to prod the memory of Major Horie or to confirm the testimony given by members of Matoba's machine-gun unit. The stumbling block became the large number of repatriated Japanese no longer on the island—men who had questioned the flyers, witnessed the execution, cooked human flesh, or participated in acts of cannibalism. The other stumbling block involved the large number of innocent Japanese officers who were still on the island but would not willingly come forth to testify against their superiors or help to identify the flyers.

After several days of testimony, Rixey and Shaffer believed, but without absolute certainty, that Major Matoba, Captain Nakajima, and Lieutenant Enomoto of the 308th Battalion performed or ordered the first executions. They also believed that whatever acts the officers and men of the 308th Battalion performed were in response to orders from General Tachibana, that Admiral Mori concurred with those orders by agreeing to Tachibana's "disposal" policy, and that at least thirty Japanese officers and enlisted men may have participated in the crimes. Each deponent added more names to the growing list of potential witnesses, and though many of them had been repatriated to Japan, the names of those still on Chichi Jima filled several pages.

Having turned the investigation over to Major Shaffer, the colonel had no clear conception of when the questioning would end. Every testimony produced more names and added more confusion to the identification process. For every question Lieutenant Parcell asked in English, Fred Savory or Lieutenant Williams translated to Japanese, and every response had to be translated back into English and recorded in order to

Major Robert D. Shaffer (USMC), on horseback, led the investigation of crimes on Chichi Jima. (Courtesy of Dr. Eugene F. Poutasse. Digitally enhanced by Wendy A. Webster)

be understood and preserved as a record. Lieutenant Poutasse took his own notes and fifty-five years later still has his records. Among the persons who listened to Horie's so-called truthful testimony, Dr. Poutasse still expresses doubts regarding the major's credibility because of inconsistencies in his statements and the testimony of others.[1]

Horie continued to cooperate voluntarily and without hesitation. He warned, however, that the testimony he gave the board was "the truth as far as I know it, but some of the witnesses [who come] after me will give testimony that will not coincide with mine, but these men will talk according to the orders I [gave beforehand]. If they tell a lie, the responsibility for that lie will be on me." This statement provides a brilliant example of how Horie could excuse himself from not quite telling the truth while claiming he did. He shifted the reason for lying to others and then took the responsibility for their lies, knowing, of course, that Shaffer's board would not blame him if some deponent during the course of the investigation contradicted what he said or became his accuser.[2]

In October, during conversations on the *Trippe*, Horie had mentioned Vaughn, Dye, and Hall, and a fourth man he could not identify. He later repudiated his statement but confirmed the three names of the flyers as he remembered them. He had questioned them personally, claimed to have cared for them, and socialized with them. Rixey and Shaffer now suspected that more flyers had been captured and executed during the early months of 1945, but Horie had not mentioned other flyers. Shaffer believed the major must have known about them and would not let the matter rest.[3]

When Horie could not recall the name of the fourth flyer, Shaffer intensified the search for the man's identity. The board recalled Horie, who remembered that two flyers had been shot down during Jocko Clark's Fourth of July air raid in 1944. The navy captured both men on Ani Jima and delivered them to the naval base at Bobitai. By an agreement between Admiral Mori and General Tachibana, the navy handed the two prisoners over to Major Horie for questioning. Horie observed that one man, Lieutenant Connell, had been badly beaten, and the other, a wounded radioman with an injured leg and shoulder, needed immediate medical attention. Horie eventually sent Connell, who had been tied to a tree for eleven days, to Japan, but the unidentified and wounded radioman, according to Horie, could not travel.[4]

Lieutenant Parcell, who led the questioning on behalf of the board, asked Horie, "By whose order was Connell tied to a tree?"

Horie replied, "I was trying to have the aviator stay in my house, but there was a strong feeling among the Japanese against me . . . having the prisoners in a house . . . so I was obliged to have the flyer tied to a tree. There was a man whose son had been killed in the air raid, and he wanted me to let him kill the flyer, but I would not permit it."

Parcell shifted the questioning to the wounded flyer who had been shoved into a garage at headquarters and given a Japanese mat. "I tried to put the radioman with Lieutenant Connell, but the plane to Japan was filled. So I kept him at headquarters where I could question him."

Parcell noted that Horie now recalled the "unknown" flyer's rating and wondered what more the major might remember. "Give us a description of the radioman."

"His face was dirty and fierce," Horie replied. "He stood about six feet tall, very thin, with closely cropped dark brown hair; he had a narrow face, and he wore blue clothes."

Parcell's persistent questioning seemed to help Horie recall more about the flyer. "I kept him in the garage until August 5, 1944. After a heavy and severe bombing raid, we moved him to my new headquarters at Haken Shireibu, back in the hills of Ogiura. I now remember his name. I think it was Wolf."

"What was done with Wolf after his arrival at Ogiura?" Parcell asked.

"I do not know," Horie replied. "Two or three days after Wolf was brought to Ogiura, I went to Iwo Jima and then to Japan, and when I came back . . . Wolf was not there."

"Who was in charge of the prisoners after you left for Iwo Jima?" Parcell asked.

Without hesitation, Horie replied, "There were many officers under me and as far as I know the one that kept the prisoner was my adjutant, Captain Kimitomi Nishiyotsutsuji."

Parcell reminded Horie that he had previously stated that Wolf had been sent to Iwo Jima. "Yes," Horie said, "this is false. . . . I do not know what happened to Wolf . . . but Captain Nishiyotsutsuji knows about it."

Parcell asked Horie why he could not remember what happened to Wolf, and the major replied, "After I came back from Iwo Jima, I heard rumors that Wolf was killed at Kominato. I was afraid to ask because it was contrary to my beliefs, and I did not want to know the fact that he was killed. I was interested in protecting the flyers."

To the members of the board, Horie's response sounded incredulously hollow, so Parcell said, "That is what I cannot understand. You wanted to protect [the flyers] and yet you did not ask questions about them?"

"During that time when I came back from Iwo Jima there were a lot of rumors and I thought that if I asked about these rumors and the aviators, I would be killed by Matoba or Tachibana so I did not ask questions about the flyers."

Parcell let the statement pass, but not everybody on the board believed it.[5]

During the course of the investigation, the board discovered that Wolf was not the name of the unknown flyer. The two flyers—the man named Wolf and the unknown radioman—would cross paths at Haken Shireibu and live out the balance of their lives together. Until May 1946 the board did not confirm that Wolf's name was not Wolf but ARM2c Lloyd Richard Woellhof, USNR, Serial Number 6286511. They never learned enough about the unknown flyer, who joined Woellhof later, to make a positive identification.

Neither Horie's testimony nor all the statements that followed could reconstruct what happened to the two flyers. Only by stitching together a labyrinth of spotty testimony could the lives of Woellhof and the unknown flyer be traced during their last days on Chichi Jima.

On 4 July 1944 Woellhof parachuted from a crippled plane, though not the plane flown by Lieutenant Connell. One of the Japanese deponents testified that the two men did not know each other. Horie eventually learned that Connell came from the *Hornet*. Both men jumped at different times, and Woellhof landed on Ani Jima.

After antiaircraft fire hit Woellhof's Curtis SB2C, the plane began to smoke and lose altitude. Woellhof lost his bearings, but he knew he was somewhere over the Bonins. Having been struck by a 25mm bullet in the right shoulder, he bailed out after the pilot, and when he landed, he injured his left leg, which also had the appearance of having been grazed by a bullet or perhaps slit by a bayonet. The Japanese on Ani Jima watched Woellhof come down and picked him up near their camp. Adhering to instructions from General Tachibana, the commander of the 275th Battalion on Ani Jima asked Woellhof a number of questions concerning the movements of Task Force 58 and then transported him across the mile-and-a-half strait to Chichi Jima. At the naval base a doctor dressed Woellhof's wounds while a corpsman removed the flyer's bloody clothes, washed them, and helped "Wolf" climb back into them.

Connell arrived at Haken Shireibu about the same time as Woellhof. Connell wore cuts and bruises on his face from a beating at the navy base, but in the end, he fared much better than Woellhof. A civilian noticed Connell tied to a tree and stopped at Horie's headquarters to get permission to kill him. Horie sent the civilian away.

On 16 July instructions came from Imperial General Headquarters to transfer the flyers to the mainland. Woellhof could not travel because of his injuries, so he remained under Horie's care at Haken Shireibu. According to Horie, he retained Woellhof at his headquarters because "there was no more room on the plane." On 17 July a motorcycle with a sidecar took Connell to the Susaki airfield, where witnesses observed him board a twin-engine Douglas transport headed for Yokosuka.[6]

At 11:00 P.M. on 4 August 1944, Japanese antiaircraft fire shot down an American B-24 over Futami Ko. The bomber crashed into the water near the navy base. One American flyer swam to the pier, climbed out of the water, and stood watching as boats from Bobitai pulled four of his comrades out of the water and the wreckage and brought them ashore. Three flyers were already dead. The fourth suffered from burns and mortal injuries. He died soon after sailors moved him into the navy sickbay. Nobody knew his name. The Japanese buried the flyer and the three dead crewmen in the Japanese Botanical Gardens behind the navy base.[7]

Lieutenant Commander Minoru Yonehara and Lieutenant (jg) Taketoshi Hasegawa proceeded to interrogate the sole survivor, the flyer on the pier whose identity will remain for the rest of his life as "unknown." His captors bound him hand and foot, tied him to a tree, and left him in the bushes near the entrance to the tunnel where Fred Savory had recently worked as a *gunzoku*. The interrogators could never decide whether the prisoner was an officer or an enlisted man because his clothes were scorched. After the initial interrogation, the Japanese left him tied to a tree outside while light cruisers and destroyers from Jocko Clark's carrier group shelled the navy base. In between raids the Japanese reminded the prisoner of their irritation over the air attacks by slapping him, the traditional Japanese method for delivering an insult.

That afternoon Admiral Mori sent the unknown flyer to Tachibana's headquarters. There a sergeant picked him up in a truck and drove him to Horie's headquarters at Haken Shireibu. Woellhof now had company—a battered radioman like himself with a name unknown except to him.[8]

Horie kept the two men outside his headquarters, using Woellhof as his English teacher. He tied the unknown flyer to a tree but not Woellhof, for "Wolf" could not wander far because of his wounds. On occasion soldiers passed Haken Shireibu and noticed the "unknown" tied to the railing leading up the stairs to Horie's office. They remembered him because he was short—about five feet four inches tall—and had a round face like themselves, but unlike his captors, he had curly red hair and wore a dirty khaki uniform.[9]

In early August Horie received orders to fly to Iwo Jima to meet with General Kuribayashi, the division commander. During his absence, Horie put the prisoners in the care of his adjutant, Captain Nishiyotsutsuji, and instructed him to keep the flyers at Haken Shireibu because he was not finished questioning them. The captain remembered Woellhof as being very weak from his wounds and always in considerable pain. When he was not resting on a mat, he sat on a chair, rarely standing or walking. Woellhof stood about five feet ten inches tall and had long auburn hair, hazel eyes, and a fair complexion. "Wolf," Nishiyotsutsuji recalled, "came from the carrier *Yorktown*. When the two flyers were not with Major Horie or tied outside, they stayed in a garage adjoining headquarters at Haken Shireibu."[10]

Neither flyer received harsh treatment at Haken Shireibu, where they enjoyed each other's company. Horie assured both men no harm would come to them, and according to his statement, he promised to send them to Japan as soon as transportation could be arranged. The two flyers spent most of the day tied at the waist, sprawling outdoors on mats and chatting under the eaves of Horie's headquarters. While there, nobody bothered them. Woellhof was still on the mend but well enough to make the trip to Japan. According to Sergeant Major Shigeo Hasegawa and Captain Nishiyotsutsuji, the two flyers reminisced about their lives back home, their families, and their sweethearts. They chatted about baseball and fishing and the fun they had growing up. They talked about the future with optimism, and they waited, one day upon another, for the promised plane that would take them off the island. During the first day of Horie's absence, Captain Nishiyotsutsuji looked after the prisoners, bringing them water and biscuits and an occasional cigarette, and then the good times ended.[11]

On the day after Horie departed for Iwo Jima, Captain Seiji Higashigi, General Tachibana's senior adjutant, phoned Horie's headquarters and demanded the two prisoners. Nishiyotsutsuji spoke with Captain

Kyuryo Isoda, the military police chief, asking if any boats had come to take the prisoners. Isoda did not think so, but he reminded Nishiyotsutsuji that prisoners must be treated in accordance with international law, emphasizing that the two flyers must be held at Haken Shireibu until transportation to Japan could be arranged. Nishiyotsutsuji did not know what to do in Horie's absence. He could not ignore an order from Tachibana's headquarters, even though he technically reported through Haken Shireibu to the division commander at Iwo Jima. Finding himself in a quandary and pressed by Higashigi, Nishiyotsutsuji felt he had no alternative but to comply with the order, but he asked that the flyers be returned to Haken Shireibu. Higashigi made no promises, loaded the two flyers on a truck, and drove away.[12]

When Woellhof and the unknown flyer learned they were being transferred to brigade headquarters, they accepted the change with enthusiasm. Woellhof believed they were going to Japan because Horie had implied as much. The two flyers probably, though quietly, celebrated their good fortune. They would be thankful to be gone from the island. They did not know that General Tachibana had waited until after Horie departed to activate his plans for their "disposal."

Higashigi knew the fate of the flyers when he called Horie's headquarters. He had already informed Lieutenant Colonel Kikuji Ito of the general's wishes and told the colonel to arrange for the flyers' executions. During a sake party after Horie's departure, Captain Katsuya Fukuda observed Higashigi approach Ito and say that he was going to detail an officer to execute the flyers in the morning. Ito recalled Higashigi coming to him and saying, "It has been decided that the prisoners should be executed by bayoneting." Later on the evening of 6 August 1944, Ito learned that his command, the 307th Battalion, had been selected to perform the execution. Higashigi also said he would "send one noncommissioned officer and one superior private as executioners." Ito did not expect to personally perform the execution, but Higashigi approached him again in the morning and asked in a most official manner, "Mr. Ito, will you please do the beheading?" Ito considered a request from Higashigi as coming from the general and bowed without challenging the request.[13]

Higashigi told a different story, leaving the matter for the Board of Investigation to determine who was lying. Higashigi claimed that the request to dispose of the prisoners came from Captain Nishiyotsutsuji, who could not have made the request without an order from Horie. Dispose, in the vernacular of the Japanese, meant execute. That night, during a sake party at Tachibana's quarters, the general said: "The 307th Battalion [Colonel Kato's unit] will handle the disposition of the prisoners." Higashigi told the board he had nothing to do with the orders.

Lieutenant Colonel Kikuji Ito was among those involved in the execution of American flyers. (Courtesy of Dr. Eugene F. Poutasse. Digitally enhanced by Wendy A. Webster)

He denied giving them to Lieutenant Colonel Ito, though he most certainly did.[14]

While Higashigi and Ito laid plans for the next day's executions, Woellhof and the unknown flyer held their last conversations in the 307th Battalion guardhouse. What the prisoners discussed that evening will never be known, but until the morning of 7 August 1944 they had no reason to believe they had seen their last sunrise. Both men must have felt a rush of anxiety when they learned that no transport had arrived to take them to Japan. They probably wondered why they had been so abruptly moved to another location after Horie had promised to keep them under the protection of his Haken Shireibu headquarters. Each man must have tried to bolster the anguished spirits of the other. At least they had the company of one another. At Horie's headquarters they felt safe, but here in the Kominato area their treatment changed, and they felt nothing toward them but hostility and the curious and expectant expressions on the faces of passing soldiers.

The night must have passed slowly, and neither man would have slept well on their Japanese mats. Nobody came to give them a blanket, and the summer nights became chilly in the hills. Woellhof still felt pain. His wounds had not completely healed, but now he could walk.

After sunrise a guard removed them from the jail and took them to a nearby pavilion. Another soldier brought them breakfast, a few biscuits and a little water, nothing more. As the flyers ate, they could hear men of the 307th Battalion practicing on the nearby firing range, and then the clatter of rifle fire stopped.

At 9:00 A.M. Lieutenant Colonel Ito came to the pavilion, spoke sharply to the guards, and led the flyers to a road winding up the mountain. As they stepped into the bright morning sunlight their hearts must have leapt into their throats when they observed a squad of soldiers marching toward them from the firing range. Ito pointed to a spot in front of the soldiers, and the guards shoved the prisoners forward. Woellhof still walked with a limp, and the unknown flyer offered his arm as they hiked to the top of Nakayama Toge, a high cliff overlooking a large cove on the western side of the island. From the heights the flyers could look down and see part of Susaki airfield and the broad expanse of the Pacific Ocean. When two soldiers came forward with towels and blindfolded the eyes of the prisoners, the flyers might have wondered whether they had seen their last glimpse of life. Woellhof and the unknown flyer probably shared a single thought: they had been brought to Nakayama Toge to be shot. But the Japanese did not consider humanity when they decided upon the method for killing Woellhof and his companion.[15]

The two flyers waited, breathing heavily. They stood silently in the summer heat, perhaps sweating from the uphill hike, listening for sounds, waiting for the click of bullets snapped into the chamber, waiting for death. They had seen men with shovels, men with sledgehammers, and men with rifles. Then they probably wondered: Were they to be shot or bludgeoned to death? Or was this a Japanese ploy to fill them with terror to make them talk? They could hear a shuffling of feet nearby and smell the presence of several men. They could not see Leading Private Hisao Shimura standing nearby. Shimura could hear the two flyers talking, but he could not hear what they were saying, so he asked another Japanese soldier who spoke a little English to move closer to hear what the two flyers were saying.[16]

One flyer spoke softly to the other, asking, "Are you there?"

"Yes," the other replied.

"What is happening?"

"We are going to die."

"What can we do?"

"Nothing."

The flyers did not understand a word Ito said when he turned to his soldiers and asked in Japanese, "Who out of you are expert at handling the bayonet? Those that are expert, hold up your hand."

Captain Higashigi had already assigned a noncommissioned officer, Corporal Moriki Okamoto, and a superior private as one pair of executioners. He chose carefully, selecting two men who had lost friends during the last American air raid. Ito picked his executioners from a group of volunteers, Superior Privates Matsutaro Kido and Hisao Shimura. Ito's two executioners waited beside Higashigi's two executioners while men from the battalion drove stakes into the rim of an old hollowed-out machine-gun nest.

The two flyers recognized the sound of stakes being sledgehammered into the ground, but they did not know the reason until two Japanese soldiers took each of them by the arms and led them to the sound. As the flyers stood waiting, two soldiers kicked at the back of the prisoners' knees until both men slumped to a squatting position. They felt their arms being tied around the stakes. If the flyers were good Christians, they would have prayed through the night. If they were poor Christians, they would be praying now. Sergeant Moriki Okamoto noticed the flyers' lips quiver, perhaps as they silently reached for God and asked for salvation. Moriki did not want to kill the prisoners, but Colonel Ito ordered him to pick six more soldiers and arrange them in such a way that five men armed with bayonets would face each flyer.[17]

In the crowd of spectators, no longer visible to the prisoners, stood Colonel Takemune Kato, the battalion commander, with First Lieutenant Shigeo Ikawa and First Lieutenant Soji Hiroise. Kato, the highest-ranking officer on the hill, made no effort to stop the execution. Instead, he listened with interest when Lieutenant Colonel Ito faced the execution squad and said, "Acting on orders, we are now going to execute these two prisoners."

Ito drew a fountain pen from his pocket, walked to the prisoners, and inscribed on the flyers' shirts a circle around their hearts. Beside the first circle he drew another near the center of the flyers' chests. Before the Board of Investigation Ito explained his reasons, saying, "I did this because I did not want the executioners to bayonet the prisoners in a place which would make them suffer," but Ito lied. He wanted the executioners to bayonet the prisoners in the smaller circle first. That way the initial blows would miss the heart.

Ito ordered each group of executioners to bayonet one of the flyers, not simultaneously but one at a time, slowly alternating the thrusts. Sergeant Okamoto balked. He lowered his bayonet and backed away, but Lieutenant Ikawa ordered him to do his duty. Private Shimura also wavered. Ito merely said, "First aim at the middle, second aim at the heart."

Woellhof and the unknown flyer could hear the discussion, but they knew nothing of its contents. Neither flyer knew how they would die or which of them would die first. They still must have remembered the rifle squad and envisioned the faces of the gloating little devils raising their pieces and aiming at their hearts. What they could not see were ten Japanese soldiers, each with bayonets, standing before them ready to thrust. All they could hear was a shuffling of feet and crisp but scrambled orders in a language they did not understand.

Nearby a Japanese officer spoke sharply, like a man growing impatient. Then the flyers heard movement. One could have heard the other groan with pain as a bayonet sliced into his chest. And then the other flyer knew why as the point of a bayonet struck his ribs. He would feel it go through his body and back out again. And the man beside him groaned again, this time less audibly, and again he felt a blade go through his own body. He could no longer scream or think or wonder because in a few fleeting seconds his life went black.

Each prisoner received five bayonet wounds, four in the small circle penned on his chest, which would not kill him, and the other in the heart, which took his life.

Ito came forward and pressed his fingers to the flyers' necks. He felt no pulse and said, "They are dead."

The flyers slumped forward, their heads dangling from the stakes. Blood poured from their wounds. Shimura and Okamoto testified they heard the flyers groan and knew they were both still alive because "their bodies were still twitching." Okamoto believed it was possible, for when he thrust his bayonet he purposely did not break the flyer's skin but stopped the thrust three inches short. He suspected that others might have done the same. Ito drew his saber and in two swift slashes beheaded both flyers. He wiped the saber clean and slid it into its scabbard.

Then he turned and walked away, looking neither to the right nor to the left.[18]

On 15 April 1946 Major Shaffer brought Ito before the board for questioning. Lieutenant Parcell asked, "Why did you behead them?"

Ito offered a prepared statement and said, "In the Japanese Bushido, when a man is executed, it is a sign of honoring him that he be beheaded and although I was stepping beyond my actual orders, I honored the two prisoners by beheading them. In the Japanese Bushido you have to wrap the head in a white cloth and bury it in a different place than the body. [Instead], I took two sheets of white paper and wrapped the heads in them and buried them [in the machine-gun nest] with the bodies, and on the grave I put a stick as a marker."[19]

The Board of Investigation did not believe Ito.

ARM2c Lloyd Richard Woellhof went to his death on or about 7 August 1944. The few Japanese who questioned him thought his name was Wolf. On the same day and at the same moment his friend, the unknown flyer, went to his Chichi Jima grave without a name. Of eight other unidentified pilots whose names appear in some obscure way through hundreds of pages of investigative testimony, none of them were shot down during a time that might qualify them for consideration as the unknown flyer.

An interesting twist occurred during the latter stages of the investigation of the two executions. Captain Shigeo Ikawa, who was a lieutenant at the time and also an involved observer, blamed the executions indirectly on Major Horie for "not carrying out [his] duties properly. . . . If they [meaning Horie's headquarters] would have sent the prisoners to Iwo Jima or Japan, no one would now be involved in such a case." Ikawa proved not a very reliable witness, blaming Horie because the Japanese army might now be charged with war crimes, but his testimony suggests that Horie might have been able to send the prisoners to Japan, which directly conflicts with Horie's statement. He also blamed Captain Kimitomi Nishiyotsutsuji, Horie's adjutant, stating that the captain "could not find any unit to execute the flyers," so Ryodan Shireibu (Tachibana's headquarters) took it upon themselves to have them executed. There is nothing in Nishiyotsutsuji's statement to validate Ikawa's allegation, but the conflicting testimony continued to muddle the board's efforts to find the truth.[20]

During this period of time, Captain Kyuryo Isoda, the military police chief, spoke with Nishiyotsutsuji, who asked what to do with the prisoners. Isoda replied, "There are rules in the Japanese Army and Navy concerning the treatment of prisoners of war," and he referred to the Rikusen Hoki, which the Imperial high command claimed to have compiled from the Geneva Convention. Isoda advised Nishiyotsutsuji to not issue any order regarding the final disposition of the flyers but to hold the prisoners until they could be transported to Japan. During his testimony, Isoda told the board, "I believe that General Tachibana never read International Law; and therefore, I think that he acted contrary to International Law."[21]

Toward the end of Isoda's testimony, he dropped a bombshell on Rixey's investigation. When asked how many flyers had been executed on Chichi Jima, the military police chief implied at least ten and perhaps a dozen more. Shaffer and his board had not been able to understand why the four flyers whose identities they sought had so many conflicting physical characteristics. It suddenly became clear twenty days into the investigation that more than four flyers disappeared into the abyss of Chichi Jima. To Rixey, the news came as a mild blow because it meant that the Board of Investigation would have to start over again and months might pass before all the answers could be found.[22]

When the investigation began in earnest on 1 January 1946, seventeen months had already elapsed since the execution of Woellhof and the unknown flyer. Those giving testimony jumbled dates as well as events and descriptions of what they observed, heard, or did. The case of the unknown flyer falls into the category of multiple possibilities. When on 4 August 1944 the B-24 carrying the unknown flyer crashed into the harbor near the navy base, Lieutenant (jg) Hidehiko Noomi talked with him on the pier. "I remember hearing the name Verb," Noomi said. "I did not see the name spelled, but the name was pronounced something like Verb. He said it was a part of speech. I think the flyer came on a Navy plane from Saipan, but I do not think he was telling me the truth." In a search of the flyers missing in action on 4 August 1944, the only radioman with a name resembling a "part of speech" was ARM2c Kenneth J. Powl, whose last name could be mistaken for "vowel." Shaffer's investigation team never made this connection.[23]

On 16 and 17 January 1946 Second Lieutenant Robert N. Frazer took a detail of Marines and exhumed two graves in the Kominato area. In the northern grave the excavators found one human vertebra. In the southern grave where they hoped to find the remains of Woellhof and the unknown flyer, they sifted through the soil and found only a small amount of rope and a few pieces of wood from broken stakes. Sergeant Okamoto formed part of the excavating party. He knew exactly where the two bodies had been buried. Then he was led to a third grave, one he knew nothing about, and expressed surprise that another life had been taken. "I have always wanted to know," he said, "where the third one came from."[24]

Five days later Colonel Rixey ordered the B-24 carrying the unknown pilot to be raised from the harbor and the remains of the three dead crewmen excavated. The only identification found on the aircraft was the

From a B-24 bomber crash in the harbor, Second Lieutenant Robert N. Frazer (USMCR) and Lieutenant Eugene Poutasse (USNR) attempt to assemble the bones of the flyers so they can be boxed for shipment. (Courtesy of Dr. Eugene F. Poutasse. Digitally enhanced by Wendy A. Webster)

engine tag and number. The Japanese had burned the bodies of the dead flyers before burying them. Lieutenant Poutasse, the medical representative on the Board of Investigation, reassembled the bones of the flyers to determine their cause of death and to match them to the man. Other articles found in the grave included the flyers' life preservers, a belt, two buckles, buttons, a fingernail file, a corroded officer's bar, shoes, and thirty-six cents in change. The only clue to the identification of the crew of the B-24 was a man whose name may have been Verb.[25]

On 14 May 1946 the Board of Investigation received confirmation that Lloyd Richard Woellhof was indeed the man the Japanese called Wolf. On 14 July 1942 he had entered the Navy in Salina, Kansas, and went through training at the Aviation Radio School and Naval Air Gunner School. Sent to the Pacific, he became part of Bomb Squadron One on Task Force 58. The Navy did not terminate his active service until 4 February 1946, though he had been missing in action for nineteen months. The Navy never explained what happened to ARM2c Woellhof and simply listed his place of separation as Chichi Jima, Bonin Islands.[26]

In the long list of naval casualties containing the names of flyers re-ported as dead or missing in action against the Bonin Islands on or about 4 August 1944 there was no Verb, or any person whose name faintly resembled Verb. What scraps were found of the remains of the uniden-tified flyers from the B-24 were sent to the U.S. Army on Iwo Jima and reinterred in a special grave for the unknowns.[27]

They are still there.

CHAPTER 7

The Flesh Eaters

After August 1944 American bombing raids became less frequent, and with the exception of Rear Admiral Ralph E. Davison's air and cruiser/destroyer strikes on 31 August–2 September, Chichi Jima remained relatively peaceful until February 1945. Lieutenant George Bush made his near-fateful sortie over the Yoake Wireless Station on the morning of 2 September, and had fighter-bombers from the USS *San Jacinto* not shot up a pair of approaching enemy patrol boats, he may never have been rescued from the clutches of the enemy.

In preparation for the Iwo Jima amphibious assault, heavy American air attacks resumed in mid-February. Their objective: to disable Susaki airfield, knock out the island's vast communications center, destroy shipping in the harbor, and render the First Mixed Brigade on Chichi Jima unable to reinforce or support the Japanese defending Iwo.

Admiral Mitscher's Task Force 58 consisted of eleven fleet carriers, four escort carriers, eight battleships, eighteen cruisers, and seventy-five destroyers. The armada struck Tokyo on 16-17 February and on the following day began working south through the Bonins. With the carriers *Lexington* and *Hancock*, Admiral Radford's Task Group 58.4 remained off Chichi and Haha Jima for three days, pulverizing the airfield and cutting up the naval base. Raids on the Yoake Wireless Station knocked down communications towers and disabled generators, but bombs could not reach the sensitive sending and receiving equipment sheltered inside the mountains.[1]

On the morning of 18 February 1945, two American flyers parachuted into the water near Ani Jima. Their plane crashed a few seconds later between Nisha Jima and Hitodama Jima. A strong falling tide carried

On 2 September 1944, four SB2C Navy "Helldivers" from the USS *San Jacinto* (CVL-30) pass over the Japanese naval base on Chichi Jima after dropping their payloads on the Yoake Wireless Station. (Courtesy of National Archives)

the two flyers into the strait between Chichi Jima and Ani Jima. During the afternoon a Japanese air patrol spotted the flyers in the water and radioed naval headquarters.

Corporal Fukuichiro Maikawa, who was lying in an air raid shelter and nursing a stomach ailment, received a call from 308th Battalion headquarters to pick up the downed airmen. At 4:30 P.M. Warrant Officer Saburo Soya joined the corporal, and together they pushed a fishing canoe into the water and hauled the flyers out of the strait. While Soya warmed the prisoners at a fire blazing on shore, Maikawa phoned the battalion for instructions. Captain Yoshiharu Kanmuri told him to bring the prisoners to headquarters for questioning. The youngest of the flyers, a man over six feet tall with dark brown hair and blue eyes, had shed his clothing and wore nothing more than his long white woolen under-wear, boots, a knife strapped to his waist, and a gold graduation ring crested with a shield. The older flyer stood about five feet ten inches, carried a pistol, and wore a green jacket and green-colored dungarees. He had reddish brown curly hair, a long slim face, and a fair complexion. When Maikawa pulled the flyers from the strait, they were "half paralyzed" from the chilly water and "on the point of sinking. Their lips were blue," said Maikawa, "and they shook from the cold."[2]

Later in the afternoon Warrant Officer Soya delivered the two flyers and their weapons and personal articles to Captain Kanmuri, Matoba's adjutant. Because the 308th Battalion had no place to keep prisoners, Kanmuri secured them for the night in the air raid shelter. He questioned the prisoners through two interpreters but made no effort to record their names. Tachibana expected his brigade to be attacked and wanted to know the strength of the American force. He wanted the information from the prisoners and did not care how he got it. In the morning Kanmuri delivered the flyers to Captain Tadaaki Kosuga, one of the general's adjutants, who ordered the prisoners tied to a tree. Captain Harashima and Captain Jegehei Sato resumed the questioning, adding slaps in the face to induce a faster response. During the interrogation American bombers struck the island, and Harashima, Sato, and Kosuga started to guide the prisoners to the nearby air raid shelter. General Tachibana, convinced that the flyers made poor informants, stopped Harashima and Sato on their way to the shelter and ordered the flyers tied to a tree outside the cave and "not given shelter, food, or water." After the air raid ended, Tachibana laconically observed that neither flyer had been injured and sent them to Haken Shireibu to be questioned by Major Horie.[3]

Horie received both men and identified the pilot with the reddish brown hair and ruddy complexion as Ensign Floyd Ewing Hall, a name easy for him to remember. When giving testimony one year later Horie could not remember the name of the other flyer in the white woolen underwear because he had difficulty pronouncing "Mershon." Nor could any of the other Japanese, who vaguely remembered his name as "Marchand" or "Marchant." Petty Officer Marvie William Mershon served as Hall's radioman on what Horie described as a Navy Helldiver. When arriving at Haken Shireibu, both men were famished, and Horie gave them water, biscuits, and blankets. While Hall and Mershon ate their biscuits and washed them down with water, guards brought two more prisoners into Haken Shireibu late that night. Horie refused to have his sleep disturbed, and the two newcomers, AOM3c Grady Alvan York and Aviation Radioman Third Class (ARM3c) James Wesley Dye, spent the night tied to trees near Hall.[4]

In the morning Horie questioned Hall and Mershon and learned they were from the carrier *Bennington*. Horie never mentioned much about Mershon because he preferred the company of Hall. Horie and Hall talked often, leaving the impression at Haken Shireibu that they enjoyed each other's company. "Hall came from Missouri," Horie recalled, as his memory began to return;

and his mother operates a beauty parlor. He had a beautiful older sister. He was still single because he had postponed his marriage on account of the war. He looked forward to going home and marrying his sweetheart as soon as the war ended. He said that if I ever came to the United States, he would guide me everywhere. I told him that if I lived to return to Japan and if he ever came there I would have him sleep at my home and guide him everywhere.

"We were having many air raids at the time," Horie recalled. "Under such conditions he consoled my heart and gave me comfort more than anything else could do. I can never forget him."

How much of the rest of Horie's story is true nobody will know, but the major said that in early March a communication from the mainland told of a submarine transport on its way to Chichi to pick up the prisoners. Horie said he hoped to put all four prisoners on it. The veracity of the statement can be questioned in light of what happened next.[5]

Horie held on to Hall, whom he liked, but spent little time with Mershon, whose name he could not pronounce. Major Matoba eyed the number of pilots held at Horie's headquarters and made arrangements to turn one of them over to Lieutenant Jitsuro Suyeyoshi, commanding officer of the Imperial Japanese Navy's 8th Antiaircraft Battery (in Japanese terminology, Suyeyoshi Tai). Mershon had the misfortune of being a less-worthy opponent because he wore no uniform, only dirty white long underwear and boots. He created an unseemly spectacle around Horie's headquarters, and when Matoba sought to hand over a prisoner to Suyeyoshi Tai, Horie decided to give him Petty Officer Mershon.[6]

On or about 22 February 1945 Lieutenant Suyeyoshi and a sailor arrived at Horie's headquarters to pick up the petty officer. Mershon had been moved about before and slapped wherever he went. He felt uncomfortable leaving Haken Shireibu, where he had been treated well and enjoyed the camaraderie of being among other American flyers. Mershon did not know why he was being taken to Suyeyoshi Tai. He did not know that Matoba had decided to execute a prisoner as a morale builder for the unit. Matoba would later testify that the execution had been Suyeyoshi's idea, and Suyeyoshi would lay the blame on Matoba. Which Japanese officer promoted the killing made no difference to Mershon. He would never learn that soon after his rescue Lieutenant Suyeyoshi had claimed one of the two prisoners—he cared little about which one—because his unit had captured them.[7]

Months later Fred Savory translated the following order found among Matoba's papers:

Lieutenant Suyeyoshi, Company Commander of Suyeyoshi Tai, receive a Prisoner of War from Adjutant Kanmuri. Execute this prisoner on the plateau to the

Marvie W. Mershon as he appeared in his flight gear before his ill-fated sortie over Chichi Jima. (Courtesy of National Archives)

East of your company area. Get the details regarding the method of execution from Kanmuri.

Major MATOBA
Commander of Army and Naval Forces
Northern Section
Time: 1400 February 22, 1945

The order specified that the execution, when completed, be reported to Major General Tachibana and Rear Admiral Mori. Though Lieutenant Suyeyoshi refused to admit the role he played in obtaining Mershon or planning the execution, he instigated the killing with the blessing of Admiral Mori.[8]

After Suyeyoshi picked up Mershon, he drove to the 8th Antiaircraft Battery and turned the flyer over to Lieutenant (jg) Hironobu Morishita, advising him "the 308th Battalion has sent the flyer to the Suyeyoshi Tai for disposal." Suyeyoshi later lied in an effort to transfer his complicity in Mershon's execution from himself to Morishita. Suyeyoshi did not expect any trouble from blaming a subordinate officer who had already been returned to Japan.[9]

Major Matoba, though never a trustworthy deponent, may have clarified much of the confusion propagated by Suyeyoshi's lies and Major Horie's deceptions. On the subject of Suyeyoshi's involvement, Matoba said, "The responsibility for the delivering of prisoners of war to naval units lies on General Tachibana, but the rest of the responsibility lies with Admiral Mori." Lieutenant Suyeyoshi actually asked naval headquarters for permission to execute a flyer and received the approval of Mori, who seemed to go along with every directive that had the appearance of coming from Tachibana's headquarters. "Admiral Mori thanked me," said Matoba, "for letting him have a prisoner for execution." Concerning Horie's involvement, Matoba said, "I believe it was Major Horie's idea to return the flyers to the units which captured them and to encourage them to capture more, and the flyers were returned as a reward to the units." Matoba and Horie did not like each other, and whenever one of them was in a position to condemn the actions of the other, they did.

As soon as Mershon arrived at the 8th Antiaircraft Battery, Suyeyoshi delivered him to Lieutenant Morishita, who had been designated to perform the execution according to the rules of Kendo. When asked why he chose Morishita to perform the execution, Suyeyoshi merely shrugged as if he knew nothing about it and said, "Morishita was the next superior officer in my unit. He took care of all duties of the company, other than that of battle commands. . . . I was not really concerned with the question of war prisoners." But according to Ensign Junko Uzaki, there was another side to the story. Uzaki testified, "At the time Lieutenant Suyeyoshi

Lieutenant General Yoshio Tachibana did not have lavish quarters. He lived in a small hut, which was rather well concealed among the hills near Ogiura. (Courtesy of Dr. Eugene F. Poutasse. Digitally enhanced by Wendy A. Webster)

and his officers were opposed to each other," implying that the lieutenant ordered Morishita to do the execution because he "disliked" him. As time passed, the board would discover that men like Tachibana and Matoba chose their executioners for exactly the same reason.[10]

Petty Officer Nobutani Iwakawa, a member of Suyeyoshi Tai, witnessed Mershon's execution and, by doing so, also contradicted his commander's testimony. Before Morishita led Mershon up the hill and into the Daikonzaki Army Cemetery at Omura, Suyeyoshi spoke to a gathering of his unit and said, "If you men are captured, you must be strong and as collected as this enemy." Iwakawa remembered bringing a detail to the cemetery with shovels to dig the flyer's grave. He stopped near Mershon, noticing that the flyer did not look so strong or particularly brave in his underwear, but he understood that Suyeyoshi wanted to build morale by demonstrating the courage of an enemy about to be killed.[11]

As the flyer walked among the markers in the cemetery, he would have seen Iwakawa's work party digging a solitary grave. From the glances of the workers, he must have suspected that the grave was intended for him. If he wanted to fight to the last breath, he could not, for his hands were tightly bound behind his back. With death imminent, he had one last opportunity to take a long look at life. In the wintry heights of the island, a chilly breeze would be blowing off the ocean in February. It probably tormented his thin-clad body with a cold he barely felt. A pair of guards turned his body to face the wind, which blew off the ocean. Below lay the white-capped bay, sparkling in the late afternoon sunlight. A hand cocked his head back and his eyes stared upward, toward the sky, where scattered clouds pushed by the breeze moved slowly over a carpet of blue. As Morishita approached with a blindfold, Mershon must have known that he had witnessed his last glimpse at life. A towel wrapped around his head shut out the last light. One of the guards noticed a spasm ripple through the flyer's body. Mershon turned pallid. Sweat oozed from his pores, though he was shivering in the cold.

The guards led him closer to the sounds of the digging, and then the noise of scraping shovels stopped. Petty Officer Iwakawa, in charge of the work detail, stood aside and ordered his men to stand at attention and watch. Mershon instinctively stopped. He must have known he had reached the killing site. He must have felt a sudden rush of nausea, a sickness that would grip his stomach and flow to his throbbing temples. Hands pressed him toward the direction of where the digging sounds had come. Morishita kicked at the back of his knees and made him squat. Mershon must have known that his back was to the grave, though he could not reach to feel the ground with his hands. There were no sounds, only a sharp winter breeze blowing off the bay and the subtle scraping of a saber as it slid from its scabbard.

Morishita spoke, but Mershon could not understand what the Japanese lieutenant said when he told his men to move away "because the blood will spurt in all directions." Then Morishita raised his saber and cut through Mershon's neck with a single blow. "The flyer did not cry out," said Iwakawa. "However, I heard a slight groan."[12]

Petty Officer Haruichi Yoshida witnessed the execution and said;

The prisoner's head was not completely decapitated. It was hanging by the skin of the throat. [Morishuta] cut almost completely through the neck. After the flyer was sabered the body tipped forward, and then kind of stretched and fell backwards into the grave. The corpsman straightened the body and covered it with dirt.[13]

The following day Major Matoba went to General Tachibana's headquarters and reported Mershon's execution at Suyeyoshi Tai. Tachibana grunted satisfaction and served a round of drinks—sometimes sake and sometimes rum made from sugarcane. The conversation turned to the Japanese forces fighting on Bougainville and New Guinea, and the general mentioned that troops that were running out of provisions had to eat human flesh. During the discussion Captain Shigeo Ikawa came into the room, and the general offered him a glass of sake. Matoba poured Ikawa a drink and then filled his own glass, saying, "I have been drinking for three days to prepare for battle." The general turned to Ikawa and began a convoluted discourse on the defense of the airfield. During the discussion an invitation came from Colonel Kato at 307th Battalion headquarters for the general and his guests to join him for a party.

"We walked to Colonel Kato's quarters," Matoba recalled, "and when we arrived, we found that Colonel Kato did not have enough food or sake to have a good party." This disturbed Matoba, who was already intoxicated, and he shouted for more drinks. As the afternoon lengthened into evening Matoba became more incensed when dinner arrived without enough meat to go with the vegetables.

Tachibana raised the issue of "where to get something to eat in the line of meat." The question emanated from the corpulent general's insatiable appetite. Though he was among the smallest men on the island, he was also the fattest. Having recalled the recent execution at the army cemetery above Omura, he turned to Matoba and in hushed tones asked him to get some meat and more drinks. Matoba called 308th Battalion headquarters and ordered his adjutant, Captain Kanmuri, to exhume Mershon's body, remove his liver and some flesh, and have it delivered to him at Kato's headquarters.

"I overheard Matoba telephone the 308th Battalion for meat," said Captain Ikawa, "as it was general knowledge that Matoba ate human flesh. Colonel Kato ate his supper and left the table because he knew what was coming." Matoba became furious when Kato and others attempted to leave and shamed them for the insult. During the squabble a fresh supply of sake arrived, and the group settled back to enjoy the drinks.[14]

Mershon rested in peace for barely more than twenty-four hours when First Lieutenant Tadashi Teraki and Sergeant Kasutoshi Kanemori arrived at the Daikonzaki Army Cemetery with a bag of surgical instruments and a work party carrying shovels. At first Kanemori believed the surgeon intended to dissect the body for cremation. When Teraki told him that he planned to remove the liver and a piece of thigh for meat, Kanemori argued vehemently against doing it because it had been in the ground long enough for decomposition to begin. Teraki grunted and told Kanemori to shut up and follow orders.

"I passed the instruments to Doctor Teraki," Kanemori said, "and he did the actual dissection. I helped to remove a piece of flesh from the flyer's thigh about four inches wide and a foot long, but I was not expert enough to remove the liver." Kanemori observed that Mershon had been bayoneted or stabbed in the chest, but he could not tell whether this happened before or after the beheading. "I came to the cemetery with bandages," said Kanemori, "because I thought that Teraki had been dispatched to care for a wounded man. Before leaving, for reasons I cannot explain, I bandaged all the incisions on the flyer's body before reburying the remains."[15]

Teraki wrapped the liver and the flesh in white cellophane paper and started back toward the battalion. At the entrance to the cemetery he met Sergeant Akira Sugiyama, who had been sent by Matoba to pick up the flesh. Sugiyama stressed the urgency of getting the meat to 307th Battalion headquarters, which was located about five miles away on the opposite side of the bay. At about 9:00 P.M. he returned to 308th Battalion headquarters and obtained a car to expedite the delivery. Some of the officers at Kato's party must have been particularly hungry for human flesh because Matoba met Sugiyama outside the kitchen and scolded him for being so slow. Sugiyama recalled that the package weighed about three and a half pounds and that Matoba did not think it would be enough. Whether Matoba sent someone else back to obtain more of Mershon's flesh Sugiyama did not know, but before leaving Kato's sake party he looked inside and observed General Tachibana in an elevated state of intoxication.[16]

Colonel Kato came into the kitchen, spied the package on the table, and went outside. He called to Sugiyama, who was returning to the car, and asked if the package just delivered contained human flesh. Sugiyama dodged the question and did not answer. Matoba overheard the conversation and came out the door. He ordered Sugiyama to be off and then turned on Kato, saying, "Why do you treat your guests in an improper manner? We are hungry."

"Colonel Kato did not like Matoba for his flesh eating habits," Ikawa recalled. "Then the colonel called for me. I went to him, but Matoba grabbed me and said, 'Hurry and get the meat!' "

Ikawa opened the package and placed the flesh between the fire and the pot on the table. He cut the flesh into small pieces and put part of it into the pot. Before the flesh had time to cook, Matoba and the general demanded that it be served. "Give some to Colonel Kato," Matoba said. "You have to eat this kind of meat to become a strong fighter."

Kato refused the flesh, saying that he had eaten earlier and wanted no more food. Ikawa took Kato's plate and scooped the flesh back into the pot. Matoba and Tachibana continued to eat, but Kato got up and stepped outside. Ikawa followed a few paces behind, but Matoba grabbed him and again said, "This is no way to treat guests," and ordered him to put the rest of the flesh into the pot.

At that moment bugles blew, signaling another air raid. Kato and Ikawa headed for the shelter, but Kato stopped and ordered Ikawa to go back and get the general. Ikawa obeyed and led the weaving general to the shelter. "Matoba did not come," Ikawa recalled, as he said that bullets and bombs would not hurt him. He kept eating from the pot. After the air raid ended General Tachibana was too drunk to be moved. He stayed in the shelter for two hours until a car arrived from headquarters. Major Matoba remained in the house where Colonel Kato lived and slept until morning. The colonel never bothered to cover him with a blanket, and he was left like that until the next day.[17]

Matoba, though a major, did not hesitate to inveigle superior officers to do his bidding, the exception being General Tachibana. When drunk, Matoba became the most unpredictable officer on Chichi Jima and a feared tormentor. He did not like Ikawa, and the feeling was mutual. After the arrests on Chichi, and well before the investigation got into full swing, Matoba and Ikawa shared the same tent in the stockade. Matoba warned Ikawa to never reveal his presence at the 307th Battalion's sake party. If he did, Matoba promised to kill him.[18]

Under the circumstances, Matoba's first testimony before the board on 14 January 1946 became a litany of lies and denials. By 6 March the truth became manifest through the testimony of others, so Matoba began to confess his role in the atrocities, but he repudiated part of Ikawa's testimony with his own.

According to Matoba, Kato's personal cook prepared the flesh, but Captain Ikawa did the actual cooking at the table. Contrary to Ikawa's testimony, Matoba testified that five officers, besides himself, ate the flesh of Mershon—Tachibana, Kato, Ikawa, Captain Tadaaki Kosuga, and Captain Genzo Enjo of the Japanese Imperial Navy. Two of the 307th Battalion's company commanders joined the party, but Matoba could not recall if they ate flesh or not. "I believe that each man ate a few pieces, or just a single piece, and I believe that most of the flesh was left over. What happened to it I do not know." Leftovers from the officer's mess, however, often reappeared in the soups served to the Koreans.

Lieutenant Parcell, who led the questioning of Matoba, asked if General Tachibana ordered the cannibalization of prisoners of war. Matoba replied, "At a conference at division headquarters on February 17, 1945, General Tachibana said that supplies would diminish and ammunition would run short, and in the end men would have to fight with rocks, and they would be forced to eat their own comrades, but the flesh of the enemy should be eaten first."

"Who was present at this meeting?"

"Every battalion commander. Not only once or twice, but several times the general said this."

Matoba implicated everyone in the army from Tachibana to Major Horie, stating the general's edict demanded that all prisoners be executed and eaten. Matoba also implicated Admiral Mori, who tried to extricate himself from any culpability in the executions and the general's flesh-eating directive. "Admiral Mori was in command of the island," Matoba said,

and I think it was impossible [for General Tachibana] to issue such orders without the approval of Admiral Mori. That edict included all the men in army and navy headquarters, including Haken Shireibu [Horie's headquarters]. Admiral Mori personally thanked me for letting him have a prisoner for execution. When Major Horie handed over the prisoners after examination, they were all to die.[19]

This conference occurred at the time when Allied forces were attempting to destroy the defenses of Chichi Jima in advance of the invasion of Iwo. Tachibana believed that because of the intensity of the bombing raids Chichi Jima might also be assaulted. The general said, "This would be the last battle prior to the invasion of Japan, and we must fight even though we have no supplies and no food, and that while we fight, we must live on the flesh of our comrades." Once again Tachibana referred to Americans as *kichiku*, meaning "beastly," a word used by Imperial Japanese Army headquarters to discourage soldiers from surrendering because their remains would be used to add meat to the contents of American cooking pots.[20]

Mershon went to his death having never heard the word *kichiku*. Nor during his short life was it likely that he had ever met a bestial American. Men of that sort all seemed to be Japanese officers congested on Chichi Jima where they bonded together to become a proud group of flesh eaters.

Lieutenant Frazer, in picking through the gravesites, never found the remains of Ensign Marvie William Mershon. If a bone or a tooth still existed in February 1946, they would be among the unclassified remains that were sent to Iwo Jima and reburied in an "unknown" grave with those of other flyers. From Shaffer's investigation, the Navy eventually updated the flyer's service record. Mershon had entered the service at Los Angeles on 28 July 1943, went through Naval Air Gunnery Training, and at the time he parachuted into the sea near Chichi Jima, he served with Torpedo Squadron 12. Consistent with the findings of the investigation, on 19 February 1946 ARM3c Mershon became officially dead. When naval administrators referred to Chichi Jima as the place of Mershon's "separation," they did not intend to ascribe to such a common word the actions taken by Lieutenant Teraki at the flyer's gravesite.[21]

Upon discovery of Mershon's execution, Major Shaffer summoned twenty-two-year-old Lieutenant Morishita, the flyer's executioner, and learned he had been repatriated to Japan. In March the summons arrived at Morishita's residence in Wakayama City. At 11:40 P.M. on 17 March 1946 Morishita swallowed "a small quantity of white powder with a cup of Japanese tea." Pretending that he was suffering from a cold, he went to bed. Ten minutes later he lay dead. Dr. Masuke Takeda examined the body and ruled it a suicide, committed "by taking violent poisonous substances."[22]

A year after taking Mershon's life, Morishita took his own.

CHAPTER 8

The Execution of Floyd Ewing Hall

On 18 February 1945, when Hall and Mershon were captured in Ani Jima Strait, Mershon lived four days before being taken to Daikonzaki Army Cemetery to be beheaded. Ensign Hall fared much better under Horie's care, mainly because the major liked him. But by Tachibana's decree, Hall could not remain indefinitely under the protective wing of Horie at Haken Shireibu. Hall probably never learned of Mershon's execution, but he certainly must have wondered what had happened to his friend. He might have queried Horie, who would not tell him, and when two other flyers were brought into Haken Shireibu, they, too, mysteriously disappeared.

On 9 March 1945 Hall's status suddenly changed after General Kuribayashi committed suicide on Iwo Jima. The Japanese Imperial Army reorganized the 109th Division and placed Tachibana in charge, elevating him to lieutenant general. Ryodan Shireibu (Brigade Headquarters) and Haken Shireibu (Horie's headquarters) were combined to form the Shidan Shireibu, the new division headquarters. After Horie lost Kuribayashi as his boss, he became chief of staff to General Tachibana, an unpleasant relationship for both men but especially uncomfortable for Horie. Because of his lenient treatment of prisoners, Horie had developed a reputation among battalion commanders as being "not a true Japanese," and some of Tachibana's staff privately referred to Horie as a "double-crosser." It also became known that Horie, contrary to Tachibana's orders, had attempted to make arrangements for sending Hall to Japan. Soon after Horie became directly responsible to Tachibana, a phone call came from the 308th Battalion ordering him to hand over Hall. Horie obeyed but asked Captain Kanmuri, Matoba's adjutant, to not treat Hall inhumanely. This was asking a lot because Tachibana had issued orders for all prisoners to be beaten, deprived of food, and executed.[1]

Captain Kanmuri remembered the conversation differently. He claimed that Horie initiated the call and asked that someone from the 308th Battalion come to headquarters and pick up Hall. Kanmuri recalled that "Major Horie said not to *kill* Hall in any inhumane way because Hall was very much in his favor. Thus taking into account the general feeling of the time, I understood that Hall was to die but to do the job as humanely as possible." He also confirmed that neither Tachibana nor Matoba ever allowed Horie to have any authority or preference over the prisoners, and this statement was probably true, but not until General Kuribayashi committed suicide and Tachibana was elevated to command of the division. According to Kanmuri, who attempted to protect himself, all orders for executions came from Kuribayashi, Tachibana, or Admiral Mori, and Horie merely did what he was told.

Kanmuri probably shortened Hall's life on earth by reporting his phone conversation with Horie to Matoba. If Horie wanted someone treated humanely, Matoba could be expected to do the exact opposite. He did not like Horie, and the feeling was mutual.

By then Matoba had lost track of the number of American flyers executed on Chichi Jima. His estimate ran as high as eleven, but he demonstrated a very poor memory for names, probably because he never cared or was always too drunk to remember.[2]

Fred Savory cleared up the discrepancies in the testimony by rifling through Matoba's order book and translating another of the major's orders, this one to Kanmuri:

First Lieutenant Kanmuri have the American Prisoner of War Lieutenant (junior grade) Hall executed at someplace fronting the headquarters at 10 A.M. on the 9th of March, 1945.

> Battalion Commander: Major Matoba
> Time: 9 A.M. March 9, 1945
> Place: Mikazuki Hill Headquarters

Place to Report after Completion of Order:
  Brigade Commander: Major General Tachibana.
  Chief of Staff of Detached Headquarters, Major Horie.[3]

Savory found a second order right behind the above that read: "The Battalion wants to eat the flesh of the American Aviator . . . Hall." The order indicates that Matoba could remember names. He assigned the job of rationing the flesh to Kanmuri, and the removal of Hall's liver and gall bladder to the medical corps. He ordered Kanmuri to inform Tachibana and Horie when the flesh had been extracted so a special dinner could be prepared and guests invited.[4]

When Hall left Haken Shireibu, he lost his protection. Mershon never returned from the 308th Battalion, nor had the other flyers who had greeted him when they arrived. Rumors of executions might have caught Hall's notice at Horie's headquarters. Whether Horie told Hall he would be executed will never be known, but the young ensign, as he hiked to Matoba's battalion with Sergeant Furushika, probably held little expectation of ever seeing his home in Missouri.[5]

Matoba arranged for the flyer's execution several hours before Hall arrived. Captain Kesakichi Sato, who had just returned from an inspection of island defenses, spent part of the morning with Matoba receiving instructions on how and where to perform the killing. After departing from battalion headquarters Sato looked into the noncommissioned officers mess and was surprised to hear Sergeant Major Seiji Wada, Sergeant Sawaumi, and Sergeant Sugiyama already chatting about who would be chosen to kill Hall. One of the NCOs turned to Sato and asked, "Are you to kill the flyer?" Sato replied, "No." What Sato avoided saying was that Matoba had ordered him to supervise the execution and that Sergeant Furushika had been chosen to do the killing.[6]

All during the morning, before he went to Haken Shireibu to pick up Ensign Hall, Furushika prepared his sword. He wiped it, sharpened it, and wiped it again, honing the cutting edge to razor sharpness. When the call came to get Hall, he put the sword away and went to Horie's headquarters. Perhaps Hall's friendly smile or his few words of Japanese shattered Furushika's resolve, because the sergeant took the ensign to battalion headquarters, left him there, and "got cold feet and could not be found." Captain Sato failed in his search to find Furushika, so he began looking for Leading Private Yukuchi Yoshino, another good man with the sword, to perform the execution. Both soldiers were attached to Kariya Tai, a company that had lost ten men during a recent bombing raid. Sato believed that either man would relish the opportunity of beheading Hall, but when Sato sent for Yoshino, he could not be found. Frustrated by delays and perhaps fearing Matoba's wrath, Sato became impatient and clamped onto Corporal Shigenobu Nakamura. Nakamura said he did not want to execute Hall and that the colonel should find Furushika. Sato became furious and ordered Nakamura to keep his mouth shut and carry out his orders.

Bomb craters had become the place of choice for beheadings, and on the morning of 9 March 1945 Captain Sato took Ensign Hall from the guardhouse, tied the flyer's hands behind his back, and walked him to the execution site. Word had circulated through the unit that a beheading would occur at 9:30 A.M., and a large crowd of spectators followed a few steps behind Sato and Hall. Nakamura walked among the crowd, sword in hand, to the designated crater near Kariya Tai, some 300 yards south of battalion headquarters. As Nakamura approached he saw Hall standing a few yards from the bomb crater, smoking a cigarette and apparently chatting with the guards. Drawing nearer, he noticed Captain Sato waiting impatiently nearby with Lieutenant Teraki, the medical officer. Beside the surgeon stood two corpsmen gaping at the flyer. "Teraki wanted to give these corpsmen a lesson in dissecting a human body," Nakamura recalled, "and they were all waiting for someone to kill the flyer."

Captain Sato, Doctor Teraki, and the two corpsmen from the naval base fell in with Nakamura and followed him to the crater. As Nakamura approached, one of the guards gave Hall a drink of whiskey. The flyer drank it and felt the alcohol burn his dry throat. He looked Nakamura straight in the eye, and the corporal looked away. Sato noticed the exchange and told a guard to blindfold the flyer. Hall's body stiffened as a dirty towel closed over his eyes.

Teraki did not like Hall's position and tried to make him squat. Hall uttered not a word. He no longer wore a friendly smile. His lips trembled slightly, and Teraki, who understood a little English, thought the flyer was offering a final prayer. He picked up a few words, like "The Lord is my . . ." but he could not understand what probably followed—". . . my Shepherd, I shall not want," but at this tragic moment, Hall did want. He must have wanted more life, to set the clock back, and if he was going to die, he must have wanted to say good-bye to the mother and father who loved him, to his brothers and sisters, and to the girls he left behind. Like all men about to die, he must have wanted to change time, to go back to Missouri and rearrange the life that deposited him on Chichi Jima and delivered him to the executioners on Nakayama Toge.

Captain Sato pushed the doctor aside and said, "This is not the proper way for the flyer to sit." He wanted Hall to bend his legs and squat on the balls of his feet, but Teraki said that foreigners could not sit in that position. While the two men argued, Hall breathed heavily, his head pounding and wet with sweat, his stomach wrenched with nausea. He could probably hear the sounds around him, but they were words he could not fathom. He could do nothing but wait unsteadily in a crouch for the sword to strike.

The doctor won the argument, and Sato allowed Hall to squat like a catcher waiting to catch a baseball. Then the doctor, who could speak a little English, bent over and told Hall that he was about to be executed. Hall said nothing. He already knew. All he could hope for now was to have it done quickly.

Sato turned away from Hall to address the soldiers standing nearby and said, "The man who is going to bayonet the flyer, get ready." Sergeant Yasumasu Mori stepped forward and waited, perhaps grateful the flyer would be dead when he drove the bayonet into the body.

Nakamura stepped up to Hall, raised his saber, and with one blow slashed at the ensign's head. The dull blade penetrated partway. As blood spurted from the wound, Nakamura turned and paused, feeling a sudden rush of nausea. Hall's body twitched and made gurgling sounds. Blood gushed from the wound. Nakamura fell back, unable to raise his sword.

Sato turned to Mori and said with disgust, "All right, go ahead."

Mori borrowed a guard's rifle and buried the bayonet close to the flyer's heart. Hall's body jerked with spasms, and Sato shouted, "Again!" Mori thrust once more, and with his bayonet dripping with blood, he looked blankly at Sato. The captain nodded and waved Mori away.

"I did not know the reason behind the order," Mori said. "It was public and in front of the enlisted men, and although I did not like to do it, I did it anyway. I still do not know why I was made to bayonet a dead body."

Mori returned the rifle to the guard and hurried from the scene. With him went Nakamura. They returned to the barracks and sat on their mats. "I did not feel so good," Nakamura recalled. "Neither did Sergeant Mori."

Sergeant Kanemori stretched the flyer on the ground, removed his blood-soaked clothing, and exposed his chest and abdomen. He stood aside, waiting and watching with the corpsmen as Doctor Teraki took a two-inch scalpel, cut open Hall's chest and stomach, reached inside, and extracted the liver. A corpsman standing nearby took the warm liver, wrapped it in cellophane paper, and handed it to Kanemori.

Teraki went to work on the opened body. He split the flyer's ribs, cut through the bones and cartilage with scissors, lifted out the heart and lungs, and handed them to the corpsmen to examine. Then he lifted out the stomach, drolly explaining the intestines in anatomical terms, and handed the corpsmen the flyer's organs. An hour later he wiped his hands on a blood-soaked towel and vanished down the hill.

Before the corpsmen shoved Hall's body into the crater, Kanemori returned. He cut off pieces of flesh from the flyer's thighs, working the knife down to the bone and stripping away huge gobs of meat. He gave a large piece to Yoshino of the Kariya Tai and a smaller piece to a carpenter from Kariya's second company. Then he packaged the remainder in waxed paper for the battalion. When Kanemori finished removing the flesh, the corpsmen returned the heart, lungs, and stomach to the body, pushed the remains into the bomb crater, and covered it with dirt.

A day later Nakamura observed pieces of liver strung on a wire to dry beside the house of Superior Private Shinosuke Konishi, Major Matoba's cook. Sergeant Mori saw the slices hanging in the galley a few days later. Some of it had been eaten. As each day passed, the liver slowly disappeared, piece by piece.[7]

Matoba and Tachibana believed that liver provided special curative powers for those who practiced the finer art of Bushido. The Japanese gave it a pharmaceutical name—Seirogan—and considered it a good medicine for alleviating gastric disorders. When Matoba learned that Hall's liver had been delivered to his orderly's room, he had it sliced in half. Konishi, the cook, prepared one half for a party at battalion headquarters that night and gave the other half to Superior Private Saburo Asano for drying. "Major Matoba wanted the other [dried] half for medicinal purposes," Konishi said. The cook recalled another liver coming to Matoba's headquarters about the same time. He had no knowledge of who brought it or from whose body it had been removed. The fresh liver could not have come from Mershon; he had been dead for more than two weeks.[8]

Matoba's parties lacked the lavish spread of culinary delicacies provided at official military banquets, but he believed in the importance of warriors eating the flesh of their enemy. He invited officers whom he knew would eat Hall's liver, and he invited others for the personal satisfaction of compelling them to eat human flesh against their will. On the day of Hall's execution Matoba invited Captain Sato, Warrant Officer Soya, Sergeant Major Wada, Captain Kanmuri, Captain Nakajima, and Captain Kariya. He served them each a piece of liver fried in soy sauce and mixed with vegetables, and he provided them with enough drinks to dull their senses. Second Lieutenant Ono rejected the offering. "I am a Christian," he said, "and I cannot eat the flesh." Matoba snorted and pushed him out the door.

First Lieutenant Toshio Kurosawa had the misfortune of being summoned to Matoba's party without knowing the menu. He learned that human liver would be the entrée while sitting next to the major. He refused to eat anything on his plate, but Matoba insisted. Kurosawa picked at a few vegetables away from the liver. "Then I became nauseated and left the room," he said, "vomiting up the food after I got outside. When I returned to the party later, Major Matoba grabbed me in a headlock and struck several blows on the top of my head."

Second Lieutenant Gunji Isogai also attended the liver party, but he admitted being so drunk that he had no recollection of what he ate. In the morning Matoba told him that he had eaten a flyer's liver. Matoda shamed all his guests for their squeamishness, asserting in a loud voice: "Eating human liver is good stomach medicine." Several of the officers who tasted the flesh and vomited would not agree.[9]

Matoba derived sadistic pleasure from watching his brother officers wince as they picked or nibbled at human flesh. On several occasions he purposely did not tell his victims the source of the meat until after they swallowed it. After watching for several days one of the livers in the galley dry, he decided to take it over to the navy base at Bobitai. His cook prepared the liver by cutting it into smaller slices. Then he plunged a bamboo stick through each morsel and fried the liver to a crisp in soy sauce sukiyaki style. He wrapped Hall's skewered remains in paper—like he had done many times before with goat meat—and handed it to the major. Lieutenant Isogai drove Matoba and his dinner offering to the navy base, which was located about a mile away. On the way to the party, Isogai asked Matoba if the package contained human flesh. Matoba replied, "Sometimes you may be right." Isogai said, "[I]f this [is] human flesh and my mother heard of it, she would faint because it was against her religion." Matoba ignored the comment. He did not care about such foolery as religious beliefs.[10]

Upon reaching Admiral Mori's headquarters, Matoba entered drunk, coatless, and bearing a gift to test the human palette. "I brought you the liver as promised," Matoba said to Mori.[11]

Lieutenant (jg) Miyuki Iijima remembered the conversation differently, recalling that Matoba entered during dinner and said, "I have brought you some delicacies." Either way, drunk or sober, Matoba would have his fun.

According to Matoba, Admiral Mori thought the idea a great trick on the men and colluded to keep the source of the meat secret. Mori and Matoba started the affair by reheating a serving over the fire and registering gastronomic pleasure over its tastiness. Each guest took a stick of liver and added more soy sauce as the meat began to sizzle. Lieutenant Commander Ichiro Shinoda attended the party and did not know what he was eating until later. "After Major Matoba told us it was human flesh, nobody ate it. He thought it a great practical joke and left the party as soon as everyone stopped eating." Isogai admitted eating some of the liver but said that Matoba would have beaten him if he had refused.

According to Matoba, Admiral Mori scoffed at his officers, reminding them that during the Sino-Japanese war Imperial troops dined regularly on human flesh, using it as a medicine to make them invincible in battle.

Why Admiral Mori, who ranked several grades above Matoba, would participate in such a bad joke is an indication of the power the major exerted over the navy. Matoba commanded the northern end of the island, and in it were several naval units. Mori felt that if the navy did not treat Matoba with respect, it would become difficult for the two services to get along. As Commander Shinoda observed, "Although nobody liked him, we treated [Matoba] as a guest."[12]

As for the flesh cut from the thighs of Ensign Hall, the pieces disappeared into the messes of the 308th Battalion. The cooks used it to add ballast to the soup of the enlisted men the night after Hall's execution. A large portion of the flesh went to feed the Koreans, and many of the men in both messes rejected their supper that night. Major Matoba only wanted the liver. As Captain Kanmuri observed, the major munched on human liver whenever he had it available.[13]

Japanese corpsmen buried the body of Ensign Hall in the bomb crater where he was executed. After the war the Japanese exhumed Hall's remains, cremated them, and reburied them in Omura's Daikonzaki Army Cemetery next to Mershon. On 19 February 1946 the Navy listed Hall's casualty status as "presumed dead." The ensign was not positively identified until 8 March 1946 when the War Crimes Office matched his name with a person listed as "missing in action—Station: Torpedo Squadron 12."

When captured in Ani Jima Strait, Hall wore none of his medals, which consisted of the American Area Campaign Medal, the Asiatic-Pacific-Area Campaign Medal with one Bronze Star, World War II Victory Medal, the Air Medal, and the Purple Heart. The Navy officially reported Hall's date of death as 19 February 1946, thereby extending his short life, at least on paper, by eleven months.[14]

Born 12 June 1920 in New Lebanon, Cooper County, Missouri, Floyd Ewing Hall was the second of Edward and Margaret Hall's five children. The family lived at 666 East 13th Street in Sedalia. In May 1939 Hall graduated from Smith-Cotton Junior-Senior High School and went to work as a machinist's apprentice for the Missouri Pacific Railroad. On 16 December 1941 Hall enlisted in the U.S. Naval Reserve with five other young men from Sedalia and decided he wanted to become a pilot. He learned to fly at the Naval Air Training Center in Corpus Christi, Texas, and at the Naval Air Station in Fort Lauderdale, Florida.

On 22 July 1944 Ensign Hall joined Torpedo Squadron 12 and was attached to the USS *Randolph*. On 18 February 1945, during a glide-bombing run, Hall flew into heavy antiaircraft fire over Susaki airfield and Futami Ko but stayed in the air long enough to aid in the sinking of a Japanese cargo ship before making a water landing in the strait. He and his crew were officially listed as shot down over Ani Jima and Chichi Jima.

On 13 January 1946 Lieutenant Frazer exhumed Hall's remains and found a combination of charred bones and ashes. Frazer's detail gathered everything into a box and marked the contents as possibly Hall's. The lieutenant sent the box to Iwo Jima, where the U.S. Army reburied it in a common grave. The remains of two flyers, Hall and Mershon, who knew each other so briefly during their final days of life, finally came to rest together, buried in the bloodied sands of Iwo Jima in a special spot reserved for "Unknowns."

On 20 January 1946, U.S. Occupation Forces on Iwo Jima received Hall's remains and buried them in Grave 2228, Row 25, Plot 1, of the 4th Marine Division Cemetery. On 2 July 1948, Hall's remains were permanently reburied in the Santa Fe National Cemetery, Santa Fe, New Mexico.

Major Shaffer's Board of Investigation made important strides reconstructing the last days in the lives of Ensign Hall and Petty Officer Mershon, but their work had barely begun.

CHAPTER 9

The Flyers from the *Bunker Hill*

In tracking the fate of Hall, the board learned that as many as five men had been tied to trees outside Major Horie's headquarters during the mid-February American bombings. They could account for Hall and Mershon, as both had been together at Haken Shireibu when guards late at night brought two more prisoners to Horie's headquarters. The board could also account for the unknown flyer killed with Woellhof at Kominato. But none of these flyers were named Vaughn or Dye, which were the only other names given to the board by Horie during his so-called truthful testimony. Little did they realize that in the search for Dye they would find yet another flyer, an unnamed ordnance mechanic who eventually materialized through the investigative process as AOM3c Grady Alvan York. York would bring the number of flyers disappearing on Chichi Jima to seven, three more than the number Horie originally admitted. Shaffer believed that Horie had either never seen all the prisoners or he was still hiding something.[1]

On 16 February 1945, three days prior to the Iwo Jima assault, Admiral Radford's Task Group 58.4 sailed to the Bonins and launched fighter-bomber strikes against Chichi Jima and Haha Jima. On 18 February two more carrier task groups, one under Admiral Davison and the other under Admiral Sherman, tore up Susaki airfield, shattered ground fortifications, and took a heavier-than-usual toll of life among the Japanese units on the ground. At 3:30 P.M. that day two American flyers parachuted from a three-man Grumman Avenger (TBF) and landed on Ani Jima. One was ARM3c James Wesley Dye, and the other was Grady York. They had flown off the carrier *Bunker Hill* with Task Force 58, Torpedo Squadron 82. York's identity would remain obscure for more

How many of these men (members of Flight 191, Naval Air Station, Melbourne, Florida) may have lost their lives during operations over Chichi Jima will never be known. Ensign Grady A. York, squatting second from left, flew off the USS *Bunker Hill* with James Wesley Dye (not pictured) and shared a mutual fate on Chichi Jima. (Courtesy of National Archives)

than four months. The pilot whose name may have been King would never be found. As the plane began disintegrating in the air, Dye and York bailed out, but the Japanese did not take notice of where the aircraft crashed. They later discovered a wreck in Takinoura Bay.

One flyer landed on the northern side of Mikauri Mountain, and the other landed on the western side. Both men were captured and taken to battalion headquarters on Ani Jima for questioning, but none of the Japanese could speak intelligible English and the interview failed. A call came from brigade headquarters on Chichi ordering that the flyers be sent to Horie's headquarters. Major Naoji Takenaka, commanding the 275th Battalion on Ani Jima, put the two men on a diahatsu, together with their jumpers, personal effects, notes, and names, and forwarded everything to Ryodan Shireibu. Takenaka could not differentiate between the two flyers because they were both nineteen to twenty years of age with light brown hair, fair complexions, and about five feet six inches tall. Captain Jiro Takeda remembered that the two flyers' names were short—having only three or four letters—and that one was a radioman

Major Naoji Takenaka commanded the battalion of Ani Jima that captured a pair of American flyers. Gene Poutasse recalled that the Japanese always had "ivory cigarette holders ready, but nothing to go in them, until we got there." The "OK" painted on his jacket meant that he and his personal belongings had been in-spected and approved. (Courtesy of Dr. Eugene F. Poutasse. Digitally enhanced by Wendy A. Webster)

(Dye) and the other a mechanic (York). Both men had graduated from high school, Captain Takeda recalled, and he remembered that the mechanic wore a black leather jacket and blue trousers and carried three pictures of girls on his life jacket.[2]

When Second Lieutenant Nichio Tamura captured Dye and York on Ani Jima, he treated the two flyers as conventional prisoners of war. Major Takenaka treated them with passive curiosity, Captain Takeda had been friendly, and nobody had punched or slapped them. As they approached the harbor of Chichi Jima, they expected more interrogation but no harsh treatment. They probably congratulated each other for their safe landing on Ani Jima and deliverance into such hospitable hands. They had not heard of Major Matoba, Admiral Mori, or General Tachibana.

During the air raid, Captain Takeda noticed a lot of firing in the vicinity of Nishi Jima, a small island where Tachibana had not posted any troops. At first he did not understand the firing. He later learned that a number of American flyers had ditched off the island and that Admiral Mori had sent out a squadron of diahatsus to search for them. American planes, hovering above the downed pilots, sank one of the boats and drove the others off. Takeda watched signal flares coming from around the island and later learned that an American submarine had rescued all the downed flyers. Dye and York were not so lucky.[3]

The two flyers came ashore in the area controlled by the 308th Battalion and at 9:00 P.M. reached brigade headquarters (Ryodan Shireibu) on the other side of the bay. On instructions from General Tachibana, Tamura shuttled them over to Horie for questioning. Tamura found the major in bed and woke him up. Horie said that he would question the prisoners in the morning, and to put them in the air raid shelter with the others, those being Hall and Mershon. Neither man had eaten since the previous morning and both were thirsty. Nobody fed them, but they spent their first night of incarceration with two comrades from the carrier *Bennington*. None of the flyers slept well. They shared experiences and discussed their capture. Hall looked fresh, but Mershon showed bruises and welts around his face. Dye and York expected the same treatment in the morning. If they discussed escape, they had no place to go. There were no "friendlies" on Chichi Jima—just Japanese, Koreans, and an unhappy number of conscripted prostitutes with babies and medical problems.

In the morning Horie called for his interpreter, Cadet Sergeant Oyama, and the questioning began. Toward evening on 20 February Marine pilot Second Lieutenant Warren Earl Vaughn joined the four flyers at Horie's headquarters. Horie now had more prisoners than he could handle. He interrogated Dye and York periodically over a span of three days. By 23 February he realized that neither man could tell him anything of importance, so he called Ryodan Shireibu and informed Captain Kosuga, the general's adjutant, to send someone for two prisoners. At the time, it was understood between Horie and Tachibana that all prisoners, after being questioned, would be sent to brigade headquarters for "disposal." Horie first said that disposal meant debarkation to Japan, but he later admitted that disposal meant, according to General Tachibana's definition, execution.

Kosuga kept Dye and York tied to a tree outside Tachibana's office at headquarters. He claimed he fed the flyers food and water against the general's orders, but being directly under the eye of Tachibana, it is unlikely that Kosuga would take such risks. By then the two flyers may have heard rumors about the disappearance of Mershon at Suyeyoshi Tai but not the details.[4]

Tachibana peered through a window at the two flyers tied outside his headquarters and decided to dispose of Dye first. Sometime during the afternoon of 22 or 23 of February, Dye and York parted company forever. Tachibana informed Captain Kosuga that he wished to have Dye killed with bamboo spears by the 307th Battalion. "You must have an expert bayonet man do the job," Tachibana said, "so you had better take Privates Hidano and Kido to do the executing." Kosuga obliged and ordered Superior Private Matsutaro Kido to have two spears made. Dye had no idea that spears were being made to kill him, but while Kido shaved the bamboo to a sharp point, Commander Yoshii arrived from the Yoake Wireless Station and said he needed a radioman to help decode intercepted American messages. Tachibana said, "All right," and Dye lived to see another sunrise.[5]

Giving Dye to Yoshii created a small problem for General Tachibana. He had promised the 307th Battalion a prisoner because they had lost the most men during the recent air raids. So instead of Dye, he ordered Kosuga to give the battalion York. The general did not care who got killed first because he intended to execute all of them. Kosuga called the 307th Battalion and told Captain Ikawa to come and get the prisoner. He reiterated Tachibana's instructions to "let the men from the companies that lost personnel through American bombings get satisfaction." Ikawa located and informed Colonel Kato, the battalion commander. Kato was not at the base but overseeing some additional construction work to improve the defenses at the airfield. Hearing the general's directive, Kato replied, "I do not know what to do."[6]

Kato phoned his clerk, Sergeant Ichitaro Nakada, and ordered him to find out which companies lost the most men in recent raids. When Nakada returned with the tally, Kato selected six men—two from the first infantry company, two from the third infantry company, one from the machine-gun company, and one from the Ito mountain-gun company.[7]

During his absence at Susaki airfield, Kato turned the arrangements for York's execution over to Captain Masao Yamashita. Because the selected executioners served at different locations on the island, Yamashita needed time to locate and assemble the men at battalion headquarters.

Inside the 307th Battalion guardhouse the days passed slowly for York. Military police noticed that the prisoner could not sleep, and every slight disturbance seemed to unnerve him. York complained of hunger, but when the soldiers brought him biscuits and tea, he could not eat. Perhaps he noticed the knotted expressions of curiosity on the faces of every passing soldier who stopped and peered into the room to see the prisoner who was about to be executed. No one came to interrogate him. No one asked his name. No one cared, for the death writ had been issued. So York waited, no doubt counting the hours and the minutes, listening for the footsteps that would come to take him away.

Yamashita caused the delay. He waited four or five days for Colonel Kato to come from the airfield. After Kato returned to the battalion he wasted no more time. He contacted Yamashita and said, "Send the men to get the prisoner for execution." York finally heard the dreaded footsteps at the guardhouse door, and he probably knew they had come to kill him.

At 2:00 P.M. on or about 28 February, Captain Akeichi Asakawa and three soldiers tied York's hands behind his back and led him from the guardhouse to battalion headquarters. A number of soldiers and six sailors stood nearby. Kato looked at the short, sandy-haired flyer and nodded. Then he turned to Yamashita and said, "Take him to Nakayama Toge and kill him." Nakayama Toge held a special meaning to Captain Yamashita, for it was there above the beach at Kominato that Lieutenant Colonel Ito supervised the execution of Woellhof and the unknown flyer. Ito expressed some relief that this execution had been turned over to Yamashita.[8]

Superior Private Takekazu Oshida and Leading Private Shoichi Morito of the Asakawa (Third) Infantry Company fell into step behind York. They carried bamboo spears and followed the procession to Nakayama Toge. Four other infantrymen carried rifles with fixed bayonets. They trailed Captain Yamashita and six sailors up the hill. No one spoke.

While the guards prodded the flyer to walk faster, York probably mulled over the purpose of the bamboo spears. He could see their sharpened tips, and he probably wondered whether they would try to kill him with those flimsy lances, or perhaps they were ingenious Japanese tools of torture. He probably asked himself: Will I die quickly or will I suffer? Like most Americans in the same situation and believing they were about to be killed, York probably wanted to die quickly. Officers on the *Bunker Hill* had heard the gut-wrenching stories of Japanese torture, spoke of them during mission conferences, and had told flight crews not to expect any kindness if they fell into the hands of the enemy.

York kept stumbling as the guards prodded him up the mountain. Twice he fell to the ground. The guards grunted, gave him a kick, and hoisted him to his feet. York probably never expected to die when he joined the Navy. Nobody ever did. He probably never expected to be shot down over some godforsaken island in the Pacific. Every flyer knew the risks, but York probably never expected *this* to happen to him. He was not a pilot, just a simple ordnance mechanic who operated the cockpit gun. His nineteen years of life had passed swiftly, and he probably felt cheated. Any other nineteen-year-old would feel the same way. As men face death, they lament over a life unfulfilled. The pictures of girls pinned to York's life jacket may have represented his hopes of the future. The Japanese had taken them away and discarded forever that part of his life, and now they wanted to the rest.

All that goes through the mind of a young man about to be executed can only be hypothesized. Perhaps he prayed for an air raid, one that would blast the little brown bastards off the face of the mountain. There was always a measure of satisfaction knowing that if you were to die, your killers died with you. He might have sucked in the air, perhaps thinking that the one deep breath may be his last. If he could take his own life perhaps it would deprive the bloodthirsty devils of their pleasure, but his hands were tied, and he had no way of doing it. Such thoughts probably made him angry and perhaps built his courage, but he did nothing. In minutes or maybe hours it would be over; he could not know which.

The guards retied his hands to a telephone pole overlooking the landscape. Before him lay the rugged terrain of the pockmarked mountain and below the breakers rolling in from the ocean. When a soldier approached with a blindfold, York took his last look at life. Captain Yamashita barked an order, a towel slipped over his head, and he could no longer see the Japanese soldiers who began to form in front of him.[9]

The guards and sailors fell into pairs, each with fixed bayonets. They stood solemnly at the ready, waiting for Captain Yamashita's order. Leading Private Shoichi Morito and Superior Private Takekazu Oshida moved to the front with their sharpened bamboo spears and leveled the points at York's chest. Yamashita turned to Morito and said, "Spear the prisoner!" Morito studied the prisoner and wondered whether his thrust would penetrate York's leather jacket. As a bayonet man Morito ranked among the best on the island, but he did not feel confident killing a man with a bamboo spear. He stepped up to York, took his stance, and thrust. York groaned, and Morito stepped back. The sharpened tip showed blood, but the spear did not go through the flyer's body. Morito paused at the ready, waiting for his partner, Oshida, to make the second thrust.

Captain Yamashita became impatient. He turned to Oshida and said, "Hurry up and spear him!"

Oshida thrust at the bloody puncture where Morita's spear had penetrated York's leather jacket. He missed the spot but felt the tip go into the flyer's body. He heard York groan again and withdrew the spear. Oshida felt a touch of nausea and stood aside, slowly backing away. He stopped several yards down the hill, his eyes pasted on the flyer gasping for breath as a froth of blood poured from his mouth. Oshida stood aside and watched as Yamashita, four soldiers, and several sailors stepped up and thrust bayonets into the flyer's body. Yamashita kept waving his arms and yelling, "Spear his heart! Spear his heart!" The whole scene became a melee of soldiers and sailors thrusting at the dead flyer's body. York's leather jacket became a mass of blood, and Oshida turned away and hastened down the hill, for the flyer was dead.[10]

The guards untied York and removed his bloody jacket, tearing it into pieces for souvenirs. Then they tore off his shirt, ripping it into more souvenirs, and dropped the body into a hole near the telephone pole. The soldiers covered the grave with dirt and returned to the battalion, satisfied they had done their duty. Nobody remembered the exact date of Grady York's execution, whether he died in late February or early March of 1945, for on Chichi Jima, days, weeks, and time no longer mattered.[11]

After the war ended, but before the Marines arrived, General Tachibana issued an order that the men responsible for the executions in the Kominato region exhume the bodies and destroy all evidence of the flyers.

"We went in the night," Oshida said, "Sergeant Takano, Morito, Gyokurin Nakamura, and myself, to 307th Battalion headquarters to get Captain Ikawa. He ordered us to go to Nakayama Toge, where the flyers were executed, and to wait there." Ikawa came along later with a fifth man and together they dug up the graves. "I thought at the time that there was only one flyer buried there, but when we got through we found four bodies and four skulls." The work party stayed on the site most of the week, pouring oil on the bones until nothing remained but ashes. They carried the flyers' ashes to Ogiura—the ashes of Woellhof, Hall, York, and the unknown flyer, and buried them in a trench. Lieutenant Frazer with a detail of Marines eventually found the ashes of the four flyers, marked them, and sent them to Iwo Jima for burial in an "unknown" grave.[12]

On 16 January 1946 Fred Savory led a party of Marines to Nakayama Toge. Nearby he spotted a ten-foot telephone pole with three indentations made by the tips of bayonets. Around the pole were circular scuffmarks, the kind that would have been made by a rope. No one in the party could identify York's remains, but they had located the place of his death.[13]

By General Tachibana's orders, the prisoner originally marked for execution with bamboo spears had not been York but "Jimmy" Dye. Dye won a reprieve when Yoshii, the diminutive, sour-faced commander of the Yoake Wireless Station, learned that the flyer was a radioman. He talked the general out of killing Dye on the premise that he could use a flyer to teach his radiomen how to decode American transmissions. When soldiers came to take York away, Dye never knew that a substitution had been made, nor would he have cause to celebrate.

Dye's first indication of a change in his status came when a car from Yoake containing an officer and several men arrived at Ryodan Shireibu and separated him from York. The two flyers said good-bye, unsure of whether they would meet again. By then, both flyers knew that the men taken from Ryodan Shireibu or Haken Shireibu had never been returned.[14]

As the car bumped up the serpentine road to the radio station, Dye could not have guessed where he was being taken or why. He arrived at a gray concrete building situated on a small plateau nestled among rocky heights on the eastern side of the island. Nearby he could see a tall radio antenna made of angle iron, and along the crest of Mount Yoake and Mount Asahi he could see several more. When the car came to a stop by the building, the guard gave him a nudge and Dye got out. He followed the guards as they ushered him through the building, which was filled with spare parts, and into a long radio receiving area inside a cave. Power lines and cables ran across tapered walls into a long bank of radio receivers arranged in a row on tables, each having a chair and a headset. There he met Petty Officer 1/C Fumio Tamamura, who had been born in San Francisco, lived for thirteen years in California, and spoke perfect English. Tamamura intercepted American radio calls from aircraft and listened to short-wave radio broadcasts, and though he understood what was being said, he could not decode the messages. That, Yoshii said to Tamamura, was to be Dye's job.[15]

Relieved that he had finally found a Japanese enlisted man who spoke English, Dye appealed to Tamamura to have York brought up to Yoake. The petty officer said he could do nothing about York, but he tried to make Dye feel comfortable and lodged him in his room. Dye did not know that York's execution had already been decided.

Commander Yoshii expected Tamamura and Dye to get to work immediately, but Dye behaved "in a nervous state of mind," Tamamura said. "I knew he could not do any work, so I let him sit in front of the receiving set, and we talked a lot." Dye kept pulling on a scarf wrapped around his neck, and Tamamura asked him where he had gotten it. The flyer replied, "It was a gift from my sweetheart."

For the first time since his capture, Dye spent a comfortable night slumbering in the generator room at the receiving station. He liked Tamamura, and if he could settle his nerves, he said he might be able to

High on Yoake Yama were the important radio towers commanded by Captain Shizuo Yoshii. These are part of the communications system bombed by Lieutenant (jg) George H.W. Bush on 2 September 1944. It is also the site where James Wesley Dye was executed. (Courtesy of Dr. Eugene F. Poutasse. Digitally enhanced by Wendy A. Webster)

help the radioman. But Dye did not know anything about American naval code—only what the jargon meant that bounced back and forth between the aircraft, the squadron, and the carrier.

In the morning Yoshii came to the radio station and asked whether Dye had helped. Tamamura replied, "No. Not yet." A little later Yoshii returned to the receiving station and said, "We cannot keep Dye. We must dispose of him."

Tamamura looked puzzled, but Yoshii knew the petty officer's American lineage and said, "You may have your own ideas, but I have mine, too. You have silly ideas about war, and you must get those ideas out of your head." To emphasize that he meant business, he added, "Since the prisoner cannot help you, he will be executed."

The remark startled the men operating the radio equipment. Yoshii noticed their reaction and angrily said, "I must kill this flyer to instill more fighting spirit in all of you." Then he whirled about and departed from the cave.[16]

Tamamura did not have the heart to say anything to Dye about Yoshii's declaration. "I did not feel so good," Tamamura recalled, so he and the flyer sat together all morning and talked. They shared a meal and chatted about Japan and about America, and Tamamura noticed that Dye began to relax. He watched as the natural spirit of the flyer's young life began to revitalize. Dye began tinkering with the radio set and asking questions because he wanted to learn and to help his new friend. Tamamura went through the exercise of explaining to Dye whatever he asked. Time passed quickly, and Dye soon picked up the scuttlebutt coming from the ships lying off Iwo Jima.

About 2:30 in the afternoon Yoshii's orderly came into the room and in Japanese told Tamamura that the commander was about to announce Dye's execution. Then he turned to the flyer and through Tamamura told Dye to take off his leather jacket and his scarf, as the commander wanted them. The orderly departed, leaving Dye and Tamamura alone, and so they sat together a little longer and talked of things past and of good memories before the war. Tamamura liked the flyer, and he could not bring himself to say, "You are about to die."

While Dye and Tamamura conversed in the radio room, Yoshii called a general assembly. Most of the men came outside and fell into line by the fuel storage building. Others had heard about the executions on Nakayama Toge and made an effort to remain invisible. Tamamura came alone, leaving Dye in the receiving room. While the men stood at attention, Yoshii, who tended to squint and never wore a pleasant expression, sent a pair of orderlies into the cave to get Dye.

For the last time in his short life, Dye walked into the afternoon sunlight. He did not know where he was being taken because Tamamura had said nothing. As he stood between the orderlies with his hands tied, he could see fresh, upturned soil and a gravelike hole that had been dug nearby. Then he heard Commander Yoshii deliver a prayer, one he could not understand, and when everyone bowed his head, he did so, too. Dye did not know that Yoshii's message included the announcement of his own execution or that Yoshii said to his men that the American flyer's fate today might be their fate tomorrow. He ordered all the men in the unit to "watch carefully."

Yoshii's arrangements for Dye's execution had been made during the morning. When he selected Lieutenant (jg) Minoru Hayashi to perform the beheading, he did so intending to expunge the lieutenant's timidity and cast off any vestiges of the young officer's civilian-bred humanity. Hayashi did not know whether he could behead the flyer because he had never performed an execution. He did not like the task imposed on him by Yoshii, and when he objected to the assignment, Yoshii scowled and said, "You know what happens to an officer who refuses an order." Hayashi knew it well. Disobeying an order meant execution or life imprisonment, so he bowed to acknowledge that he would behead the flyer. As Hayashi stepped forward with his sword, Yoshii again ordered all the men in the unit to "watch carefully," but Hayashi peered nervously at the flyer and hesitated, for Dye was looking at him square in the eye. Then Yoshii remembered the blindfold and called for his orderly to bring a towel.

Tamamura stood about five feet away from Dye when the orderly approached and wrapped a towel around the flyer's eyes. He observed Dye begin to shake. The flyer's chin quivered like a person forcing back tears. Dye knew that Tamamura stood nearby and asked, "What are they going to do to me?" Tamamura could not tell him the truth and said, "You are just going to be questioned." Dye nodded his head as if to say, "Okay," but all the blood had run from his face, and beads of perspiration dripped from his light brown hair. It must have seemed odd to Dye to have his hands tied and his eyes covered to be questioned.

"I felt sorry for him," Tamamura recalled, "and I thought if he was going to die, it would be better without the mental pain."

Commander Yoshii called to Tamamura and said in Japanese, "Tell the prisoner to kneel."

Tamamura complied. He noticed that the radioman was close to losing consciousness, and he told Dye to sit still while the commander questioned him. Dye felt someone move his body closer to the freshly dug hole, close enough that Dye probably realized that he was sitting on its rim. He no longer asked Tamamura questions. He now knew he was about to be killed.

Yoshii turned to Hayashi and nodded. The lieutenant came forward, unsteadily raised his sword, and swung it for a killing blow. The blade cut into Dye's neck about an inch, breaking into the nape of the neck just above the flyer's backbone. Dye winced and groaned and tried to lift his head. With his spinal cord severed, he could probably sense a feeling in his arms and legs but not be able to move them. His head would swim, transporting through his semiconsciousness a myriad of dazzling lights as his nervous system searched to find its circuits. Hayashi took one look at the blood spurting from the back of Dye's neck and dropped his sword. He dove among the crowd and sprinted away. Others followed. Dye slumped forward, his head nearly touching the ground. Then he tried to straighten himself but could not move his body. He was not dead, yet nothing about his body felt alive.

A second man, Lieutenant (jg) Shinichi Masutani, stood by with a sword, but when he saw blood pouring from the cut on Dye's neck, he backed away. Yoshii snapped an order, and Masutani raised his sword, but he froze and could not bring it down. Yoshii hollered, "Cut and finish him," but a man slumped over, his face turned to the side on the ground, could not be properly beheaded. Masutani handled the sword clumsily, using the blade to hack rather than smoothly cut. After two slashing blows, Dye's head, still held by a thin strand of skin, dangled over the pit. More blood spurted from his neck, and slowly Dye's body stretched out on the ground and leaned forward. His head rolled into the grave, and his trunk and legs tumbled in behind it.

Yoshii said nothing to Hayashi or Masutani, but he looked angry. He called for the surgeon, and Doctor Sasaki plunged through the astonished spectators with his bag of surgical instruments. Men began to move away, some hurrying back to their work. Others followed the doctor toward Dye's body, puzzled by what miracles the doctor intended to perform on a decapitated corpse. Sasaki stared into the grave, saw the messy result of a clumsy execution, and shook his head grimly. He looked disparagingly at Yoshii, who growled, "You know what to do."[17]

Sasaki reached for his scalpel, and a few men crowded around to watch the bloody work. The surgeon cut away Dye's shirt and made two long incisions, one vertically into the stomach and the other horizontally. He peeled back the flyer's skin and cut out the liver, placing it on sheets of paper. The Officer of the Day stood by and dolefully watched, but when the surgeon began slicing off flesh, he cried out, "Do not cut any more!" Yoshii reprimanded the officer and told him to mind his own business. He sent the other men away and waited while Sasaki removed the flesh. When the surgeon finished cutting through the thighs, Yoshii called for the burial detail and said, "Cover the prisoner."[18]

A sailor delivered Dye's liver, wrapped neatly in paper, to Petty Officer Second Class Kazunori Suzuki, Commander Yoshii's cook. Suzuki did not know what the package contained. He put it aside in the galley and went about preparing the commander's usual supper. Later that evening Yoshii called for the package. Suzuki brought it to him and unwrapped it. "It was very dark colored flesh," Suzuki recalled. "I did not know that human liver looked like this, as I had never seen one before."

Yoshii scowled at his cook and said firmly, "Do not tell this to anybody."

Suzuki bowed and departed. He wanted nothing more to do with human liver.

Alone in his room Yoshii cut a slice from the slab, cooked it, ate it, and took the remainder to a party just getting started in the main building at the radio station.[19]

When Yoshii arrived two parties were already under way—one on the second floor, which contained the officer's mess, and the other on the first floor, where the enlisted men ate. A galley on each floor served the two dining areas. After Yoshii reached the second floor he opened the package of liver. A few of the navy officers took a quick look and bolted from the table under the pretext of being on duty. During the course of the evening Yoshii fried the liver in the galley, sliced it, added garnishes, and brought it to the table to eat. He ordered his officers to eat a slice, but some of them refused. Others, reinforced by liberal amounts of sugarcane rum and compelled by duress, joined the commander and dined on pieces of Dye's liver. About 8:00 P.M. an air raid disrupted the party when a pair of American hecklers flew over Chichi. Men ran for the cave but not Yoshii. He remained behind to store some of the uneaten liver in the galley's icebox. The remainder he took back to his quarters for personal consumption.[20]

While the officers drank rum and temporized over eating Dye's liver on the upper floor, another serving of flesh occurred at the enlisted men's party on the lower level. In accordance with Yoshii's instructions, Doctor Suzuki had wrapped all the flesh removed from Dye's body in paper and sent it to the cooks at the enlisted men's mess. The sailors had become accustomed to seeing whale meat in their soup, but on this night they observed new meat from an unknown source bobbing about in their nightly concoction. Word soon spread that anyone who wanted to eat human flesh could do so at the first floor mess. Among enlisted men, only noncommissioned officers were permitted to drink rum. Sobriety reduced the number of flesh eaters despite Yoshii's directive that everyone, officer and enlisted man alike, partake of the flyer's body.

When the bugler sounded the air raid, not all the men took shelter, for they had been through heckler raids before. One Korean *gunzoku*, Shoshoku Arai, used the raid as an excuse to leave the party. While he crouched in a dugout a lieutenant from the supply office jumped in beside him and confessed that for the first time in his life he had eaten human liver. Arai asked him how it tasted, and the lieutenant said, "Different." When the air raid ended, Arai returned to his barracks. He found most of the Koreans on their mats grumbling that they "would rather die than eat human flesh."[21]

Petty Officer Tamamura seldom bothered to take shelter. He usually stood on the front steps of the main building to watch enemy planes bomb the island. "When the big planes came you had to duck in a hole, but when the carrier planes came over, they had a specific target and one did not have to go in but could stand out[side] and watch."[22]

By morning heads cleared and the men at the radio station began comparing notes. Some thought they had eaten human flesh but could not remember. Others knew they had but would not admit it. A few sailors, learning the character of the meat, rushed outside, shoved a finger down their throat, and tried to vomit.[23]

Sometime during the month of June 1945 a Japanese work party exhumed Dye's remains, built a fire, and cremated the bones. They put the ashes in a box and reburied them in the same hole. In late January 1946 Lieutenant Frazer's Marines excavated the site of Dye's grave and found several unburned bones and a small amount of brown hair. Frazer presumed that the bones belonged to Dye. He boxed the flyer's remains, marked the container, and shipped it Iwo Jima. The U.S. Army reburied the box in an "unknown" grave in the 3rd and 4th Marine Division Cemetery.[24]

The board's discovery of Dye's remains closed another case of missing flyers over the Bonin Islands. ARM3c James Wesley Dye of Glouchester, New Jersey, had entered the Navy on 17 February 1943 at Philadelphia, Pennsylvania. He had already earned four campaign medals and a Purple Heart before flying over Chichi Jima on 18 February 1945. Another member of Torpedo Squadron 82 saw Dye's plane shot down and reported the crew dead. He did not see Dye parachute, and his report caused the Navy to put the flyer in the "presumed dead" category. Dye lived five or six days before being executed at the Yoake Radio Station.[25]

Commander Yoshii's rush to execute Dye cannot be explained in the context of the American concept of morality. Yoshii behaved much like his counterpart in the 308th Battalion, Major Matoba—the difference being that Yoshii was seldom drunk, and Matoba was often drunk. Yoshii executed American prisoners not because he craved human flesh but because he believed that war was coming to the island, and he expected it to be brutal. Matoba seemed to enjoy the taste of human flesh and took every opportunity to acquire it. To face American bestiality, Yoshii and Matoba believed that their men must be hardened to fight *kichiku* with more fanaticism. They also believed that human liver gave those who ate it inner as well as spiritual power and that soon the entire division on Chichi would be faced with the need to eat their own dead in order to survive and continue the fight. Eating a few dead Americans now would make the practice more palatable when the ground war came to Chichi.

When Colonel Rixey formed the Board of Investigation, he ordered Major Shaffer "to administer an oath to each witness," thereby compelling them to tell the truth or face the consequences of perjury. Americans understood the power and the validity of the oath, but few Japanese were Christians, and if they told the truth, it was not because of the oath. Rixey, being a good Marine, intended to run a proper military investigation whether the Japanese understood the oath or not, and Shaffer obliged. Among the 123 Japanese who testified, only Commander Yoshii connected the oath to the faith of Westerners because his wife was a Christian.[26]

During the investigation, Shaffer brought Yoshii before the board and made him swear to tell the truth. Yoshii turned out to be a tougher customer than the board anticipated. Though a practicing Buddhist, he had spent twenty years studying philosophy and Christianity. He also knew something about freedom of religion in the United States, so he refused to testify and threw the Bible back in the face of Shaffer's board. Yoshii took the position that though the United States won the war,

Americans had also committed atrocities when they dropped the A-bomb on Hiroshima and Nagasaki and were now only interested in prosecuting the defeated Imperial Japanese Empire. To make one of many points, Yoshii read from Matthew, Chapter Seven: "Judge not, that ye be not judged. For with what judgment ye judge, ye shall be judged, and with what measure you mete, it shall be measured to you again." He continued reading, chapter and verse from scripture, demanding that the board explain to him why he should be tried when the Bible advocates forgiveness. Yoshii concluded his statement by saying, "Until this is explained, I refuse to be tried, because it is against my religion. I will not answer a single question."

Lieutenant Parcell replied that the board did not intend to answer philosophical questions, nor was Yoshii on trial. The board only wished to learn the truth so the innocent would not be falsely accused. Having made his statement, Yoshii refused to say more until the board replied to his philosophical question. The session ended in deadlock, and Yoshii, having delivered his rejoinder, went back to the stockade.[27]

Having once eaten human liver, men like Yoshii and Matoba in particular showed signs of becoming addicted. They craved more, but the massive air raids stopped, and the flesh eaters began to run out of flyers. Yoshii knew of another aviator, a pilot named Vaughn. Because Major Horie still sheltered Vaughn at Haken Shireibu, Yoshii made a case for bringing him to the radio station, thereby cutting out any claims for the flyer by Matoba. Such fierce rivalry among flesh eaters set the tone for outright competition whenever a flyer fell among the Bonins. Men like Yoshii and Matoba had no reason to believe that the supply of American flyers would quickly end. Just as the remains of Hall and Dye were beginning to flavor the cooking pots of Chichi Jima, Matoba and Yoshii learned that Horie had another flyer. This one happened to be a Marine.

CHAPTER 10

Semper Fi

On 23 February 1945 a chill wind blew off the ocean and into the face of Superior Private Fukutaro Ishiwata. He stood by his gun position on Fukuro Misaki near Kominato and scanned the sky for incoming American aircraft. Recent air raids had been intense and severe, but on this day everything remained refreshingly quiet. By his own account, Ishiwata shivered because the cold winter wind penetrated his light clothing. Huddling into his jacket he probably snugged his chin into the collar, lowered his head, and looked straight down the cliff and into the bay. An unusual object caught his attention, and he spied a man swimming toward shore among the breakers. He knew the man would be an American flyer who had parachuted into the ocean.

Ishiwata felt no fear when he dropped down to the beach and threw a rope to the flyer struggling in the surf. Suffering from exhaustion and hypothermia, the airman grabbed the line and stumbled onto the beach. He could barely stand. His lips were blue, his teeth chattered, and he shook too much to speak. Other men came down from another antiaircraft position on the cliff and helped build a fire. Ishiwata seemed pleased that he had captured an American and gave the flyer a cigarette. Twenty-three-year-old Second Lieutenant Warren Earl Vaughn, the only Marine pilot to seek refuge on Chichi Jima, had made it to shore after nearly a day in the water.

For an hour Ishiwata and Vaughn communicated by sign language. When color returned to the flyer's features and his wet clothing had warmed, Ishiwata gave him another cigarette and motioned that they must move on. Vaughn would have observed the high hills and the densely foliaged island as he began the trek up the winding dirt road that led to Ishiwata's company headquarters. Along the way they met Lieutenant Shigenori Tanaka, and instead of going to company headquarters, Ishiwata and Tanaka took Vaughn to Colonel Kato's 307th Battalion headquarters at Kominato.

Tanaka had seen American flyers before, but never one quite so impressive as Vaughn. Being more than six feet in height, Vaughn towered over Tanaka. Unlike the sandy-haired flyers Tanaka had watched as they were led to their executions on Nakayama Toge, Vaughn wore his black wavy hair long, and he had a dark complexion and a strikingly handsome face. When Vaughn offered his life jacket to Tanaka, the Japanese lieutenant noticed a gold ring with a red crest on the flyer's finger. Had Tanaka not made these observations, Shaffer's board may never have been able to discover and confirm the identity and fate of Lieutenant Vaughn.

Captain Shigeo Ikawa, operating under orders from General Tachibana, called Ryodan Shireibu at Ogiura and informed brigade headquarters that the battalion had captured a prisoner. A few minutes later Vaughn was back on the inland road that connected the battalion with Ryodan Shireibu. He appeared to be physically spent and very tired. His clothes were still wet, and he began to shiver in the wintry breeze. Ikawa looked at him indifferently and snorted an order to a guard who produced a rope and tied Vaughn's hands. At brigade headquarters Lieutenant Kosuga came outside, gave Vaughn a quick look, and ordered a guard to keep watch on the prisoner until he could locate an interpreter. Ishiwata never saw Vaughn again.[1]

Soon Captain Kanji Harashima, one of General Tachibana's adjutants, arrived at Ryodan Shireibu with Corporal Hajime Hiroishi, his interpreter. An air raid alarm interrupted the interrogation, so Harashima took Vaughn into an air raid shelter near a bank of electrical generators to finish the questioning. The Marine said he came from Texas, but between the noise of the generators and Vaughn's southern dialect, Hiroishi could neither pronounce the pilot's name nor understand his answers.

When the raid ended, Kosuga called Haken Shireibu and asked Horie to send someone to brigade headquarters to pick up the flyer for further questioning. Horie dispatched Corporal Fujiwara, a small man who looked quite insignificant next to Vaughn. As the Marine approached Haken Shireibu he noticed four other prisoners under guard outside Horie's headquarters. In the morning all were gone but one. Only Ensign Hall remained, and he told Vaughn that Dye, York, and Mershon had been taken away. Vaughn probably probed his friend for more information, but Hall did not know, though he had his suspicions.[2]

Vaughn had not eaten for more than twenty-four hours when he reached Haken Shireibu, but Horie was more interested in questioning the flyer than feeding him. The interview went poorly because neither man could understand the other. Horie finally called Ryodan Shireibu and asked brigade headquarters to lend him Sergeant Oyama to help interpret. Of all the flyers brought to Haken Shireibu, Horie remembered Vaughn as being the most impressive, both in stature and appearance. "He had Indian blood in him," said Horie, "and was over six feet tall. The pronunciation [Texas dialect] of Lieutenant Vaughn was strange, and I had a very hard time interviewing him. He was a quite handsome man, and his complexion was very dark."[3]

Horie learned little from the interview, only that Vaughn had been called up from Ulithi as a reserve pilot, made his way from a destroyer to the escort carrier *Bennington*, and was shot down over Chichi flying an F4U Corsair on his first bombing sortie. If Vaughn knew any of the other flyers, he did not tell Horie, though some of them came from the same carrier.[4]

For several days Vaughn stayed at Haken Shireibu with Ensign Hall. The two men enjoyed each other's company, for they had become the only two living American prisoners left on the island. They probably asked Horie what had happened to Dye, York, and Mershon, but the major would not tell them.

Commander Yoshii drove down from the Yoake Wireless Station and asked Horie for another prisoner to help decode American messages. Because Yoshii had executed Dye, Horie refused to give up Vaughn or Hall. Yoshii returned a day or two later and demanded one or the other. Horie claimed to have been using the two flyers as English instructors. Because the Marine pilot spoke with a puzzling southern dialect, Horie gave up Vaughn with the understanding that "the flyer would not be ill-treated and . . . returned to me in person." According to Horie, Yoshii promised to return Vaughn, and Horie testified that he believed him. The statement made good rhetoric, and Horie probably knew how far he could stretch the truth without overly straining his believability.[5]

The so-called agreement with Yoshii to return Vaughn raises more questions about the credibility of Horie's testimony. Lieutenant Poutasse never believed half of what Horie told the board, but the major had become the investigation's star witness, and Rixey did not want Horie's cooperation jeopardized. Yet everyone on the board knew that Tachibana commanded the brigade and had issued "disposal" orders, meaning that all prisoners were to be executed, and that Horie clearly understood the meaning of "disposal," though he did not like to discuss it. To comply with orders from General Kuribayashi's division headquarters on Iwo Jima, Tachibana merely loaned the prisoners to Horie for questioning. Admiral Mori functioned as supreme commander in the Bonin Islands with headquarters at Bobitai, and Commander Yoshii served under Mori. Horie could not have retained Vaughn under any circumstance. He kept

Hall only because Kuribayashi, Tachibana, or Mori agreed to let an American prisoner teach Horie better English. Yoshii could not have demanded Vaughn without the concurrence of Admiral Mori, and because Mori sanctioned Tachibana's edict that all prisoners be executed, Yoshii would be under no obligation to return Vaughn to Horie. Major Horie knew that he could do nothing to change this agreement. He had already relinquished at least three prisoners knowing they would be killed. Much of Horie's testimony before the board had been self-serving, and his so-called efforts to save Vaughn from Yoshii fell into the same category.

In early March Yoshii traveled down to Horie's headquarters in a car to pick up Vaughn. Yoshii exchanged a few words with Horie, supposedly promising to return the flyer, and departed for the Yoake radio station. He said nothing to Vaughn as the car entered the zigzagging dirt road that led to the plateau near the top of Yoake Yama.

As the car chugged up the bumpy road, Vaughn might have noticed the first signs of spring, and as the car wound higher, he might have witnessed a dazzling view of the island from the thousand-foot-high mountain. He did not know that a few days earlier nineteen-year-old James Dye had passed up the same muddy road and seen the same sights for the last time. During the short trip Commander Yoshii squinted out the window without saying a word or displaying the least interest in his surroundings.

Yoshii deposited Vaughn at the receiving station and handed him over to Petty Officer Tamamura. "I did not like the idea," Tamamura said, "because I knew what he had done to the other flyer." But the petty officer had no choice in the matter and took the flyer into the bombproof that contained the station's wireless sets. When Vaughn discovered that Tamamura had been born in San Francisco and spoke perfect English, he felt an immediate sense of relief, for here was a person with whom he could communicate. The two men established a warm but guarded friendship, and Tamamura soon began calling Vaughn by his nickname—Cherokee.[6]

Like with Dye, Tamamura exercised full control over Vaughn, but only inside the receiving station. He played the role of host and treated Vaughn more as a guest than a prisoner of war. The flyer shared Tamamura's quarters, ate meals with him, and slept in the radio room with him, but Tamamura never mentioned Dye. When a number of enlisted men became drunk and tried to break into the receiving room to beat Vaughn, Tamamura hollered for help and restrained the hecklers at the entry. Chief Petty Officer Kagaya arrived on the scene and said, "God damn you, stay out of here and let the prisoner alone." The intruders complained to Yoshii, who castigated Tamamura for not letting the sailors have a little fun. "I want you to find out everything this pilot knows," said Yoshii, "so be quick about it." The petty officer returned to the

Second Lieutenant Warren E. Vaughn became the only Marine flyer captured and executed on Chichi Jima. He was part Indian, and one of his captors recalled his nickname, "Cherokee." (Courtesy of National Archives)

receiving room chastised, but he would not allow anyone into the area but the radiomen who worked there.[7]

For about a week Vaughn enjoyed his days at the radio station. There were no more attempted assaults by drunken sailors. He showed Tamamura his graduation ring from Southwest Texas Teachers College (now Southwest Texas University) and talked about his life in Texas. While in college he had joined the Marine Corps Reserve because they promised to make him a pilot. When the two men were not talking about their lives, they sat together and listened to the bank of short wave radios. Tamamura asked questions whenever they picked up American transmissions, but Vaughn said, "I know more than what I can tell you. You can kill me, but there is certain information I will not give you." He spoke openly to Tamamura, telling him that he flew a single cockpit plane, but Tamamura could not remember whether it was a Grumman or a Corsair. Vaughn once described how he had taken part in sinking a Japanese cruiser. Such statements could have brought the Yoake death squad. Tamamura recalled, "I did not tell Commander Yoshii because I knew that Vaughn would be mistreated." Tamamura chose his words carefully when giving testimony, substituting the word "mistreated" for "beheaded."

Vaughn also impressed Private Nobuaki Iwatake, an unwilling Japanese transcript who, like Tamamura, spoke fluent English. Iwatake had attended high school in Hawaii, and the two men struck up a friendship. He remembered Vaughn's sense of humor and his positive outlook on life. Iwatake recalled that one night a group of young kamikaze pilots came into the radio station and asked Vaughn what he would do if they got on his tail. Vaughn stood up, and towering over the young pilots, said that he would roll up, loop to get behind them, and shoot them all down. The kamikaze flyers bowed politely, shook his hand, and wished him luck as they departed.

Vaughn might have missed his chance to escape, though on Chichi there was no place to go but into the resourceless wilderness. One night Iwatake smuggled him out of the wireless station to a Japanese bathhouse on the island. On the way, Iwatake stumbled into a bomb crater six feet deep. Instead of dashing into the brush, Vaughn offered Iwatake a hand and lifted him out. "That's the way he was," Iwatake recalled.[8]

Yoshii continued to press for information, and Tamamura deflected the commander's questions by dribbling out bits of information having no real importance.

"I know that Vaughn knows more than what you are telling me," Yoshii said one day.

"I have told you everything I know," Tamamura replied. But during his testimony, Tamamura stated that Vaughn told him many things that he would not tell Yoshii, like how the Navy used code names and how

the call number was painted on the aircraft so the plane could be identified with its carrier.[9]

Yoshii thought for a moment and said, somewhat quizzically, "It is
odd that the lieutenant does not know more."[10]

Two or three weeks passed, and Tamamura became suspicious that
Yoshii did not care whether Vaughn divulged information of importance
or not. Major Horie claimed that he confronted Yoshii and asked why
Vaughn had not been returned. The commander replied, "The flyer is
working very hard in the wireless station. Let us keep him a little bit
longer." Horie had no authority to order Yoshii to return the pilot, so
Vaughn stayed with Tamamura at Yoake.[11]

About the same time the dreaded news came over the wireless that
Iwo Jima had surrendered, Iwatake had begun colluding with Vaughn
on methods of escape, but they had waited too long. That morning Yoshii
called Tamamura outside and said, "Get Vaughn ready. We are going
to give him to the Torpedo Boat Squadron." Yoshii needed a case of
dynamite, and Mori's Second Torpedo Boat Squadron agreed to furnish
it in exchange for the flyer. Vaughn asked Tamamura why he was being
moved. Tamamura believed that the flyer was to be executed, but he
would not tell Vaughn. Instead, he said that the navy probably needed
his help at the other wireless station near the navy base. Vaughn turned
to Iwatake and said, "They're taking me away. Good-bye and take care,
my friend."[12]

An hour later Lieutenant Yasuo Kurasaki arrived with several men
from the Torpedo Boat Squadron. They entered the receiving station and
removed Vaughn. Not one of them offered a word of explanation. They
shoved the flyer into a car, wound back down the mountain road, and
headed for the seaplane base at Kurasaki Butai. The car passed navy
headquarters at Bobitai, and for a fleeting moment Vaughn must have
reflected on the possibility that the navy was sending him to Japan. Horie
had said that a boat might come for him any day. He also implied that
the other flyers—Hall, Mershon, Dye, and York—only appeared to have
disappeared but were actually safe in Japan.

The driver paused briefly at the crossroad to the pier, but only to kick
the transmission into a lower gear before turning into the road leading
up to the Kiyose area. The car stopped at a cavernous bombproof near
a bridge close to where the Omura-Ogiura road formed a junction with
the Emperor's Way. A Japanese guard motioned, and Vaughn followed
him into the massive cave. Lieutenant Osamu Okubo looked after
Vaughn for three days, making sure he received food and whiskey.
Vaughn did not know why he had been sent to Kurasaki Butai. No one
put him to work, and none of the enemy assigned to guard him could
conduct a conversation in English.[13]

If Horie is to be believed, Yoshii did not inform him of the transfer of

Vaughn to Kiyose, though it is doubtful he could have prevented it. On 24 March the U.S. Marines secured Iwo Jima, General Kuribayashi committed suicide, and General Tachibana succeeded as commander of the 109th Infantry Division. Horie now reported to Tachibana as chief of staff, and no longer could anyone on the island interfere with the general's policy of executing Americans.

According to Lieutenant Okubo, the Japanese gave the Marine a "feast" on the day of his execution. Despite the language barrier, Vaughn had picked up many words in Japanese. He charmed some of his captors and made many acquaintances. He probably enjoyed the opportunity for having a fine meal, though the guards never mentioned the reason. The whiskey warmed him and probably made him a little mellow. For the Japanese warrior, it was good to die in a state of happiness. A Bushido often feasted before committing suicide, and though Vaughn had no plans to take his own life, Lieutenant Kurasaki did.

During the afternoon Kurasaki stopped at navy headquarters and joined Commander Yoshii and Admiral Mori, who were talking in hushed tones. Yoshii did not like Mori, but he probably needed the admiral's approval for Kurasaki to kill Vaughn. During the discussion the three men shared a bottle of sake. When Kurasaki departed from headquarters, he felt vibrant. Perhaps a pep talk from the admiral combined with a glass or two of sake strengthened his resolve. He clutched his saber, wondering whether to perform the execution himself or to choose someone else. He still had time to decide.[14]

About 4:30 P.M. a detail of guards entered the tunnel and brought Vaughn into the late afternoon sun. The flyer might have squinted at the sudden brightness, and he probably wondered where they were taking him now. Because Horie had once intimated that ships would come to pick up prisoners, it would be natural for Vaughn to latch onto that one last hope.

From the hill at Kiyose he could see the harbor. There were no large vessels in old Ten Fathom Hole, just a number of battered wrecks along shore that American carrier planes had shot to pieces. A large crowd had gathered, but if Vaughn had searched to find a friendly face, he would not have seen one. Horie had said not to worry, that Yoshii promised to return him to headquarters. The major was not among the crowd, but Commander Yoshii had come down from the mountain. He stood apart from the crowd, talking to Lieutenant Kurasaki, his eyes pasted on Vaughn. One observer noticed that Yoshii and Kurasaki never took their eyes off Vaughn. They appeared to be involved in an intense discussion about the flyer.

Vaughn probably recalled his last conversations with Hall, who would have spoken in speculative tones about executions, cannibalism, and the disappearance of American flyers. The thought must have occurred to him that the crowd had gathered to watch him killed. The reality of imminent death would come as a sudden jolt and after the jolt would come the rage. Being a Leatherneck, Vaughn probably thought, The hell with them. I will show those sons of bitches how to die like a Marine. He would not disappoint them.

Jeffrey Gilley, a relative of Fred Savory and a navy *gunzoku* with the 209th Construction Battalion, observed a large number of men hurrying toward the Torpedo Boat Squadron. He stopped a sailor, who told him that an American flyer was about to be executed. Gilley joined the throng and jogged toward the bombproof where Kurasaki's unit billeted. He spotted a tall, soldierly Marine standing outside the cave and observed that the condemned man showed no fear of death.[15]

Lieutenant Okubo of the Special Naval Landing Force in the Kiyose sector had urgent business with Lieutenant Kurasaki. He had not heard about the flyer's execution, but as he approached the Torpedo Boat Squadron he found himself among a large crowd. He observed Kurasaki in a private conversation with Yoshii. They seemed to be animated or arguing, so Okubo stood aside and blended into the crowd so he could watch.[16]

Gentai Kanaumi, a Korean *gunzoku*, passed through Kiyose on his way to the naval base at Bobitai. He saw a large crowd collecting near a bomb crater and became curious, so he stopped to investigate. As he melded into the assemblage he saw a tall, dark-haired American being led from the tunnel to a bomb crater several yards away. The sight of the proud, upright flyer striding without fear to his death transfixed Kanaumi to the spot. He stopped because he had to see it through.[17]

When Vaughn reached the bomb crater, Gilley noticed that the flyer cast a look of defiance at Kurasaki and Yoshii. The eyes of Kurasaki shifted away, but Yoshii's icy black eyes never wavered. A guard tried to tie Vaughn's hands, but the Marine waved him off. The last thing Vaughn probably saw during his twenty-three years of life was Yoshii nudging Kurasaki to go forward. Then a man behind him wrapped a towel around his eyes and made Vaughn kneel on a mat at the lip of the crater.

Kurasaki came forward and addressed the crowd. Vaughn could hear him but could not understand what he said. Kanaumi heard every word when the lieutenant stepped forward to speak. "We are now going to execute an American flyer," Kurasaki said, "and maybe one day you all will be in the same situation so have a good look at it and remember the details." Then Kurasaki approached and told Vaughn in English that he was about to be beheaded.

"Are you prepared to meet death?" Kurasaki asked.

"Yes," Vaughn replied.

"Do you want to say anything?"

Gilley thought he heard Vaughn say, "Go to hell!"

"Then goodbye," said the lieutenant.

"Semper Fi!" Vaughn shouted.

Gilley had never heard those words before. Nor had Kurasaki. The lieutenant hesitated, surprised by an outburst he neither expected nor understood. He drew his saber and raised it over his head. When Vaughn heard the saber come out of the scabbard, he arched his back, reached up with his hand, and turned down his collar to expose his neck. The movement unnerved Kurasaki, and because he was somewhat intoxicated, he almost lost his balance. He lowered the saber, stepped back, and shouted for Lieutenant (jg) Takao Koyama, who was an expert at Kendo. Koyama came forward, but when the lieutenant told him to execute the flyer, Koyama balked. Kurasaki became angry and demanded that his order be obeyed. "You are the best swordsman in the squadron," Kurasaki said sharply, "and you must behead the flyer."

Koyama still hesitated, but Lieutenant Kanehisa Matsushita, the surgeon, came forward and handed Koyama his personal saber, a very old sword with a good blade. Koyama now had no choice. He stood before more than 150 officers and men, all with their eyes fastened on the sword, and they all waited for Koyama to raise it.[18]

During the interregnum Vaughn waited in darkness, listening to the unintelligible exchange between Kurasaki and Koyama. He probably wanted to tear off the blindfold and cry out, "Good God, get it over with!" but he kept his silence. Then the crowd grew still. He could have heard the faint rustle of footsteps to his side and known the time had come.

Koyama spread his legs, raised the saber with both hands, and took a deep breath. He stared at the nape of the flyer's neck and measured the blow, for the cut must be clean. He remembered his years of training, but he had never killed a real man before, only the dummies provided by the master. The flyer kneeling before him was not a dummy but a brave and helpless enemy. He neither twitched nor quivered. Koyama let the air flow out of his lungs in a piercing cry as he swung the blade into Vaughn's neck. A gush of blood spurted into the air. Koyama threw down the sword and turned away as the flyer's body tumbled into the pit. He had made a clean cut. He did not have to look to see that Vaughn's head still hung by the skin of his throat, for that was the way of Kendo.[19]

The crowd did not cheer, but everyone began talking at once. Most of them had never witnessed an execution. Then they saw Commander Yoshii standing over the flyer's body and shouting for the surgeon. Lieutenant Matsushita came forward and a quiet discussion ensued. The surgeon objected to Yoshii's request, but the commander reeled back and said, "Split him open!"

Matsushita looked at the body, nodded, and pulled from his jacket pocket a sharp knife. He rolled the flyer's body onto its back, the head still dangling by the skin of the throat. Then he peeled away Vaughn's shirt and plunged his knife into the flyer's stomach, making two incisions, one vertically and the other horizontally. Jeffrey Gilley, who had stumbled upon the execution by accident, turned away. He could not watch as the surgeon dug through the flyer's intestines to remove the liver. The Korean Kanaumi stayed a little longer and watched as the doctor removed a second object, perhaps the gall bladder, but he could not see what it was.[20]

Matsushita wiped off his knife, picked up the liver, and carried it into the Torpedo Boat Squadron's headquarters, which was located directly in front of the execution site. After the surgeon departed, the body lay exposed, and Yoshii invited anyone who wished to remove some flesh to take whatever they wanted. A few men stepped forward, but not many, and Kanaumi thought they were cooks. Some time later a work detail covered the remains of the flyer's body, where it rested in a bloody and mangled heap in the bomb crater.[21]

Warrant Officer Minoru Miyashita worked in the caves as an electrician. On the day before Vaughn's execution he stopped by the flyer and offered him a cigarette. Miyashita had a long pointed beard, and Vaughn wore long hair, so the two men joked about each other's appearance. Vaughn told Miyashita that sooner or later the Americans would capture Chichi Jima, and if Miyashita would help save his life, he would return the favor by seeing that no harm came to the Japanese. Miyashita laughed and departed, for he had already heard that the 308th Battalion had arranged with the Torpedo Boat Squadron to eat the flyer.

The following day, after Miyashita received word that the flyer had been killed, he asked for some flesh for the Navy Seaplane Base. After finishing work he went to the Torpedo Boat Squadron to get the meat. The cooks shook their heads and said that most of it had been distributed to the different galleys. He could only have a little less than a pound because everyone wanted some for their soup.[22]

For the cannibals of Chichi Jima the liver remained the choicest morsel. Commander Yoshii took the largest piece back to the Yoake Wireless Station and refrigerated it in his icebox, carving a slice from the chunk from time to time and frying it in soy sauce. He gave the smaller piece to Lieutenant Kurasaki, who shared it with the officers of the 2nd Torpedo Boat Squadron.[23]

Lieutenant Osamu Okubo, an officer of the 2nd Torpedo Boat Squadron, saw much of Commander Yoshii during the last months of the war. He recalled that Yoshii behaved much like Major Matoba and that the two men influenced each other. "The commander," Okubo recalled, "was something out of the ordinary. He did not recognize ordinary men as human beings. He would do things without thinking of anything or any-one. He was sort of a bully and a despot."[24]

But Yoshii, unlike Matoba, would never admit to doing anything wrong or out of the ordinary. During the summer of 1945 he suffered a wound, and on 4 July 1945 Mori evacuated him to Japan. Yoshii never admitted to committing a crime or eating human flesh. Mori court-martialed Yoshii twice for direct disobedience to orders, both of which he ignored. "On one court martial," Tamamura said, "Yoshii . . . went down [to Mori's office] in dirty clothes and in slippers, and just walked out." Yoshii remained what he had become on Chichi Jima, "something out of the ordinary"—a Bushido warrior. Lieutenant Commander Ku-rasaki never appeared before the Board of Investigation. On 1 August 1945 he was killed in action.[25]

After the war ended, the Japanese cover-up began. The Torpedo Boat Squadron exhumed Vaughn's remains from the crater, stacked the bones in a pile, poured oil on them, and burned them to ashes. No record exists of where they took the ashes. Excavation of the crater by Marines failed to turn up a single bone. The board persisted in attempting to determine whether Admiral Mori ordered or condoned Vaughn's execution. His headquarters, being but a short distance away, made it impossible for Mori not to know about the broadly advertised execution, but he made no effort to stop it. Japanese naval personnel remained protective and voiced no statement that would directly implicate the admiral in the execution of Vaughn or any of the other flyers.[26]

In April 1946 members of the Board of Investigation traveled to Japan to question men who had participated in the execution. Some had al-ready been detained in Tokyo's Sugamo prison. In early February the board notified Lieutenant Koyama that his testimony would be required in the beheading of Warren Earl Vaughn. On 28 February 1946 Koyama took his own life by cutting his carotid artery to become, he said, "a guardian ghost of the fatherland." He wrote a suicide note admitting that he had killed an American flyer and four others. He made no effort to identify the other four, and no assumptions can be made. "Today," Koyama wrote, "after defeat in war, I realize my actions were neither moral nor humane, and, in dying, I pray that the souls of the five brave heroes may rest in peace." He condemned Kurasaki for issuing the or-ders to execute Vaughn, adding that "from ancient days, the carrying out of orders from superior officers was more important than death. . . . I believe I have done right as a military man."[27]

The ashes of Warren Earl Vaughn still remain hidden among the plants and flowers of a peaceful Chichi Jima. The Naval Records Center listed Lieutenant Vaughn as "Killed in Action" and misstated the location of his death as being Omura, probably because nobody in the record's center had ever heard of Kurasaki Butai or Okumura, for it was there that Vaughn met with death. His friends and relatives back in Childress, Texas, would miss him. He lived life as a Marine and died like a Marine because he was a Marine—always faithful.[28]

CHAPTER 11

The Search for the Unknowns

Major Shaffer's Board of Investigation continued its hunt for the unknowns, now numbering as many as nine flyers and possibly more. The many months of labor would never produce the name of the unknown buried with Woellhof on Nakayama Toge in the Kominato area. Sergeant Oyama, a member of the signal corps at Fortress Headquarters, once told the board that the unknown's name might be Verb, or a word pronounced like Verb, but Shaffer's search of the records of the missing in action could not produce a name remotely similar.[1]

In late January 1946, when Lieutenant Frazer's Marines exhumed the grave in the Daikonzaki Army Cemetery, they found a clue that led the board on another hunt: three bones and a badly discolored red and gold mechanical pencil inscribed with the name Glenn J. Frazier. The name had never been mentioned before—not by Horie or by any of the Japanese or Koreans summoned to testify.[2]

Because of the number of executions and the fragmentary and misleading testimony of deponents, it became increasingly difficult for the board to string statements together that tied any specific flyer to the events that led to Glenn Frazier's execution. Ever since 10 January 1946, when the board listened to the testimony of Corporal Fukuichiro Maikawa, they had never been able to connect the corporal's story about an American he claimed to have captured because the flyer's physical characteristics did not match any of those the board felt they had identified. This was not particularly unusual. Three eyewitnesses to Vaughn's execution described him differently. But still the board wondered: Could the flyer Maikawa described be AOM2c Glenn Frazier?

Corporal Maikawa of the 308th Battalion happened to be the same man

Lieutenant Burd McGinnes picks through a burial site on Chichi Jima in search of bones and clues that might lead to the identity of American flyers. (Courtesy of Dr. Eugene F. Poutasse. Digitally enhanced by Wendy A. Webster)

who on 18 February 1945 dragged Ensign Hall and Petty Officer Mershon out of Ani Jima Strait. Five days later Maikawa and *gunzoku* Tsutomu Yamada, who served on the battalion's fishing unit, paddled a canoe over to Tamana Kaigen beach to catch squid. They heard aircraft engines in the distance and spotted "fourteen flying fortresses" bearing for the island. Being close to shore, they stroked to the beach, hid the canoe, and concealed themselves among the rocks.

After the air raid Maikawa and Yamada hauled the canoe back to the beach, paddled offshore, and were about to resume fishing "[w]hen we looked back," Maikawa recalled, and "saw an American flyer with one of his hands in the air, standing up, and waving at us." The sudden appearance of an American came as a surprise because neither Maikawa nor Yamada had seen or heard a plane go down.

The flyer continued to beckon to the Japanese fishermen in the canoe. He frantically waved for them to come back to shore, but Yamada thought it would be better to go to his home and report the incident to the authorities because neither he nor Maikawa carried arms. If the flyer was acting as a decoy for others hidden in the brush, the Americans would take the canoe and escape. But the flyer spotted an old pier farther down the beach, walked out on it alone, and waved again to the pair of fishermen.

"We decided the flyer wouldn't shoot us," Maikawa said, "so we paddled back and Yamada helped him into the canoe." Referring to the flyer, Maikawa said, "He was a very small man, so Yamada did not have much trouble with him."

Except for his long, fiery red hair and ruddy complexion, Glenn Frazier compared in size to the average Japanese soldier on Chichi Jima. Standing about five feet three inches tall, he was quite thin but with broad shoulders, or looked so in his "new leather jacket and fur collar." Frazier carried a knife in his belt, but his two Japanese captors never attempted to disarm him because neither of them carried a weapon. Yamada offered Frazier a cigarette, and he accepted it, and when the *gunzoku* pointed to the flyer's bracelet, Frazier gave it to him.

Frazier remained docile because he was famished, exhausted, and had given up hope of rescue by the Navy. He had ditched on the island on 18 February and had for five days been in hiding. During the same period of time, American fighter aircraft sank two Japanese diahatsus cruising offshore in search of downed flyers, and submarines had rescued two Americans in the water off Chichi Jima. All Frazier needed was a little help to get into the strait where he might be seen by a friendly submarine. He no doubt hoped that Maikawa and Yamada, who were not dressed in military uniforms, were friendly natives who would help him—an occurrence more common among the islands of the South Pacific. Instead, Maikawa paddled the canoe to the beach near Miyano Hama and put Frazier into an old empty warehouse while he called battalion headquarters to report the capture. Several minutes later Maikawa returned to the warehouse and together with Yamada walked Frazier to the company barracks. There, while waiting for instructions from headquarters, they fed him biscuits and gave him water. Nobody tied his hands or slapped his face, but Frazier now knew that he had fallen into the hands of the Japanese and not friendly natives. The flyer stuffed the biscuits into his mouth as fast as he could swallow them. In an expression of gratitude for his captor's kindness, Frazier wept a few tears and handed Maikawa his ring. After the war when General Tachibana ordered all evidence of American flyers destroyed, Maikawa grudgingly pulled the ring from his finger and threw it into the ocean. Neither he nor Yamada ever learned the flyer's name, only that Frazier had been a gunner on a Grumman TBF Avenger and had parachuted onto the island several days before.

Frazier ate about half the bag of biscuits before Corporal Matsue arrived at the barracks, took charge of the prisoner, and walked him to 308th Battalion headquarters. The flyer still had the bag of biscuits in his hand when Matsue turned him over to Warrant Officer Soya.[3]

Captain Kanmuri, Matoba's adjutant, received all prisoners delivered to the battalion, and as evening approached Frazier found himself sitting on a mat outside headquarters. Kanmuri spent a few minutes with the prisoner and, experiencing the usual language barrier, sent Sergeant Major Seiji Wada to Matoba's quarters to report the capture. Wada found the major in a rollicking mood and hosting one of his nightly drinking binges. Kanmuri bowed and expressed his pleasure at announcing the capture of another prisoner. Matoba, perhaps envisioning another source for human liver, told Wada to hold the prisoner at headquarters, and he would deal with the flyer in the morning. Then he turned to Captain Kesakichi Sato, who did not drink, and to Captain Meguru Isono, who did drink, and said, "Go over to headquarters and question the prisoner, and if he does not answer your questions, beat him." Sato and Isono bowed and departed for headquarters.

As a gesture of respect, Frazier stood to greet Matoba's emissaries. Unlike Maikawa and Yamada, the two officers wore no smiles on their faces. Isono, who could not walk a straight line, careened directly up to Frazier and gave him a mighty slap. The jolt sent the flyer to the ground, but he got back on his feet and stood at attention. Sato asked him questions, but Frazier just shuddered and stammered, so Sato slapped him twice. This time Frazier stayed on the ground, his hand to his cheek, until Isono pulled him upright. Terrified by the unexpected reception, Frazier continued to shake, but he spied the friendly face of Wada returning from Matoba's party. Wada asked the two captains why Frazier was shaking, and they told him that the flyer had refused to answer their questions. Wada grunted and slapped Frazier again, knocking him backwards. The two officers returned to Matoba's party, and Wada stepped into headquarters, leaving Frazier to puzzle over the unexpected assault.

Isono noticed that Matoba, along with the majority of his officers, had now become uncontrollably drunk. Captain Noboru Nakajima knocked over a bottle of rum, and Matoba flew into a rage, turning upon the captain and chastising him for being intoxicated.[4]

Nakajima, well known for his pugilism, clenched his fist and rose from the table, but he remembered that Matoba was a martial arts master and suppressed his temper. But Nakajima, filled with fury, needed an outlet to vent his anger. He had beaten men at Suyeyoshi Tai whenever it pleasured him, and it was not his nature to control his urges to fight. Having overheard the conversation between Wada and Matoba regarding the prisoner, he stomped out the door and staggered toward battalion headquarters.

In the dim evening light Frazier could see another soldier weaving toward him, and as he watched, he probably wondered whether the man was an officer or an enlisted man. Enlisted men treated him well, and by now he sorely missed the kindness of Maikawa and Yamada. But this soldier kept coming, his approach unsteady but deliberate as if he had something working on his mind. Though exhausted from his recent ordeal and his face reddened from a series of slaps, Frazier pulled himself to his feet as if to greet in a respectful manner his next visitor.

Captain Nakajima walked up to the flyer and asked him a question. Frazier could not understand Japanese, and Nakajima could not understand English. Nakajima communicated with hand motions at the same time he spoke, and Frazier shook his head and looked confused. The impasse infuriated Nakajima, so he lowered his baton on Frazier's head. The flyer fell to the ground, half-conscious. Sato, who had followed Nakajima outside, tried to restrain him, but the captain pushed him away. A crowd began to gather as Nakajima shouted at the bludgeoned flyer to get up. Frazier could not understand a single word, which made Nakajima even madder. He raged at the flyer, raising his baton and hollering words in Japanese, delivering blow after blow until Frazier, his head a bloody pulp, lay limp and unconscious.[5]

The sight of Frazier's twitching body sobered Nakajima. He leaned over and began rubbing the flyer's chest. He sent a soldier for water and dabbed it on Frazier's head. Kanmuri heard the ruckus outside and found Nakajima with a bloody baton staring glumly at Frazier's bleeding skull. Kanmuri shook his head dolefully and gave the captain a critical glance. Nakajima gruffly said, "The flyer did not answer my questions."

"Major Horie was to question this man by orders of the general," Kanmuri said.

Nakajima shrugged and replied, "It is a general order from Tachibana that all flyers are to be killed, so I beat the flyer to death. He seemed to me to be stupid."

"Do you speak English?" Kanmuri asked.

"No," Nakajima grumbled, "I used hand signals." And then he stomped away.

Frazier died two hours later. Major Matoba learned of the killing in the morning and angrily confronted Nakajima. Matoba chastised Nakajima for two reasons: the flyer may have had important information about an American attack on the island, and he would have to explain the unauthorized execution to Major Horie. "I should kill you," he said to Nakajima, "for killing this flyer, but because this war is so close to this island, I will let you live."[6]

From Frazier's battered body Matoba might not have taken the liver, but the source of the second liver seen drying outside the major's galley had never been attributed to any specific flyer. Matoba admitted that he could not remember from what flyers the livers on display had come, nor could he remember making a statement that "the flyer [meaning Frazier] was too thin to be eaten." Matoba hosted another party the following night and for the main entrée served liver and possibly other body parts. He later testified that he thought the flesh might have been cut from Frazier's body, not that doing so made any difference to the flyer. The board worried that more flyers had been executed than they had been able to identify, and one of the trails that led to their identities was through their livers.

The following evening, after threatening to kill Nakajima in the morning, Matoba invited the captain to come to his nightly party and enjoy a serving of liver. The major admitted being drunk almost every day and finally said, "I do not know which body was eaten by the various men who came to my parties. Maybe it was Hall's body, or maybe it was the Navy man's body [meaning Frazier]. Many men came and took flesh. I don't know whether they took pieces of liver, the gall bladder, or some meat." Matoba's statement suggests that he served many forms of flesh at his parties other than liver and made whatever was left of a human carcass available to whoever hungered for a little meat.[7]

After Frazier died, no doctor or corpsman on Chichi Jima admitted to removing the flyer's liver or gall bladder. A detail buried the body in a bomb crater on Mikazuki Hill near 308th Battalion headquarters. At the end of the war the Japanese exhumed the body, cremated it, and reburied the ashes and remains at the Daikonzaki Army Cemetery above Omura. The Japanese work party that exhumed Frazier's body missed one small detail, a mechanical pencil engraved with the words "Glenn J. Frazier." The Marines eventually found three bones, a piece of rope, and a die. Without the pencil the disappearance of AOM2c Frazier would have remained forever among the island's growing number of "unknowns."[8]

On 28 July 1943 Glenn J. Frazier entered the service at Kansas City, Missouri. There is nothing in his service record to reveal his antecedents. The Navy listed him as missing in action from Torpedo Squadron 12 after Admiral Davison and Sherman's 18 February bombing mission on the Bonin Islands. AOM2c Frazier earned a Purple Heart in combat before being shot down over Chichi Jima. The Navy terminated his service a year later on 19 February 1946 without knowing that a mechanical pencil containing his name had been found in a grave on Chichi Jima.[9]

No one will ever learn how much human flesh went into the cooking pots on Chichi Jima. Leading Private Takematsu Wakabayashi, a Korean *gunzoku* from the Third Company, 275th Battalion, left a grisly account of a visit to the ice plant at Biyobu Dani for rations about the time of Frazier's, Mershon's, and Hall's executions. There was little meat on the island, and at the ice plant Wakabayashi saw only a little pork and the lower trunk of a man. "The lower parts of the legs were sawed off," the *gunzoku* said.

I knew it was the flesh of a human body because there were still two legs on, and the upper trunk was split in half. It was still bloody, and when an axe was used to split the lower torso, it came off in bits. I saw a number of arms severed a little above the wrists. They must have come off of the bodies of at least three men.

Wakabayashi watched as the butchers in the ice plant cut one of the torsos into seven or eight pieces, wrapped them in paper, and dispensed them to cooks who arrived to collect their meat ration. He could not tell whether the flesh came from the bodies of flyers or from dead Japanese soldiers killed in air attacks, but he recalled that several American flyers had been recently executed and that several dead bodies had been removed from recent crash sites and brought to the ice plant.

When Wakabayashi grabbed a piece of pork for his quota "a big fat man with a fat face" took it back and replaced it with human flesh. A mild skirmish ensued between Wakabayashi and the fat man, but the fat man won, mainly because the soldiers guarding the ice plant wanted the pork reserved for themselves and the human flesh to go to the Koreans. Wakabayashi took the ration forced upon him back to the company galley, and when he unwrapped the package, he recognized it as flesh from a human leg. Wakabayashi had studied physiology and identified the source of the flesh immediately. Superior Private Nakagowa, the chief cook at Ryodan Shireibu, remembered the ration of flesh being soft and fresh, not at all like pork or goat meat.[10]

Hideo Ishino, a navy *gunzoku*, managed the ice plant at Biyobu Dani and denied ever storing human flesh, but he did admit that by mid-February 1945 the shortage of meat had become severe. Ishino suggested that Wakabayashi must have seen goat meat, unless he had gone to the ice plant at Omura, where most of the rationing was done. But Ishino admitted that though he managed and maintained the ice plant, he was not in charge of food storage and not always aware of what meat was being distributed to company messes. Every other person who might have been able to shed light on the matter of flesh rationing had been returned to Japan. The board struck a blind alley verifying Wakabayashi's account. Though the Koreans' statements were believable, they did not help identify the bodies, only the pervasiveness of cannibalism on Chichi Jima.[11]

Had it not been for Colonel Rixey's Board of Investigation, two other flyers would have vanished into the oblivion of Chichi Jima's mountainous interior. On or about 5 August 1944, when carrier-based planes raided the island, Japanese antiaircraft fire shot down an SB2C Helldiver during a strafing run at a ship in the harbor. The plane crashed on Bull Beach. First Lieutenant Hyonosuke Hayakawa saw the Helldiver come

Lieutenant Burd McGinnes (left) and Fred Savory walked much of the island looking for the remains of flyers from downed aircraft. (Courtesy of Dr. Eugene F. Poutasse. Digitally enhanced by Wendy A. Webster)

down and two hours later inspected the wreckage. He found a flyer dead beside the wreckage and estimated his age at nineteen or twenty. Captain Nishimoto sent a detail to Bull Beach with orders to bury the body near the site of the crash. Of the flyers shot down on the Bonins, how many contributed their flesh to the cooking pots on Chichi Jima will remain, like the flyers themselves, unknown.

On 8 January 1946 Second Lieutenant Burd S. McGinnes, USMCR, took a Korean work party to Bull Beach and began excavating the Helldiver. As they pulled it out of the sand, they found the name B.J. Brotton stenciled on a piece of wing. They found no bodies, but Hayakawa came along and showed them the location of the flyer's grave. McGinnes collected a number of bones strewn about the gravesite and among them a watch, a GI belt, and an identification bar bracelet bearing the name John Cavanaugh. They had found the remains of Lieutenant (jg) John A. Cavanaugh, USNR, but they never found a flyer named Brotton. By dying in the crash, Cavanaugh fared much better than the flyers executed and eaten on Chichi Jima. His bones were later forwarded to Iwo Jima and reburied in a grave marked with his own name.[12]

During a bombing raid in November or December 1944, a B-24 took antiaircraft fire over Futami Ko. The plane began to smoke and crashed into the cliffs above Maruen Wan on the south side of Chichi Jima. Part of the aircraft landed on top of the cliff, and the rest fell to the beach. After the crash Captain Fumio Kudo sent a search party along the beach, but they could not reach the aircraft on the cliff and assumed that the flyers were dead.[13]

On 5 January 1946 Roger and Willie Savory approached Lieutenant McGinnes and volunteered to guide a party to the crash site. From their boat they could still see pieces of the aircraft clinging to a nearly perpendicular cliff. As they climbed the escarpment, they found more scattered pieces from the aircraft, including a mixture of personal articles and four pieces from old letters addressed to S/Sgt. William J. Farrell, 42d Bomber Squadron (H), 11th Bomb Group. They also found a baseball cap bearing the name Farrell and pieces of clothing with his name sewed inside. Nothing remained to identify the other members of the crew.[14]

After identifying Cavanaugh and Farrell, other trails became increasingly difficult to follow. On or about 12 August 1944 an American flyer parachuted into the area of the 17th Independent Battalion (also known as Iida Butai) behind the Yoake Wireless Station. A search party from the 2nd Battalion, commanded by First Lieutenant Hiroyoshi Kono, went into the mountains to find the flyer but could not track him down until evening. After they cornered him in a small area on Jorin Yama, the flyer fired into the search party. Japanese soldiers returned fire, aiming at a rock to the side of the flyer to force his surrender. The search party said a bullet ricocheted and killed him. They removed the flyer's personal effects and sent them to brigade headquarters. Papers on the flyer, written in ink, had been blurred by moisture, and the name at the top of one sheet used as a wrapper for the others contained a name that looked like "Fell," "Fellow," or "Feld." In January 1946 Lieutenant Frazer's Marines searched for the remains of the flyer but found nothing.[15]

Other leads led nowhere. During the board's investigation, they ran across names, fragments of names, or mispronunciations of names of other flyers. Lieutenant Frazer scoured the mountains of Chichi Jima in search of more evidence. Stories told by Japanese and Korean deponents suggested that cannibalism existed on a much broader basis than the few cases the board identified.

The investigators added more names to their list: Ensign Rudolf Fre Rolfing, ARM2c Carroll Curtis Hall, Joseph Edward Notony, and others with names such as King, Todd, Verb, and Moseley, never knowing whether they were first names, nicknames, last names, or not names at all. On 4 July 1944 a flyer named Lieutenant William C. Moseley, Jr., was reported missing in action against the Bonin Islands. Could this be the Moseley whose remains could not be found? Could Lieutenant (jg) Carroll L. Carlson, shot down over Chichi Jima on 7 September 1944, be the man one Japanese deponent remembered as Carroll Curtis Hall? Could Lieutenant (jg) Therolf E. Thompson, shot down on 11 November 1944, possibly be Ensign Rudolph Fre Rolfing? Could ARM2c Kenneth J. Powl, missing in action on 4 August 1944, be the radioman the Japanese called Verb? Or was he the unknown flyer executed near Kominato with Woellhof? Even less is known about Todd or King. There is no evidence to show that flyers shot down during 1944 were eaten. The cannibals did not become voracious until the Iwo Jima campaign when supply ships from the homeland could no longer reach the Bonins.[16]

Japanese units raised their own vegetables and formed fishing details, but for the exception of an occasional goat, wild pig, or whale, they no longer had meat. More than 100 U.S. Navy flyers went down in the vicinity of Chichi Jima. Only 10 of them were ever identified. How many bodies of the others flavored the soup of the Japanese on Chichi Jima will never be known. Because Tachibana and Horie had selected thousands of soldiers to be sent back to Japan before the investigation began, and because many of those men could have provided harmful testimony, other executions may remain hidden forever. Deponents before the Board of Investigation gave accounts of flesh being removed from the bodies of flyers not executed but killed in action, and others described captured flyers that could never be accurately identified. The *gunzokus* recalled human flesh appearing in their soups for many days after heavy air raids. Cooks claimed they could not identify some of the meat they received from rationing and distribution centers. Was it fact or just fiction fanned by the flames of rumor and exaggerated by one or two incidents of admitted cannibalism, or had dozens of American bodies gone into the pots?[17]

Many crashes occurred on Chichi Jima. Though the island covered no more than ten square miles, the rocky, mountainous terrain made some areas almost inaccessible. In March 1945 a TBF plummeted to the ground in the Furisaki Mountain area. The Japanese buried the flyers' remains a short distance from the wreckage. Lieutenant Frazer could not identify the three flyers. Also in March a P-51 crashed into the hills near the Yoake Wireless Station. The pilot was crushed "to bits" in the cockpit, and again the Marines never found his remains. Lieutenant Frazer located the wreck of an F6F near the beach on Ani Jima, but no remains of the pilot could be found. At one time hogs ran wild on Chichi Jima. A small amount of human flesh may have gone into making pork.[18]

When the board concluded its investigation on 6 June 1946 they had positively identified the names of ten flyers and the causes of their deaths. The Japanese had executed all but two—Lieutenant (jg) John A. Cavanaugh and Staff Sergeant William J. Farrell, who died when their aircraft crashed.

CHAPTER 12

The Criminals of Chichi Jima

An investigation into Japanese atrocities on Chichi Jima that began on 13 October 1945 came to an end on 6 June 1946 when Colonel Rixey turned more than 1,200 pages of testimony and exhibits over to ComMarianas at Guam. When he formed the Board of Investigation under Major Shaffer on 21 December 1945, he expected conclusions to be reached in a month or two. What began as a search for four flyers developed into a six-month intensive ordeal for the men assigned to collecting the testimony. There may never have been an investigation had Fred Savory and his clan not returned from Japan and alerted the colonel to rumors of atrocities on Chichi Jima.[1]

The exhaustive search for criminals never got under way until New Year's Eve when Major Horie confessed that his first statement had been a lie. Using the investigation as a fact-finding vehicle, Colonel Rixey hoped to learn more about the fate of four flyers—Hall, Dye, Vaughn, and an unknown flyer whose name no one on the island could remember. The colonel already knew that the Japanese fighting on the islands in the South Pacific, reaching all the way back to Wake Island and Guadalcanal, did not want to hold prisoners, so they tortured them for information and killed them. He did not expect to find the same acts of "disposal" occurring on Chichi Jima because the island had never been invaded by American troops and prisoners of war could be readily transported by aircraft or by ship to Japan. What took him by surprise was not so much the discovery of executions as the rumors of cannibalism and the difficulty of rooting out the guilty because of General Tachibana's nearly successful attempt at concealment.

While questioning more than 120 Japanese and Koreans, the board discovered they were dealing with a crafty cast of characters. Some of the deponents told the truth, some told half-truths, and some articulated the finely tuned cover-up strategy and continued to lie months into the investigation. The most reliable source of information came from the enlisted men, but only after they no longer feared reprisals from their superiors.

The board withheld taking General Tachibana's testimony until 20 May 1946, mainly because they wanted to collect and collate all the facts before questioning the architect of the cover-up. "Old Tachy" did not disappoint them. He tried to pin the blame on two men he disliked, Admiral Mori and Major Horie.

During the latter days of the investigation, Major Shaffer summoned the general before the board. Lieutenant Parcell, who had been most effective in conducting the questioning throughout the investigation, had packed his bags and returned to the United States a few days before the board summoned the general to testify. First Lieutenant Wilburn Caskey, USMCR, who had been a member of the investigation team since its inception, replaced Parcell as the lead examiner. Parcell was an attorney, Caskey was not, and the investigation lost a little of Parcell's pragmatic professionalism.

When Tachibana appeared before the board, he had nothing to lose by lying and nothing to lose by being forgetful. He had arrived on Chichi Jima on 26 June 1944, eleven days after two American flyers, Petty Officer Doyle and Lieutenant (jg) Terry, parachuted onto the island during the first bombing raids. He replaced Major General Osuga, who went to Iwo Jima, and took command of the First Mixed Brigade at Fortress Head-quarters (Yosai Shireibu). In a self-serving effort to exonerate himself from any criminal culpability, he shifted the responsibility for violating the rules of war to Admiral Mori, who had been in rank longer than Tachibana and was, at least on paper, the general's superior. Tachibana blithely said, "At a joint Army and Navy conference in Tokyo, it was decided that in the defense of any island garrisoned by Army and Navy units, the supreme command would be taken over by the senior officer on the island." Tachibana failed to mention that this arrangement applied only if enemy forces invaded the island. When asked the same question again, Tachibana replied, "All official matters had to be ordered by Admiral Mori, except matters regarding the land defense plans. Mori was in charge of issuing orders to all combat units in case of invasion." Tachibana indirectly admitted that Mori did not have to issue orders for executions and that the army could do with prisoners much as they pleased.[2]

In practice, Admiral Mori abrogated many of his responsibilities and exerted little, if any, influence over Tachibana or his battalion commanders. Even Commander Yoshii, who reported to Mori directly, recognized the admiral's weaknesses as a leader and, when he chose, ignored him.

On paper, all the naval units on the island reported to Mori, but those on the northern end of the island also reported to Major Matoba, who commanded the 308th Battalion. Every naval officer in the sector stated that Matoba exerted more influence over their units than Mori because they performed duties involving artillery and antiaircraft, which were directly in support of the army. Whatever Matoba controlled, Tachibana also controlled, and even before the loss of Iwo Jima, Tachibana more or less controlled Mori. When asked what orders he received from Mori of an administrative nature, Tachibana blandly replied, "None, except signals for air raids." Quickly realizing that he may have incriminated himself, Tachibana made a vain effort to qualify his statement by adding, "Regarding the defense of Chichi Jima, my immediate senior officer was Admiral Mori." Such an answer might have drawn a chuckle from the board. Putting the two statements together suggested that Mori, the senior officer on the island, gave General Tachibana, the second officer on the island, no instructions. Tachibana recognized the mistake and as a second thought added, "However, I took orders from General Kuribayashi also," who at the time of Tachibana'a testimony had been dead for more than a year. When asked about Kuribayashi's orders, Tachibana said the orders from the commanding general came through Major Horie. He implied that he never knew whether those instructions actually came from Kuribayashi and suggested that Horie could have issued them himself because, "It was not my business to question it."[3]

About ten days after Tachibana landed on the island, he moved Fortress Headquarters from Omura, which had been located about a mile from the navy base, to Ogiura, on the far side of Futami Ko. Tachibana claimed to have made the move for strategic reasons and to be closer to the island's airfield. He established his new headquarters in the center of the island at Ryodan Shireibu, thereby removing himself from direct physical contact with the admiral while providing himself with better cover in a more secluded and wooded area. Tachibana may have wanted to distance himself from Mori, but the real reason he moved had more to do with American air raids. Sorties flown from carriers had destroyed Fortress Headquarters, and Tachibana wanted to get out of Omura and into the mountains of central Chichi Jima, where he could be close to Susaki airfield.

After the move to Ryodan Shireibu only one problem stood in the way of Tachibana enjoying complete autonomy: General Kuribayashi, to whom he directly reported. Kuribayashi commanded the 109th Infantry Division from Iwo Jima, but he maintained a satellite headquarters on Chichi Jima at Haken Shireibu, where he had placed Major Horie in command. As long as Kuribayashi lived, Tachibana treated Horie with a degree of deference. Horie provided the division with transportation, communications, and supplies, and he controlled, or was expected to control, matters involving prisoners of war. As long as Kuribayashi remained alive and operational, Horie shipped prisoners either to Japan or kept them at Haken Shireibu. Horie had no facilities for holding prisoners, and after returning three flyers (Connell, Doyle, and Terry) to Japan, he claimed he lost all forms of transportation for sending more.

The fate of prisoners began to change when Kuribayashi called Horie to Iwo Jima for a conference. Tachibana, using Matoba as intermediary, sent Mershon to Suyeyoshi Tai for execution. The arrangement for protecting prisoners of war disintegrated altogether after American forces attacked Iwo Jima and Kuribayashi committed suicide. Tachibana became lieutenant general on 23 March 1945, and Mori became vice admiral on 1 May 1945. Therefore, beginning on 23 March, Tachibana outranked Mori, and this occurred about ten days after Vaughn's execution. The general needed a scapegoat, and he clearly understood the inconsistency of his testimony when he attempted to divert the responsibility for the army's executions to Admiral Mori. Of the eight known flyers executed, the army killed five, and the navy killed three, all of them during Mori's tenure as senior officer. Tachibana insisted that he had nothing to do with the executions and that they could not have occurred without a directive or the concurrence of the admiral. Matoba's letter-book, however, showed that the orders came from Tachibana and not from Mori.

In the matter of handling prisoners of war, Tachibana did not follow the Geneva Convention. Instead, he claimed to have conformed to the rules laid down in Japan's Sakusen Yomurei, a document combining the principles of strategy with rules and regulations. "The book gives you the rules on how to question prisoners of war, how to deal with them, and," said Tachibana, "when you are through with them to take the quickest method for handing them over to higher authority." The general denied being the so-called higher authority and shifted that responsibility to Major Horie, who at the time reported to General Kuribayashi. "On Chichi Jima," Tachibana said, "the Haken Shireibu was of a higher echelon than any other headquarters. Nobody questioned the doings of the Haken Shireibu." Tachibana was clearly trying to deflect responsibility for the executions to Horie as well as to Mori. Horie refuted Tachibana's statement, claiming that he never had the authority to disobey or ignore an order from the general.[4]

Tachibana then attempted to shift responsibility for executions to those who performed them. He admitted hearing a rumor of two flyers being beheaded, but he dismissed the information as untrue because "to use swords for the execution of prisoners of war was against Bushido." After failing to recall a single act of prisoner abuse, he blandly said, "If executions took place, they were contrary to my orders."[5]

When Corporal Shigenobu Nakamura confessed that he had executed Hall, he explained how the command system worked. On Chichi Jima the army and the navy functioned as two separate entities, meaning that Mori did as he wished and so did Tachibana. Major Matoba could order executions without the approval of Mori but not without the approval or direction of Tachibana, and, said Nakamura, "those orders must be obeyed. You can find out from any soldier on Chichi Jima that the daily life and actions of Major Matoba is beyond words." Nakamura explained that when he received the order to execute Hall from Captain Sato, it was the same as receiving the order from Tachibana.[6]

When Tachibana expected the Bonins to be assaulted during the February 1945 bombings, the general and battalion commanders drank heavily and became deliriously intoxicated. Tachibana attended nightly sake and rum parties and ate the food served, including vegetables laced with human liver. Yet he calmly denied being at a sake party at the 307th Battalion with Colonel Kato, Captain Ikawa, and Major Matoba when the first flesh was cooked and served. "I do not remember such an incident," the shocked general declared, "and I do not believe that such a thing happened. It is impossible." Though drunk at the time, it is not likely that the general would have forgotten the festive affair's unusual entrée.[7]

The Board of Investigation, unimpressed by Tachibana's straight-faced denials, sent the fat little man back to the stockade. But the puzzling relationship between Tachibana and Mori left questions in their minds. Tachibana pointed to Admiral Mori as supreme commander of the islands, but the two men seldom spoke to each other. Tachibana said he received orders from Major Horie—never directly from General Kuribayashi—implying that Horie may have arranged some of the executions himself. The board doubted this arrangement because the defense of the island and contact with Iwo Jima depended upon close communication between the two branches of service. That was the American way. The board eventually discovered that on Chichi, as in many of the former Imperial strongholds, the Japanese army and navy operated independently. Failing to cooperate hampered their effectiveness as a united fighting force, and the internal skirmish between the two services stretched all the way back to Imperial General Headquarters.

In February 1944 Rear Admiral Mori, a short sinewy man with a long face and a pointed jaw, took command of the Special Naval Base Headquarters on Chichi Jima. Until the surrender of Iwo Jima and the promotion in March 1945 of Tachibana to lieutenant general, Mori admitted to being the ranking officer, but, he said, "Toward the end of August 1944 the Navy and the Army came to an agreement that the senior officer on the island would take supreme command of all forces only [in the event of an American amphibious assault]." Tachibana and Horie attended this meeting and agreed to the arrangement, and General Kuribayashi signed it. During the same meeting the participants agreed to turn all prisoners over to the army for questioning and "disposal."

Mori followed the same book of rules and regulations as Tachibana, the Sakusen Yomurei, but he claimed to be "relieved" when the army took responsibility for prisoners of war because "the Navy would fight more or less on the sea, and could not be troubled with the question of prisoners." On the subject of executions, Mori said, "I never gave specific orders to my men because I thought they would never be guilty of executing prisoners of war. I believed they would obey the book." Mori denied knowing anything about naval personnel involved in executions, even though Vaughn was killed in sight of the admiral's headquarters on the same afternoon that the admiral held a preexecution conversation with Commander Yoshii and Lieutenant Kurasaki.[8]

Mori could not explain how his officers could execute three flyers without his permission: Mershon at Suyeyoshi Tai, Dye at the Yoake Wireless Station, and Vaughn at Kurasaki Butai. According to Mori, neither Lieutenant Suyeyoshi nor Commander Yoshii nor Lieutenant Kurasaki conferred with him beforehand and must have ordered the executions on their own initiatives. Mori attempted to explain that none of the executions could have been committed without his approval, and if asked, he would not have approved them. Even more amazing, more than 150 spectators witnessed the execution of Lieutenant Vaughn, but not Mori, who was in clear view of the execution site from his headquarters and claimed he never saw or heard of it. "Simply because of my lack of control," Mori admitted with lamentations,

three aviators . . . lost their precious lives without [me] knowing about it. I feel morally responsible for the conduct of my men. I did not ever dream that my subordinates would bring prisoners of war, who were in custody of the army, to their units and behead them.

The admiral suggested that navy personnel must have been baited into one or more of the executions by Major Matoba, who constantly mingled with the officers in charge of Suyeyoshi Tai and Kurasaki Butai and influenced their behavior. Mori may have been telling a partial truth. Commander Yoshii paid little attention to Mori's directives, and Matoba seemed to take sadistic pleasure in compromising Mori's authority whenever he could.

Mori opened up the proverbial can of worms when he mentioned Matoba during his testimony. At one of the drinking parties thrown at navy headquarters, Matoba arrived with pieces of human liver skewered on bamboo spits. Mori ate it but denied knowing it came from an executed flyer. Matoba testified that Mori specifically asked for "some human flesh," but the admiral denied making such a request, thinking that what Matoba brought was goat meat. After Matoba informed the party they had eaten human flesh, Mori said, "This alerted me to the possibility of an execution, and gave me the idea that Matoba had killed a prisoner." When asked if he had investigated that possibility, Mori replied that such matters were out of his hands.[9]

What puzzled Major Shaffer and his board was the curious behavior of Admiral Mori in his relationship with the Japanese army. Tachibana treated the navy as a nonentity, and Mori, who outranked the general until 23 March 1945, generously accepted a subordinate role. Having established the pecking order, neither man communicated with the other. Tachibana indirectly blamed Mori for executions by fingering him as the man in charge, and Mori claimed no knowledge of executions until Matoba arrived at Bobitai with a plate full of skewered human liver prepared sukiyaki style. Mori suggested that the liver could have come from anyone and not necessarily from an American prisoner, but he could not explain how that would make a difference after eating it.

Mori continued to ramble through the questioning as one might expect from a confused sailor who had lost his bearings at sea. The admiral denied knowing anything about executions until two months after the war ended. According to Mori, in October 1945 "[t]he Koreans came to one of my officers and threatened that if the Japanese would not let them get away from the Bonins, they would tell the Americans about the execution [by the Second Torpedo Boat Squadron]. This was reported to me," said Mori, "and this is how I came to know of the execution," though the beheading took place about a city block from his headquarters. Mori declared that he knew nothing about General Tachibana's cover-up because nobody told him, nor did he believe that one was necessary. "I did not attend the [general's] meeting," Mori said, "and I heard nothing about executions until the Koreans caused the matter to be brought to my attention." Then, when questioned again about attending the sake party at which Matoba served human liver, Mori merely replied that he thought it was goat meat. Nobody asked him if it tasted like goat meat, which Koreans had testified to having a distinctly different taste and texture than human flesh. The admiral's statement disagreed with the testimony of every other deponent, but after five months of questioning, it had become clear to the board that nobody on Chichi Jima respected Mori's authority and that some of the officers blamed him for never asserting his rank to curb the executions.[10]

Colonel Rixey gave Major Shaffer the authority to investigate but not the authority to convict Japanese personnel suspected of war crimes. The responsibility for trying war criminals lay within the jurisdiction of a military court of law. Having no preconceived notion of exactly what Shaffer's investigation might uncover, Rixey let the board target the men in charge, namely Tachibana and Mori, and waited for the board's recommendations.

Tachibana became a prime suspect the day Colonel Rixey and his staff visited the Daikonzaki Army Cemetery at Omura and viewed the freshly planted cross marking the grave of four unknown flyers falsely reported as killed during an American air raid. To what extent Mori participated in the cover-up Rixey did not know, but he suspected the admiral knew more than he admitted. After months of investigation the board concluded that Tachibana through his senior adjutant, Captain Higashigi, ordered the first executions on Chichi Jima, those being Woellhof and the unknown flyer who had survived the crash of a B-24 near the navy base. The board also concluded that both Tachibana and Higashigi selected the method of execution by specifying bayonets. Despite Mori's testimony to the contrary, the board found the admiral responsible for the executions performed by three naval units, Suyeyoshi Tai (Mershon), the Yoake Wireless Station (Dye), and Kurasaki Butai (Vaughn).[11]

Major Shaffer, Lieutenant Poutasse, and First Lieutenant Caskey recommended that Tachibana be tried by a military commission on four charges: murder, cannibalism, neglect of duty, and violation of the Geneva Convention. They also condemned the general for "ordering a cruel and unusual method of execution" by demanding that bayonets and bamboo spears be employed to execute Hall.

The board recognized the existence of two factions on the island. General Tachibana influenced a small knot of officers composed of Commander Yoshii and Lieutenant Kurasaki of the Imperial Navy, and Captain Higashigi and Major Matoba of the Imperial Army, all of whom believed in executing prisoners of war and eating their flesh as an example of courage to the men in their commands. Major Horie led a much larger group of junior officers who believed that the other faction carried the treatment of prisoners to extremes but did not have the authority to prevent it.

The board experienced difficulty in pinning charges of murder against Admiral Mori because the bulk of the evidence pointed to Tachibana. They let Mori off easy, accusing him of cannibalism and neglect of duty. The latter charge emanated from his apparent indifference to the executions performed by his own naval officers and his unwillingness to challenge a subordinate officer, General Tachibana, for command of the Bonins.[12]

Having dealt with Tachibana and Mori, the board turned to the murders of the other six flyers.

Colonel Takemune Kato reached Chichi Jima on 27 June 1944, twelve days after the first heavy carrier raid, and took command of the 307th

Battalion at Kominato. He tried to deny responsibility for the execution of Grady Alvan York. He witnessed the execution of the flyer and later admitted that the directive for killing York with bamboo spears came from Tachibana. Kato did not want the flyer's blood on his hands, so he used his adjutant, Captain Ikawa, to make arrangements with Lieutenant Yamashita to perform the execution. Doubting whether bamboo spears would kill York quickly, Ikawa added a detail of men with bayonets to finish the job. At first Kato denied involvement, but subordinate officers and enlisted men implicated him by their testimony. The board recommended that Kato be charged with the murder of York and the desecration of the flyer's body to feed the cannibals.[13]

Captain Shizuo Yoshii, formerly a commander, arrived on Chichi Jima on 9 August 1944, two days after the execution of Woellhof and the unknown flyer, and took command of the Yoake Wireless Station. He instigated no executions until 23 February 1945 when he obtained James Wesley Dye from Horie and a day later ordered the flyer beheaded. Driven by the warped theory that human flesh strengthened a person's courage in battle, he ate part of Dye's liver and served the rest of the flyer's flesh to his unit. The board recommended that Yoshii, who had been wounded on 4 July 1945 and evacuated to Japan, be tried for murder and cannibalism. Yoshii never admitted to the charges and refused to stand trial, not that he had any say in the matter.[14]

On 21 April 1946 Yoshii issued a statement accusing the United States of "inventing" war crimes trials "to grind Japan under its heels," which, he stated, "cannot be accomplished without exterminating every living Japanese." He justified the execution of prisoners because "it was too difficult and practically impossible to send them to Japan." He also implied a reluctance to feed prisoners because "men were dying from starvation at their battle stations from lack of supplies and enemy bombing raids." He said nothing about cannibalism, nor did he mention the large cache of provisions Marines later discovered stored in caves. "Therefore," he added, "War Crimes Trials are a stupid fantasy" originated by Americans. Such bluster would not help Yoshii, but as his subordinates once said, "The commander is not an ordinary person."[15]

Yoshii never implicated his two executioners, but others did. Lieutenant (jg) Hayashi at first refused to behead Dye, but Yoshii shamed him in front of the enlisted men and forced the killing upon the young man. Hayashi severed Dye's spinal chord but failed to behead him. Lieutenant (jg) Shinichi Masutani finished the job but rather crudely. The board recommended that both men be tried for murder, but in the matter of Hayashi they suggested clemency.[16]

Major Sueo Matoba had captured the curiosity of Colonel Rixey ever since he first stepped on board the USS *Trippe* to answer questions. During the session the colonel sized up Matoba as a bully accustomed to getting his own way, but even Rixey could not have guessed that the major's influence extended to admirals, generals, and colonels. Matoba eventually distinguished himself as the most conniving and voracious cannibal of the warrior caste on Chichi Jima. Corporal Nakamura, after confessing to the execution of Hall, listed a number of officers who had been so intimidated by Matoba that they should not be seated near him during a trial.[17]

In the early stage of the investigation Matoba said nothing that would connect him to executions or to cannibalism. He appeared before the board four times before he fully confessed his role as the ringleader of the executioners. Along the way he implicated Tachibana, Mori, and Major Horie. Not all of Matoba's testimony wore the badge of credibility because he harbored an obvious enmity toward Mori and Horie. Not only did Matoba confess to eating human liver on no less than three occasions; he also admitted to taking a pill produced in Singapore from human liver for the same reason as people of today take daily vitamins or antacids.

"Then, by your own admission," Lieutenant Caskey asked, "you are a cannibal?"

"Yes," Matoba replied reflectively. "I was a madman due to the war and that is the only reason I can give for being a cannibal."

Matoba made the case against himself, and the board recommended that he be charged with murder and cannibalism. The major did not seem to mind. He even looked amused, like he had perpetrated a great joke on someone and the outcome did not concern him. Matoba proved to be an interesting character with peculiar notions whether sober or drunk. He was the only battalion commander to hold the lesser rank of major, but Tachibana treated him like a colonel. The other battalion commanders were one or two grades above him, but he showed them no deference and made them subject to his whims. Matoba took special delight in bullying captains, many of whom attempted to avoid him during his frequent drinking sprees.[18]

Though Matoba masterminded some of the executions, Tachibana began the practice on 26 July 1944 when he instructed Captain Higashigi, his senior adjutant, to order Lieutenant Colonel Ito to execute Woellhof and the unknown flyer. "It has been decided upon that the prisoners should be executed by bayoneting," Higashigi said to Ito. "You are to supervise the execution." Ito did not ask questions. He assumed the order came from Tachibana. After the execution, he reported the details to the general. Tachibana grunted, feigned surprise, and said nothing.

Ito never clearly understood why he had been chosen to perform the execution. His relations with Tachibana had always been strained, and the two had recently disagreed because the general believed Ito lacked initiative. After the quarrel the general communicated with Ito only through his adjutant, which explains the general's grunt when Ito reported the execution. Ito remained puzzled over being chosen to kill the prisoners and concluded, perhaps falsely, that "Horie could not find anyone to dispose of the flyers; and therefore, the duty fell upon the Ryoden Shireibu to do the dirty work."

Before Shaffer's board had time to discover the extent of atrocities on Chichi Jima, Ito returned to Japan. Rixey issued orders for his arrest, and Ito spent a few weeks in Tokyo's Sugamo prison before being returned to Chichi for questioning. He admitted giving a speech at the scene of the execution, inscribing two bull's-eyes on the chests of the flyers, and personally beheading the flyers after they were bayoneted and thought to be dead. The board recommended that Ito be tried for two counts of murder.[19]

Captain Seiji Higashigi proved to be another shifty character, and his contradictory testimony made the board of investigation uneasy. Higashigi claimed that he received orders to "dispose" of Woellhof and the unknown flyer from Haken Shireibu, the exact words from division (Horie's) headquarters being, "Tomorrow the Ryodan Shireibu must dispose of the prisoners of war." This meant the orders had to come from either General Kuribayashi, who was on Iwo Jima, or Major Horie. At a party that night Tachibana decided that the 307th Battalion would kill the flyers. Higashigi attempted to absolve himself from any involvement in the execution, and he tried to shield Tachibana by shifting all the blame to Horie.

Lieutenant Poutasse, who took notes through the questioning, observed that Higashigi did not like either Horie or Ito and mirrored the attitude of the pro-Tachibana faction. Higashigi lost all credibility when he quoted Tachibana as saying: "The question of prisoners of war, which is an important matter as this is a good source of outside information, must be kept in mind. Prisoners must be treated kindly. They must not be killed or executed wantonly. Also they must not be mistreated in any way." Higashigi could not explain what he meant by not "mistreating" a prisoner while at the same time executing him using unwanton methods. The board knew better and recommended that Higashigi be tried for murder. They found small reason to charge men such as Higashigi with perjury because American laws meant nothing to them.[20]

Captain Noboru Nakajima represented a macabre case of Japanese behavior induced by intoxication, an affliction that pervaded 308th Battalion headquarters during the mid-February 1945 air raids. Nakajima commanded the machine-gun company and attended most of Matoba's liver, rum, and sake parties. He could not recall eating human flesh because he usually became too intoxicated to recognize it. Unlike Captain Higashigi, Nakajima recalled a verbal order from General Tachibana directing that all flyers be beaten and killed by the battalion that captured

Pictured from left to right are Lieutenant General Yoshio Tachibana, Major Sueo Matoba, Lieutenant Colonel Kikuji Ito, and Lieutenant Mitsuyoshi Sasaki as they depart for trial at Guam. (Courtesy of Dr. Eugene F. Poutasse. Digitally enhanced by Wendy A. Webster)

them. When Nakajima left Matoba's party to question AOM2c Frazier, the only impulse that permeated through the glaze of the captain's self-induced intoxication was Tachibana's order to beat American flyers. He had just been chastised by Matoba and needed to vent his anger on someone. After beating Frazier to death, he could not explain his actions. The board recommended that Nakajima be tried for murder, which he admitted, and cannibalism, which he denied.[21]

Captain Kesakichi Sato had arrived at Chichi Jima in mid-June 1944. He commanded the 308th Battalion's first company and later became a part of Matoba's headquarter's staff. He had just returned from an inspection of island defenses when Matoba ordered him to execute Ensign Hall. Sato left a vague account of the killing in an effort to not incriminate himself. He watched as Surgeon Teraki began carving up Hall's body and departed before the medical officer finished. Sato could not explain why he had been placed in charge of the execution, but the answer probably had more to do with the twisted manifestations of the devil in Matoba. Because Sato did not drink, Matoba seldom invited the captain to his parties. The major considered sobriety a weakness and probably decided to strengthen Sato's constitution, or perhaps drive him to drink, by forcing him to execute Hall. Because Sato had followed Tachibana's orders, the board recommended that he be charged with murder and the violation of the Geneva Convention for the treatment of prisoners of war.[22]

Captain Shigeo Ikawa served as adjutant to Colonel Kato. As was the custom in the Japanese army, the colonel used Ikawa to arrange for the execution of York. Tachibana wanted York killed by companies that had lost the most men in air raids, so Ikawa searched the casualty list and picked six executioners. York's death initiated another drinking party at Ryodan Shireibu. Matoba provided the meat, which most everyone expected to be human flesh. Ikawa cooked part of the meat in a pot and fried the rest in soy sauce. Ikawa denied eating human flesh, but too many of his comrades saw him chewing it. Though the captain performed no executions, he organized the killing of York. The board recommended that Ikawa be tried for murder, cannibalism, and the cooking of human flesh.[23]

Captains and lieutenants in Tachibana's First Mixed Brigade bore the burden of executing the flyers because higher-ranking officers wanted to toughen them up for the anticipated American invasion. This so-called toughening up became an excuse for everything from murder to cannibalism. First Lieutenant Masao Yamashita became entangled in the same trap when Colonel Kato, communicating to Yamashita through Ikawa, ordered him to execute York using bamboo spears. Yamashita tried to deny any complicity in the execution and succeeded only in making himself more culpable. Yamashita could not evade Ikawa's order, but this did not appease or impress the Board of Investigation. They recommended that Yamashita be tried for murder and for using a cruel and unusual method of execution.[24]

Tachibana's and Matoba's influence reached beyond the affairs of the army. Commanders of navy antiaircraft emplacements, such as Lieutenant Suyeyoshi's Number 8 Battery on Mikazuki Hill, reported to Admiral Mori. If an American amphibious assault were to occur, command of the battery would revert to the army. The Suyeyoshi Tai unit operated in the vicinity of the 308th Battalion and in the event of an attack would fall under direct orders from Major Matoba. As a consequence, Matoba became more influential with officers at Suyeyoshi Tai than Mori and constantly meddled in naval affairs.

Matoba admitted sending Mershon to Suyeyoshi Tai for execution. Lieutenant Suyeyoshi never admitted any involvement in the execution. He testified that he thought the scheme was just another of Matoba's sardonic jokes. But Suyeyoshi clearly understood that Matoba was sending Mershon to his unit to be executed and that Lieutenant (jg) Morishita had volunteered to do the beheading. In keeping with Tachibana's directives, the unit capturing a prisoner had first "disposal" rights.

Suyeyoshi did not know that Tachibana and Matoba later ordered First Lieutenant Teraki to remove Mershon's liver and flesh, nor did he participate in the feast. The board could not call Morishita to account because when they summoned him from Japan, the surgeon committed suicide. Nor could they pin Mershon's execution directly on Suyeyoshi, but they recommended that he be tried for murder and neglect of duty.[25]

After compiling all the evidence and sorting through a screen of deception to find the truth, the board recommended thirty-one officers and enlisted men be tried by a military commission. The three surgeons—Matsushita, Sasaki, and Teraki—were to be tried for the mutilation of the bodies of Vaughn, Hall, and Mershon. For eleven enlisted men and one officer charged with murder the board recommended clemency. They charged seven men with intentional cannibalism, leaving hundreds, perhaps thousands, of others to wonder for the balance of their lives whether or not they had eaten human flesh.

In early June, Major Shaffer, Lieutenant Caskey, and Lieutenant Poutasse presented their proceedings, findings of fact, opinions, and recommendations to Colonel Rixey. On 6 June 1946 Rixey forwarded the information to ComMarianas at Guam and recommended that a military commission try the accused.[26]

After eight months of investigation, Colonel Rixey shipped thirty-one officers and enlisted men to Guam for trial. Then he went home on leave to await the court's decision.

CHAPTER 13

Decision at Guam

Rear Admiral Arthur G. Robinson, USN, presided at the War Crimes Commission at Guam. Unlike the massive war crimes trials held by the International Military Tribunal for the Far East (IMTFE) in Tokyo and Yokohama, where some 980 suspected war criminals such as General Hideki Tojo and Admiral Osami Nagano waited for judgment day in Sugamo prison, Robinson's court went about its business with little notice. He and the commission members reviewed the Chichi Jima Board of Investigation's recommendations and reduced the number of Japanese nationals to be tried for war crimes from thirty-one to twenty-five. Robinson believed that twenty-five alleged war criminals were too many to be tried together, so he told the military commission to divide the prisoners into two groups and hold two trials. General Tachibana and Admiral Mori headed the list, followed by Yoshii, Matoba, Sato, Suyeyoshi, Sasaki, Matsushita, Isogai, Hayashi, Masutani, and three enlisted men, Shigenobu Nakamura, Kido, and Yasumasu Mori. The judge advocate general (JAG) at ComMarianas set the trial date for 5 August 1946. Weeks later, when Tachibana and Mori stood trial, officers such as Lieutenant Colonel Kikuji Ito, Captain Noburo Nakajima, Captain Kesakichi Sato, and Captain Masao Yamashita had already been tried and convicted. The tone of the first trial set the tone for the second trial after Shizuo Morikawa, the lead defense lawyer from Tokyo, failed to convince the tribunal that his client, former Lieutenant Colonel Kikuji Ito, deserved to be acquitted because Japanese moral standards, including acts of cannibalism, were different from those of the West.[1]

The second half of the trial held the most interest because it involved Tachibana, Mori, Yoshii, and Matoba. Two attorneys from the U.S. Naval

Reserve—Lieutenant Edward W. Field and Lieutenant Commander Donald H. Dickey—presented the opening arguments for the prosecution's case, and Lieutenant Frederic T. Suss, also from the Naval Reserve, presented the closing argument.[2]

The defense team for the thirteen Japanese defendants during the second trial contained a mix of nationalities. Shizuo Morikawa presented the opening arguments for General Tachibana, Admiral Mori, and Major Matoba. Kenro Ito represented Sato, Isogai, and Suyeyoshi. Ijichi Shigeatsu represented Lieutenant Matsushita, Corporal Nakamura, and Sergeant Mori. Masanao Toda represented Lieutenant Hayashi, Lieutenant Masutani, Lieutenant Sasaki, and Superior Private Kido. Commander Martin E. Carlson, USNR, represented all the Japanese defendants and delivered the closing argument for the accused.[3]

Without the testimony collected by Major Shaffer's Board of Investigation, there would never have been a trial. Admiral Robinson demanded discrete, supportable evidence rather than the "damning tales" espoused by the prosecution. He found all he wanted in the thorough testimony submitted by Shaffer's board and through the corroboration of witnesses who had testified before the board on Chichi Jima. Little of material significance changed from the testimony given on Chichi, though sixty-six witnesses were called and more than 3,000 pages of new testimony and exhibits created. Nothing about the original testimony changed, nor was much in the way of new content added. What did change were the denials, which became a combination of excuses and a few rare apologies to explain the motivations of the island cannibals. With the exception of two international war crimes trials—one in Germany, the other in Tokyo—the trial on Guam became the longest war crimes trial on record and one of the most important.

Prosecution and defense teams brought their own battery of interpreters, and arguments ensued continuously over differences in translations. The prosecution had the so-called ace-in-the-hole because they had the good sense to bring Fred Savory from Chichi Jima to act as one of their translators. He understood both languages—Japanese and English—better than any translator on either team, and not a word of testimony became corrupted in translation with Fred there.

General Tachibana blamed his behavior on the severity of the American bombing, claiming that it had cut off supply lines and endangered morale.

It would be difficult for us to force a survival unless we took exhaustive steps to strengthen our self-sustaining powers. We overcame these obstacles and continued our work in building fortifications, in training, and in self-sustenance day and night with a firm determination to act in a way not shameful to those seniors and colleagues who had died on other battlefields.

The general listed a litany of command problems, adding, "I did not feel the necessity to establish a special policy for prisoners." Tachibana, however, never defined his policy for prisoners. Unlike some of the officers whose testimony followed, he made no direct reference to executions or cannibalism and showed no remorse for his actions because he denied all the allegations. He remained impassive throughout the trial, as if those who refuted his testimony were discussing someone else.[4]

Tachibana's defense team, however, attempted to excuse the general's behavior because in late 1944 the delivery of food supplies ceased and created great concern on the island. The Marines who locked the general into the Chichi Jima stockade found him "fat and healthy," thereby nullifying the defense team's efforts to explain cannibalism as an excuse for survival, at least on the part of the general. After going into the stockade "Old Tachy" lost about a hundred pounds.[5]

Vice Admiral Mori, the reluctant supreme commander of Chichi Jima, rattled off a litany of excuses to justify his neglect, claiming to be too "busy with defense measures, particularly on that of the airfield, and did not have a moment's rest from planning anti-air defenses. . . . I did not have authority to issue orders except on defense and operational matters." Mori attempted to reduce his alleged involvement in any of the executions committed by naval entities by claiming to have had nothing to do with the "administration of the separate Naval units on Chichi Jima" because those units were either controlled by the Yokosuka Naval Base or by Tachibana's battalion commanders. Under such an arrangement, the admiral would have little to do but sit in his office and look out the window. Mori tried to convince the court of his obliviousness toward the acts of crime surrounding his headquarters. He now claimed having no recollection of Matoba's visit with a serving of human liver pierced with bamboo sticks, or when the major handed him the plate and said, "I have the human liver as promised." Whether Matoba used those exact words can be argued, but Mori dined that night on human flesh. "If I had known about these incidents," he said reflectively, "I would have surely reported them to the Yokosuka Naval Base." Mori's statement suggests that he would not have taken any action on the island to curb cannibalism, and his way out would have been to refer the problem to Yokosuka, where nothing could have been done because of the isolation of Chichi from the home islands.[6]

Captain Shizuo Yoshii, the fiery 125-pound commander of the Yoake Wireless Station, probably put his finger on one of the strategic mistakes that led to the rapid collapse of the Imperial Japanese military machine when he said, "I believe that one of the reasons Japan lost the war was because she did not establish a joint communication system between her land, sea and air forces, and there was no means of direct contact be-

tween them." Yoshii might as well have said that there was no communication among the army and navy on Chichi Jima with Mori and
Tachibana in charge.

Yoshii blamed his irrational behavior on the crushing American bombing raids. Surprise Japanese air attacks on Pearl Harbor, Wake Island,
China, Singapore, and the Philippines played no part in his thought
process. He only saw his comrades "being blown to bits." He believed
the forces on Chichi Jima needed to find a way to strike back. He did
not explain how killing James Wesley Dye and eating his flesh satisfied
a compulsive urge for revenge.

Yoshii refused to answer questions when summoned before Shaffer's
board, but during the Guam trial he probably unintentionally saved
Mori's life when he stated:

I received a warning from Admiral Mori not to visit with the Army and associate
with them, but I had a strong belief that it was necessary for me to get acquainted
with the unit commanders to succeed in establishing a joint Army-Navy communication system on Chichi. So I visited the Army in a manner that it was
impossible for Admiral Mori to find out. [The admiral] must have been unaware
of this until the last. That was because I was one of the senior officers in the
Navy and had absolute trust in my specialty, communication. I acted according
to my beliefs because I wanted to win the war, and as a result, I was named as
a war criminal and am now being tried as one.[7]

Yoshii might have escaped with his life had it not been for the testimony of Petty Officer Fumio Tamamura, who seemed to have disappeared into the chaos of Japan's postwar turmoil. After an unproductive
search for Tamamura in Japan, they found him living with relatives in
San Francisco and brought him to Guam. In flawless English, Tamamura
corroborated the testimony he had given before the Chichi board and
dashed the efforts of the defense team to save Yoshii's life.[8]

Major Sueo Matoba blamed his behavior on the Japanese military
handbook *Battlefront Teachings*, which stressed that a soldier must never
be disgraced by becoming a prisoner of war. The little handbook said
nothing about becoming a cannibal, but Matoba, like Tachibana, had an
enormous appetite. "The food situation became critical," he said, "and
even on half our normal rations they would last us only a few months
more. Much of our food was blasted by the bombings and before us was
death by starvation or death in action, there was only death remaining
for us." Matoba never mentioned being drunk for days on end and probably spoke for himself when he said, "Because of dire conditions on the
island, personnel became excited, agitated, and seething with uncontrol-
lable rage. These conditions affected not only physical but also mentally

the officers and men. None of us were really normal. . . . We were all definitely abnormal."

The major exaggerated the food situation because the U.S. Marines uncovered caves stacked with tons of canned fish, rice, and other provisions, and everywhere on the island were hundreds of vegetable gardens and here and there ice plants stocked with fresh fish and an occasional whale caught in the waters off Chichi. But with more than 20,000 mouths to feed, a food shortage was indeed a concern.

Matoba attempted to plead temporary insanity and became the first of the senior officers on trial to express regret. "If given an opportunity," Matoba said, "maybe mental doctors can find out what made us do the things for which we are being tried. We really are not cannibals."[9]

Captain Kesakichi Sato participated in the execution of Ensign Floyd Ewing Hall, but he never demonstrated any regret. "I was in a situation in which I had to do what was ordered," Sato said, "even if I knew it might be unjust. No matter what the situation was, we had to obey every order. Not only in this affair, but at all times I found myself in an awkward position, having to give Major Matoba's orders to my company commanders."

Sato happened to be one of the officers Matoba hoped to "toughen up" by forcing him to execute Hall and by bearing witness to the dissection of the flyer's body. Sato had never been, in a strict military sense, a professional soldier. Like many men before the war, he had been a reservist in a nonmilitary occupation and recalled to duty in 1937 during the Sino-Japanese War. While on Chichi he left four children at home with his forty-year-old-wife, and his thoughts were mainly with them and not with the Imperial Japanese army.[10]

Lieutenant Jitsuro Suyeyoshi, at Matoba's insistence, made arrangements for the execution of Marvie William Mershon on or about 22 February 1945. Suyeyoshi never admitted executing anyone or having a role in the removal of flesh from Mershon's body. He claimed to have drunk whiskey with two American pilots and being thanked by them. "Since I am a Buddhist," Suyeyoshi said, "I never did myself or ordered my men to do what might be thought cruel during several battles in which we engaged. It was my opinion that we were fighting for our country and that we fought fairly so that we need not be ashamed for our nation or for those who died at the front." Suyeyoshi did not do the beheading. He left that task to Lieutenant (jg) Morishita, who may have given Suyeyoshi undeserved shelter by committing suicide rather than testify.[11]

Lieutenant Mitsuyoshi Sasaki recalled entering the service as a surgeon and being indoctrinated into the "blind execution of orders." There was no Hippocratic Oath for Japanese doctors. "The demand was made for your death in the future," Sasaki said, "using the seductive words of

'Servitude without thought of self, loyalty to the Emperor, [and] Love of country.' "

Sasaki served under the oppressive command of Yoshii. He obeyed his orders and carved up the body of James Wesley Dye. He lamented the air raids that brought scarcity to the island, death to some of his colleagues, and fear and despair to himself. He blamed Yoshii for compelling him to perform deplorable acts. "I had no evil intent," Sasaki said. "For this reason I could not feel that I had done wrong when I was not responsible for my acts." Sasaki presented a tearful case of personal sadness, appealing to the tender mercies of the court because his mother, "who was never too strong, must be worrying. I have heard," he said, "that she is ill again." Sasaki did not pause to reflect on how Dye's mother might feel.[12]

Lieutenant Kanehisa Matsushita, who served as surgeon for the 2nd Torpedo Boat Squadron, made two slashes into the abdomen of Warren Earl Vaughn to remove the flyer's liver and perhaps his gall bladder. For being forced to dissect Vaughn he blamed Lieutenant Kurasaki, whom he described as "our absolute order giver and his guiding hand reached everywhere into our life. He used to say, 'You'll be doing all right if you model after me.' "

Matsushita said the order to remove Vaughn's liver came suddenly, and "though I asked for a reason, it was bluntly denied me. I refused two or three times," the surgeon declared,

but I was compelled to obey the order. I took it for granted that the order was both a reasonable and necessary dissection. I wanted to put the liver back, but it was gone. I saluted the body to show my respect, sewed up the cuts in the belly and neck, wiped off the body, and left in the gathering darkness.

No witnesses appeared to confirm Matsushita's final salute, but under the chain of command, the surgeon had every reason to believe the order emanated from Mori.

For Matsushita, war brought many miseries. His two brothers were doctors. One was killed on New Guinea and the other wounded from the atomic blast at Nagasaki. "I hope there will not be another war," he said, "because it is bound to take many lives, rob mankind of their reason, and subject them to war psychology." Matsushita did not explain what he meant by war psychology, but the men who investigated war crimes on Chichi Jima did.[13]

First Lieutenant Gunji Isogai killed no prisoners of war but nibbled on the liver from Ensign Hall's body. He attributed his behavior to an "unnatural state of mind." He acted every bit like a confused soldier who could not stick to a point of discussion. "I have never thought of eating human flesh," he said, but then he ate some. "At that time I used to become gay and lost my sense when I drank liquor, which made me believe the words of other people who later told me of my behavior while I was intoxicated. I could not trust myself when I drank." Isogai would have the commission believe that drunkenness made him an unwilling receptacle for human liver served during one or more of Matoba's drinking parties. "But since I liked drinking," Isogai added, "and my faults on account of it were not serious, I did not give it up." Isogai wanted the court to believe that he had not eaten human flesh but thought he did because Matoba told him so.[14]

Twenty-one-year-old Lieutenant (jg) Minoru Hayashi came before the military court as another pathetic creature of Commander Yoshii's making. "I obeyed the order of execution against my will," Hayashi declared. "I excused myself as firmly as possible, but I was obliged to obey the command, afraid of the seriousness of the crime of disobedience." Hayashi made a point. The Imperial *Rescript* taught that any order of a superior was absolute, and if not obeyed during wartime, a person could be sentenced to death or life imprisonment. According to the *Rescript* an order from a superior amounted to an order from His Majesty, the Emperor. Hayashi explained that rank among the lower officer grades was "nothing but an ornament," and "our actual authority was as little as an enlisted man's."

Hayashi's saber did not kill Dye with a single blow. He became too distraught to make a clean cut, and the blade bit deeply enough to possibly sever the flyer's spinal chord. What Dye felt halfway through the slipshod execution will never be known, but both men, Hayashi and Dye, became tragic victims of Chichi Jima's horrors.[15]

Lieutenant (jg) Shinichi Masutani became implicated in the execution of James Dye because Yosii ordered him to finish the work Hayashi bungled. Masutani proved to be as clumsy as Hayashi, requiring two blows to decapitate Dye. Both men were young officers and not trained to kill in the manner of regular navy officers, but Yoshii believed they must be hardened to fight and to "serve for the future of Japan." Designating them as executioners provided a lesson in hardening that put both men on trial for murder.[16]

The three enlisted men brought to trial at Guam became unwilling puppets of their commanders. Captain Sato ordered Corporal Shigenobu Nakamura to behead Floyd Ewing Hall. Nakamura protested but followed orders. Sato then ordered Sergeant Yasumasu Mori to bayonet the beheaded body, and Mori thrust his bayonet into the corpse. Mori made no excuses for his behavior and simply asked the court for leniency. Nakamura lamented the incident, declaring,

If I did not have duties that required me to wear a sword; if I had not been a liaison man and required to pass on the scene of the execution; if I had not

stopped at the scene of the execution and gone past, it might well be that I would
not have come to my present situation.[17]

The third enlisted man, Superior Private Matsutaro Kido, bayoneted
either Lloyd Richard Woellhof or the unknown flyer on 7 August 1944.
His partner in the bayoneting episode, Leading Private Hisao Shimura,
committed suicide and never came to trial. Nor did two other men assigned to the execution, leaving Kido to stand trial as the lone member
of the four-man execution squad. As many as six others were involved
in the execution, but they reached Japan before the investigation began
and faded entirely out of sight. Like most of the Japanese, Kido never
expressed regret for killing the flyers. He complained mostly about living
expenses in Japan, but added, "Though I did not like military service, I
had to enter the Army because it was my duty."[18]

As soon as the trial started, petitions of clemency began flooding the
system. Some came to the military commission, some went to the Commander in Chief Pacific Fleet, and a number of them went directly to
General Douglas MacArthur in Japan. Major Horie put in a good word
for Lieutenant Hayashi and blamed the order for executing Dye on
Yoshii. He also spoke kind words about Admiral Mori, asking the court
to "give him merciful judgment." Support for Hayashi and Mori came
from dozens of others—Hayashi for his reluctant role as executioner, and
Mori for his somewhat belated objections to executing prisoners of war.[19]

The most interesting of Horie's petitions for clemency pertained to
Major Matoba—the only request for clemency that Matoba received.
Horie credited Matoba as being clever and a man with initiative, but he
really never said anything good about him. He admitted that the major
had become addicted to drinking and merely suggested that Matoba be
committed to the "U.S. Medical Society concerning his violent alcohol-
ism." Matoba would have laughed at such a verdict and attributed it to
American stupidity.[20]

General Tachibana joined Matoba as the only other defendant to receive but one petition for clemency. It did not come from Major Horie
but from Major Sanichi Yokota, who served under him for a year. "His
only fault was drinking," Yokota said. "He overindulged unintentionally
because of the temper of the [sake] parties. I am so ashamed I could not
make him give it up." Yokota's clemency missed the point. Horie, who
worked with Yokota and knew Tachibana best, said nothing in defense
of the general, and his silence struck home with the court.[21]

Major Horie became the star witness for the prosecution during the
Guam trials. If he still had something to hide, no one bothered to hunt
for it, for Horie was not on trial. His testimony became a major factor
in convicting his fellow officers, though he consistently defended the

Japanese army and its code of conduct in his many trips to the witness chair.

For many of the twenty-five men on trial the Board of Investigation recommended clemency because of the mitigating circumstance of the accused being forced to perform executions and remove human flesh on orders from superior officers. The board wanted to punish the men in authority who perpetrated the crimes through their policies and practices. The two trials held at Guam lasted longer than the Chichi investigation, and the prosecution focused mainly on Tachibana, Mori, Yoshii, Matoba, Kato, Ito, and captains such as Nakajima and Yamashita who carried out the orders and joined in the practice of cannibalism. Of the twenty-five men scheduled for trial, the commission set four free and reduced the number of defendants to twenty-one.

The board incurred no difficulty in charging men with cannibalism, but the War Crimes Commission did. No international law, naval law, modern law, or the Geneva Convention provided a penalty for cannibalism or the cooking of human flesh. The delegates writing such laws never envisioned cannibalism as a potential act of war. Of the 980 Japanese charged with war crimes in Tokyo and Yokohama, only four were charged with cannibalism. There were men involved in the cases tried in Japan who were found guilty of vivisection, but charges of cannibalism proved to be unsupportable. It seemed that all the flesh eaters had been brought together on Chichi Jima.[22]

Of Chichi's twenty-one defendants, eight were charged with either eating human flesh or cooking it. Perhaps for no reason other than to establish a precedent, all eight defendants were convicted but received light sentences.[23]

As the trial came to an end, men like Major Matoba, Colonel Ito, Captain Yoshii, and Captain Nakajima confessed their crimes but did not escape the noose. General Tachibana impassively denied his guilt to the bitter end. When Tachibana learned that he would be hanged with the other four, he "seemed rather happy about the occasion as though he were glad to know it would be over soon." On 24 September 1947 U.S. Marines, under the direction of Lieutenant Colonel G.R. Newton, hanged all five men without ceremony and without publicity near ComMarianas headquarters on Guam. A sixth criminal went to the gallows with the five from Chichi—Rear Admiral Shigematsu Sakaibara, the "gentleman soldier" and "protector of the common man" who had beheaded two Americans, one by his own hand, and in 1943 shot ninety-six prisoners of war on Wake Island.[24]

Before the gibbet took the life of Captain Yoshii a Buddhist priest, Bunyu Nakajami, flew to Guam from Tokyo to provide spiritual consolation. Yoshii's Christian wife urged him to confess and pray for forgiveness, so he hedged his chances for salvation by turning to a Navy

On 24 September 1947, Major Sueo Matoba is being led to the gallows on Guam. (U.S. Navy Photo, National Archives)

On 24 September 1947, Captain Shizuo Yoshii is being led to the gallows on Guam. (U.S. Navy Photo, National Archives)

chaplain for absolution. The judgment of the court finally made it clear to Yoshii that he had done something wrong. That evening, as Yoshii ascended the scaffold, the Buddhist priest and the Navy chaplain, each in his own way, administered the last rites.

Major Matoba asked for nothing but a cigarette. He calmly smoked it and for the last time in his mortal life viewed the sun sinking low in the western sky. As he puffed on the cigarette, his last thoughts may have been similar to those of the flyers he executed, but probably not, for Matoba was Bushido. A little before sundown the Marines slipped the noose around the bull neck of the "Tiger of Chichi" and sprung the trap.

The commission could never build a strong enough case against Admiral Mori to hang him. Whether supreme commander or not, there was never enough evidence to show that Mori ordered an execution. Nor had he ever stopped an execution. His crime was neglect because he failed to control his navy subordinates or assert his rank. Mori refused to take the stand in his own defense, which may have helped his case. The rambling testimony he gave on Chichi Jima to the Board of Investigation never made much sense and struck Fred Savory as coming from a man anxious to avoid conflicts and unable to make decisions. So Mori remained inscrutably—or perhaps cleverly—silent—an idiosyncrasy of the Japanese mind little understood by Westerners. His expression never changed when ordered to spend the rest of his life in Tokyo's Sugamo prison, an unfitting end for one of Japan's most respected poets. He would, however, have company. The commission failed to find enough evidence to hang Captain Sato and ordered him to the same prison for life.

The other defendants received sentences ranging from five to twenty years. Several of them were convicted of the additional charge of "Failure to Provide Proper Burial for Deceased Prisoners of War," but those were minor penalties. The two surgeons, Matsushita and Sasaki, for which the commission collected the largest stack of pleas for clemency, were among those who received the lighter sentences.[25]

In Japan during the war, no word of atrocities ever reached the people except through the whisper of rumor. Throughout the conflict Imperial propagandists fed the populace daily accounts of benevolent Japanese soldiers treating children in occupied territories with kindness and adults with generosity and charity. Had the civilian population of Japan known of their countrymen's atrocities, they could not have done anything about it, nor would they have tried.

The atrocities on Chichi Jima lay hidden from public sight for fifty-five years. The cover-up nearly succeeded. The people of Japan escaped national embarrassment because the investigation on Chichi Jima and the details of the trial at Guam lay classified by the federal government for two generations. The Guam newspaper covered the trial, but few copies ever got off the island. Had Colonel Rixey, on 6 October 1945, not thrown out a trial balloon and asked the question, "And what became of the American flyers you captured on this island?" the criminals who had taken the lives of at least eight American flyers and had eaten of their bodies would have been repatriated to Japan to live their lives as defeated war heroes and respected members of their communities.

As a result of Rixey's investigation, about fifteen American families learned what happened to their sons. Without the colonel's investigation, the world would never have known about the hidden war on Chichi Jima.

Epilogue

For many decades after the war, Chichi Jima remained an island much the way it looked in 1945. Unlike Iwo Jima, Chichi was never cut to pieces by American bulldozers to make way for vast military installations and spacious airfields. Evidence of caves still dotted Chichi's hills, blasted gun emplacements still scarred the cliffs, and for many years the hulls of rusting ships could still be seen partially submerged in the harbor.

The Potsdam Declaration of 1945 limited Japanese sovereignty to the home islands, and Fred Savory, like his great-grandfather a century before, rekindled old Nat's dream of making the island a possession of the United States. The U.S. Navy administered the Bonins, but they closed the area and made no plans to return some 7,000 Japanese civilians who once farmed, fished, and lived quietly on Chichi Jima and the other islands of the Bonins.

Fred Savory drafted a petition to the State-War-Navy Coordinating Committee in Washington asking that the islanders be allowed to come home. The Navy approved the petition, arguing that the Yankeetown settlers deserved special attention because their Western blood had opened them to persecution by the Japanese. The Navy was especially indebted to Fred Savory and his uncles for helping to identify Japanese war criminals and bring them to justice. In October 1946 the Savorys with about 130 natives returned to Chichi Jima, and Colonel Rixey flew to the island to raise the Stars and Stripes to welcome them.

For a while the Savory clan and their friends lived in Quonset huts provided by the Navy. They regarded the island as theirs, and any Japanese boats venturing into coastal waters were met by a spatter of small arms fire.

Five years after the war the Japanese began lobbying for the return of the islands. By then the administration of the Bonins remained in the care of a single chief petty officer whom the Navy assigned to the island to help the Yankeetown fishermen put their port back into operating condition. With the outbreak of the Korean War in 1950, the Navy renewed its interest in Chichi Jima and developed a top-secret base of unknown but formidable capability. Perhaps the so-called formidable capability involved the rumored storage of nuclear bombs in the copperlined vaults in the hills at Kiyose.

The Japanese-American treaty of 1952 gave Japan "residential authority" in the Bonins but retained the islands under American administration. The Savorys did not like the arrangement. Two of them hitched a ride on a Navy plane and led a four-man team to Washington to petition for the annexation of the Bonins and a grant of American citizenship. The petition failed, and instead of the Bonins becoming an American possession, the government paid $6.5 million to the dispossessed Japanese farmers who once lived on the island, and in late 1967 President Lyndon B. Johnson took action to return the islands to Japan. He also commuted the sentences of Japanese war criminals, setting all the surviving Chichi Jima cannibals free. He did not say whether the release of convicted war criminals was intended to enhance his "Great Society." Fred Savory, who had hoped like his grandfather to make the islands of his birth an American possession, never got his wish. The Japanese renamed the island group the Ogasarawas, after the mystic sage of yore, and in 1972 declared the archipelago a national park.[1]

Fred Savory eventually settled in Guam, where the Stars and Stripes flew every day. He established a fish importing company to process and market the catch coming by boat from Chichi Jima. He built a home on a beautiful Guam beach and joined the U.S. Navy Civil Service. In the evening he took a beer to a rock overlooking the sea and watched the sunset. When nieces and nephews came to visit, Fred told stories about Matoba and the major's recipes for preparing liver.[2]

Colonel Rixey eventually went home, served the remainder of his military career in the Marine Corps, and retired in 1956 as a brigadier general. He taught for a number of years, dying in San Diego on 1 January 1989. New Year's Day would always hold significance for Rixey and his occupation force. In 1946 it became the day his Board of Investigation began lifting the lid on Chichi Jima's nasty little war against captured American flyers and bringing the guilty to trial.[3]

Nothing more need be said about the cannibals of Chichi Jima, but Major Yoshitaka Horie deserves a parting comment. Members of the board never believed that Horie was as guiltless as he claimed, and they

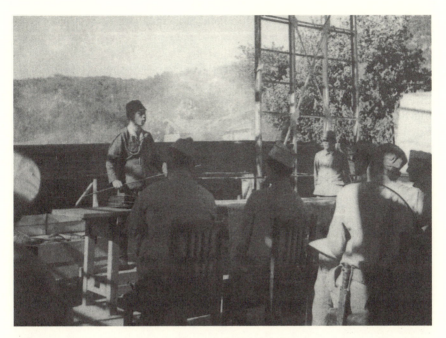

Major Yoshitaka Horie lecturing in English to a group of American officers who came to make a study of Japanese defensive methods on Chichi Jima. (Courtesy of Dr. Eugene F. Poutasse. Digitally enhanced by Wendy A. Webster)

may have been right. Whatever Horie's faults, Rixey liked him, and so did most of the members of the prosecution team during the Guam trial. Horie could not have been much older than thirty years during the investigation on Chichi Jima. When he became the star witness at Guam, he also became Westernized, right down to wearing khaki shorts and GI shoes. After the trial, Horie took his departure and returned to Japan, but before leaving he pulled Colonel Rixey aside and said,

I hope I will be permitted to come to the United States to lecture before your war colleges. Americans know how to attack but they need teachings in defensive strategy. . . . You may need my services for I believe that in five years time, America will be at war with another major world power.

Four years later the Chinese Communist People's Army struck General MacArthur's Eighth Army on the Yalu River in North Korea, broke through poorly organized Allied defenses, and sent the remnants of the general's recently victorious army reeling in retreat.[4]

Among the close calls involving flyers captured at Chichi Jima, another notable American must be remembered, a young pilot named George Herbert Walker Bush—a truly lucky man. When he ditched in the water on 2 September 1944, tidal currents carried him toward the island. He barely escaped capture after Japanese boats pushed off from Hatsune Beach to capture him. To two pilots from the *San Jacinto*, Milton Moore and Donald Melvin, Bush owes his life. The two flyers fired 1,460 rounds at the Japanese boats and drove them back to shore, giving the submarine *Finback* enough time to pull Bush from the water. Instead of flavoring the soup on Chichi Jima as perhaps another unknown flyer, George Bush, body and soul, became a permanent part of American history.[5]

The sordid side of war may never end, whether it involves a small number of crazed Japanese on Chichi Jima, an army of depraved Nazis trying to exterminate the Jewish race, or groups of suicidal Muslims addicted by their religious and terrorist leaders to slaughtering defenseless and innocent civilians of other religious persuasions.

Major Matoba many times admitted that war compelled normal people to perform abnormal acts. "None of us were really normal and knew what he was doing," he said. Then perhaps reflecting on his statement, Matoba added, "We really are not cannibals."[6]

The exposure of war crimes is never pleasant, but the truth needs to be told. The next great conflict could be worse. When Matoba said, "We are not really cannibals," he spoke the truth. But war made Matoba and many others on Chichi Jima something they never were before. The unfortunate American flyers shot down over Chichi Jima never expected to die as they did. Their last flights, by every account, were sorties into hell.

APPENDIX A

Pilots Shot Down over Chichi Jima

Executions

Woellhof, Lloyd Richard, USNR, ARM2c

Captured 4 July 1944
Executed 7 August 1944

Unknown Flyer, Radioman

Captured 4 July 1944
Executed 7 August 1944

Dye, James Wesley, Jr., USN, ARM3c

Captured 18 February 1945
Executed 24 February 1945

Frazier, Glenn J., USNR, AOM2c

Captured 18 February 1945
Executed 18 February 1945

Hall, Floyd Ewing, USNR, Ensign

Captured 18 February 1945
Executed 9 March 1945

Mershon, Marvie William, USNR, ARM3c

Captured 18 February 1945
Executed 22 February 1945

York, Grady Alvan, USNR, AOM3c

Captured 18 February 1945
Executed 28 February 1945

Vaughn, Warren Earl, USMCR, 2nd Lt.

Captured 23 February 1945
Executed 22 March 1945

Sent to Japan as POWs

Doyle, Oscar Long, USN, Petty Off.

Captured 15 June 1944
Sent to Japan

Terry, Calvin D., USN, Lt. (jg)   Captured 15 June 1944
                                                Sent to Japan

Connell, Hershel C., USN, Lt. (jg)   Captured 4 July 1944
                                                Sent to Japan 17 July 1944

Found Dead and Identified

Cavanaugh, John A., USNR, Lt. (jg)   Shot down 5 August 1944
Farrell, William J., USAF, Staff Sgt.   Shot down December 1944

Undetermined

Moseley, William C., USN, Lt.   Shot down 4 July 1944
Verb (unsubstantiated name), Radioman   Shot down 4 August 1944
Fell, Fellow, or Feld (unsubstantiated   Shot down 12 August 1944
name)

Hall, Carroll Curtis, USN, ARM2c   Shot down 18 February 1945
Notony, Joseph Edward   Shot down 18 February 1945
Rolfing, Rudolph F., USN, Ensign   Shot down 18 February 1945
Todd (unsubstantiated name)   Shot down 18 February 1945
Brotton (unsubstantiated name)   Shot down 4–6 August 1944
King (unsubstantiated name)

APPENDIX B

Key Japanese Officers and Enlisted Men Recommended for Trial

Lt. (jg) Minoru Hayashi, IJN (976)

Capt. Seiji Higashigi, IJA (975)—Tachibana's Sr. Adjutant

Capt. Shigeo Ikawa, IJA (974)

1st Lt. Gunji Isogai, IJA (976)

Lt. Col. Kikuji Ito, IJN (974)

Sgt. Kasutoshi Kanemori, IJA (977)

Col. Takemune Kato, IJN (973)

Sup. Pvt. Matsutaro Kido, IJA (977)

Sup. Pvt. Masao Kiryu, IJA (978)

Sgt. Masao Kishimoto, IJA (976)

Lt. (jg) Shinichi Masutani, IJN (976)

Major Sueo Matoba, IJN (974)—Commander, 308th Battalion

Lt. Kanehisa Matsushita, IJN (975)

Vice Admiral Kunizo Mori, IJN, Commanding (973)

Sgt. Yasumasu Mori, IJA (976)

Cpl. Shoichi Morito, IJA (977)

Capt. Noboru Nakajima, IJA (974)

Sup. Pvt. Gyokurin Nakamura, IJA (978)

Cpl. Shigenobu Nakamura, IJA (977)

Sgt. Moriki Okamoto, IJA (976)

Sup. Pvt. Takekazu Oshida, IJA (978)

Lt. Mistuyoshi Sasaki, IJN (975)

Capt. Kesakichi Sato, IJA (974)

Lead. Pvt. Hisao Shimura, IJA (978)

Lt. Jitsuro Suyeyoshi, IJN (974)—Commander, 8th AA Battery

Lt. Gen. Yoshio Tachibana, IJA, Commanding (973)

Cpl. Shinosuke Taniyama, IJA (977)

1st Lt. Tadashi Teraki, IJA (975)

Sgt. Maj. Seiji Wada, IJA (976)

Capt. Masao Yamashita, IJA (975)

Capt. Shizuo Yoshii, IJN (973)—Commander, Yoake Wireless Station

Notes: numbers in parentheses are the page numbers in the *Investigation* documents that specify the Board of Investigation's recommendations to the Guam Military Commission. Names in **bold** were those individuals accused of murder.

Notes

CHAPTER 1

1. Bill D. Ross, *Iwo Jima: Legacy of Valor* (New York: Vanguard Press, 1985), 19.

2. Theodore Taylor, *The Magnificent Mitscher* (New York: W.W. Norton, 1954), 212–13, 241.

3. Samuel Eliot Morison, *History of United States Naval Operations in World War II*, 15 vols. (Boston: Little, Brown, 1947–1962), 6:237–38; Francis T. Miller, *The Complete History of World War II* (Chicago: Progress Research Corporation, 1948), 651; Kyuryo Isoda Testimony, *Records and Proceedings of a Board of Investigation Convened at Headquarters of the Commander, United States Occupation Forces, Bonin Islands . . .* , Brig. Gen. Presley M. Rixey Papers, 376, hereinafter cited as *Investigation*.

4. Morison, *History of United States Naval Operations*, 6:239–40.

5. S.E. Smith, ed., *The United States Navy in World War II* (New York: William Morrow & Company, 1966), 783–84.

6. Quotes from Eric Hammel, *Aces against Japan: The American Aces Speak* (Novato, Calif.: Presidio Press, 1992), 1:219–20.

7. Morison, *History of United States Naval Operations*, 8:313.

8. Robert Sherrod, *History of Marine Corps Aviation in World War II* (Washington, D.C.: Combat Forces Press, 1952), 203, 261; Michael Russell, *Iwo Jima* (New York: Random House, 1974), 13.

9. Isoda Testimony, *Investigation*, 378.

10. A.R. Buchanan, ed., *The Navy's Air War: A Mission Completed* (New York: Harper & Brothers, n.d.), 219.

11. Jack Sweetman, *American Naval History: An Illustrated Chronology of the U.S. Navy and Marine Corps 1775–Present* (Annapolis, Md.: Naval Institute Press, 1984), 207.

12. Morison, *History of United States Naval Operations*, 14:67.

13. Taylor, *The Magnificent Mitscher*, 243–44.

14. Richard Washington Testimony, *Investigation*, 40–41.

15. Robert B. Stinnett, *George Bush: His World War II Years* (Washington, D.C.: Brassey's Inc., 1992), 119, 138, 140, 147, 150.

CHAPTER 2

1. Major Y. Horie, "How the Combat of Chichi Jima Garrison Should Be Conducted," Eugene F. Poustasse Papers, 1–5.

2. "Japanese Camouflage, We Penetrate a Prepared Story in the Occupation of the Bonin Islands," Papers of Brig. Gen. Presley M. Rixey, 1.

3. Samuel Eliot Morison, *"Old Bruin": Commodore Matthew Calbraith Perry, 1794–1858* (Boston: Little, Brown, 1967), 311–12; Fred Savory Testimony, *Investigation*, 2; Gilbert Cant, "Home to Chichi Jima: Yankee Trader's Descendant Welcomes U.S. Flag," *Life* (24 June 1946), 17.

4. Morison, *"Old Bruin,"* 312; Timothy E. Head and Gavan Daws, "The Bonins—Isles of Contention," *American Heritage* (February 1968), 58, 64, 69.

5. Head and Daws, "The Bonins," 63–64.

6. Rixey, "Japanese Camouflage," 5; Cant, "Home to Chichi Jima," 18.

7. Head and Daws, "The Bonins," 62; Cant, "Home to Chichi Jima," 18; Ross, *Iwo Jima*, 18.

8. Head and Daws, "The Bonins," 71.

9. Ibid., 70–71.

10. Russell, *Iwo Jima*, 9.

11. Fred Savory Testimony, *Investigation*, 2.

12. Ross, *Iwo Jima*, 19.

13. Stinnett, *George Bush*, 4, 136–39.

14. Buchanan, *The Navy's Air War*, 206.

15. Fred Savory Testimony, *Investigation*, 4; Morison, *"Old Bruin,"* 314.

16. Buchanan, *The Navy's Air War*, 214.

17. *Record of Proceedings of a Military Commission Convened at U.S. Pacific Fleet ComMarianas, Guam: Case of Yoshio Tachibana et al.*, No. 154578, National Archives, RG 125, File 370 21/29/02, Flynn Argument, F1–2; hereinafter cited as *Trial*.

18. Quoted in Ross, *Iwo Jima*, 20.

19. Quotes from Keith Wheeler, *The Road to Tokyo* (Alexandria, Va.: Time-Life Books, 1979), 41–42.

20. Yoshitaka Horie, "Explanation of Japanese Defense Plan of Chichi Jima," Eugene F. Poustasse Papers; Stinnett, *George Bush*, 119.

21. Buchanan, *The Navy's Air War*, 410; Finding of Facts, *Investigation*, 962.

22. Andrew D. Carson, *My Time in Hell: Memoir of an American Soldier Imprisoned by the Japanese in World War II* (Jefferson, N.C.: McFarland Publishing Company, 1997), 33; Fred Savory Testimony, *Investigation*, 2–8, Exhibit 1.

23. Samuel Savory Testimony, *Investigation*, 21–27; Horie Testimony, ibid., 117–21; Fred Savory Testimony, ibid., 7.

24. Horie Testimony, *Investigation*, 127–29. See also 962–63.

25. Ibid., 130–36.

26. Finding of Facts, *Investigation*, 970, 972.

27. Fred Savory Testimony, ibid., 1–2.

CHAPTER 3

1. Denis M. Frank and Henry I. Shaw, Jr., *Victory and Occupation: History of the U.S. Marine Corps Operations in World War II* (Washington, D.C.: Historical Branch, G-3 Division, Headquarters, U.S. Marine Corps, 1968), 5:460; Flynn Argument, *Trial*, F-2.

2. Rixey, "Japanese Camouflage," 1; William Monks Memoirs, 1 April 2001, in author's possession; Robert J. Gath Memoirs, n.d., in author's possession. Bill Monks now lives in Fairview, N.J., and has published his recollections in a book titled *Pearls* (New York: JJ Company, 2002).

3. Rixey, "Japanese Camouflage," 1; Richard W. Johnston, *Follow Me: The Story of the Second Marine Division in World War II* (New York: Random House, 1948), 144–47.

4. Rixey, "Japanese Camouflage," 1.

5. Ibid.; Frank and Shaw, *Victory and Occupation*, 5:460.

6. Rixey, "Japanese Camouflage," 1–2.

7. Horie Statement, *Investigation*, Exhibit 3A.

8. Rixey, "Japanese Camouflage," 2.

9. Ibid.

10. Ibid.; Transcript of Questioning on *Trippe*, *Investigation*, Exhibit 3; Horie Statement, ibid., Exhibit 3A.

11. Rixey, "Japanese Camouflage," 3; Donald D. Dickey Statement, *Trial*, JJ3; E.F.L. Russell, *The Knights of Bushido* (New York: E.P. Dutton, 1958), 55–56.

12. Rixey, "Japanese Camouflage," 3.

13. Ibid.; List of War Criminals, Eugene F. Poutasse Papers.

14. Frank and Shaw, *Victory and Occupation*, 5:103; Rixey, "Japanese Camouflage," 4.

15. Sugarawa Statement, *Investigation*, 47–49, and Exhibit 3.

16. Rixey, "Japanese Camouflage," 4–5.

17. Quoted in Frank and Shaw, *Victory and Occupation*, 5:460.

18. William Monks, "Once Upon a Time" (unpublished monograph), William Monks Papers, 39, Author's files.

19. Ibid., 39–40; Rixey, "Japanese Camouflage," 5.

20. Monks, "Once Upon a Time," 40–41.

21. Ibid., 41.

22. Ibid.

CHAPTER 4

1. Fred Savory Testimony, *Investigation*, 1; Willie Savory Testimony, ibid., 21.

2. Rixey, "Japanese Camouflage," 5; Cant, "Home to Chichi Jima," 19; Fred Savory Testimony, *Investigation*, 2.

3. Jimmy B. Savory, "My Recollections of Uncle Fred," Jimmy Savory Papers, Author's files.

4. Fred Savory Testimony, *Investigation*, 1–20A; Rixey, "Japanese Camouflage," 5–6.

5. Rixey, "Japanese Camouflage," 6.

6. Fred Savory Testimony, *Investigation*, 13.

7. Rixey, "Japanese Camouflage," 6; Fred Savory Testimony, *Investigation*, 5, 13.

8. Rixey, "Japanese Camouflage," 6.

9. Ibid.; James W. Leary Papers, Author's files.

10. John H. Monaghan Papers, Author's files.

11. Ahn Testimony, *Investigation*, 636–39; Rixey, "Japanese Camouflage," 7.

12. Rixey to Shaffer, 21 December 1945, *Investigation*, A, 292.

13. Rixey, "Japanese Camouflage," 7.

14. William Monks, "Grandpa Goes to War" (unpublished monograph), William Monks Papers, 14, Author's files; Monks, "Once Upon a Time," 43, 44.

15. Monks, "Once Upon a Time," 43.

16. Author's interviews with John Wick, William Monks, Ann Rixey Boyd, and Dr. Eugene Poutasse. See also Stinnett, *George Bush*, 122–24.

17. Monks, "Once Upon a Time," 43–44.

18. Ibid., 46–47.

19. Jerry Candelaria Letters, William Monks Papers, Author's files.

20. Robert Gath Letters, William Monks Papers, Author's files; Dr. Eugene Poutasse, interview by author.

21. James W. Leary Papers.

22. Rixey, "Japanese Camouflage," 7.

23. Testimony of Frederick, Samuel, Roger, Willie Savory, and Richard Washington, *Investigation*, 1–43.

24. Rixey, "Japanese Camouflage," 8.

25. Richard Washington Testimony, *Investigation*, 42.

26. Rixey, "Japanese Camouflage," 8.

27. Ibid.

CHAPTER 5

1. Monks, "Once Upon a Time," 49–50.

2. Rixey, "Japanese Camouflage," 9.

3. Ibid.; Horie Testimony, *Investigation*, 117–54.

4. Rixey, "Japanese Camouflage," 10.

5. Ibid.; Horie Testimony, *Investigation*, 135, 147, 152.

6. Rixey, "Japanese Camouflage," 10; Horie Testimony, *Investigation*, 133, Exhibit 3A.

7. Horie Testimony, *Investigation*, 141–42; Harashima Testimony, ibid., 773.

8. Horie Testimony, ibid., 141–42.

9. Ibid., 154.

10. Rixey, "Japanese Camouflage," 10, 11.

11. Monks, "Once Upon a Time," 42–43.

12. Ibid., 43; Sherrod, *History of Marine Corps Aviation*, 354.

13. Letter from 308th Battalion Personnel, *Investigation*, Exhibit 2.

14. Rixey, "Japanese Camouflage," 11–12.

15. Carson, *My Time in Hell*, 1, 200.

16. Sugawara Testimony, *Investigation*, 47–50, Exhibit 3.

17. Ibid., 51–52.

18. Kurimoto Testimony, *Investigation*, 53–58.

19. Hiroishi Testimony, *Investigation*, 59–63; Fred Savory Testimony, ibid., 8, 10A.

20. Hirosihi Testimony, ibid., 60, 62.

21. Ibid., 63–69.

22. Ibid., 68–74.

CHAPTER 6

1. Author's interview with Dr. Eugene Poutasse.

2. Horie Testimony, *Investigation*, 157.

3. Horie Statement, ibid., Exhibit 3A.

4. Horie Testimony, ibid., 118, 121; Finding of Facts, ibid., 962.

5. Horie Testimony, ibid., 121, 126–29; Personal Notes of Investigation on Chichi Jima, Eugene F. Poutasse Papers, 15.

6. Horie Testimony, *Investigation*, 118, 123–26; Nishiyotsutsuji Testimony, ibid., 163–64, 166; Shigeyasu Testimony, ibid., 510–11.

7. Noomi Testimony, ibid., 643.

8. Tani Testimony, ibid., 443; Miyashita Testimony, ibid., 783; Nishiyotsutsuji Testimony, ibid., 161, 166–67; Hasegawa Testimony, ibid., 457; Matsumura Testimony, ibid., 647–49; Finding of Facts, ibid., 962–63.

9. Isoda Testimony, ibid., 380.

10. Nishiyotsutsuji Testimony, ibid., 162–66.

11. Ibid., 167–68; Hasegawa Testimony, *Investigation*, 662–63.

12. Nishiyotsutsuji Testimony, ibid., 162–69; Isoda Testimony, ibid., 376–81.

13. Fukuda Testimony, ibid., 391–94; Ito Testimony, ibid., 786–87; Flynn Argument, *Trial*, F-1. Ito testified that orders came on 26 July 1944, but the date is suspicious.

14. Higashigi Testimony, *Investigation*, 867–68; Fukuda Testimony, ibid., 392–93.

15. Okamoto Testimony, ibid., 955–56.

16. Shimura Testimony, ibid., 776–78; Okamoto Testimony, ibid., 958.

17. Okamoto Testimony, ibid., 954–55.

18. Shimura Testimony, ibid., 777–78; Okamoto Testimony, ibid., 956–57.

19. Ito Testimony, ibid., 787–90.

20. Ikawa Testimony, ibid., 911–12; Nishiyotsutsuji Testimony, ibid., 161–75.

21. Isoda Testimony, ibid., 381–82.

22. Ibid., 383.

23. Noomi Testimony, *Investigation*, 646; Finding of Facts, ibid., 969, Exhibit 41; Naval Casualties, ibid., Exhibit 49.

24. Rixey G-2 Report, ibid., Exhibit 42; Okamoto Testimony, ibid., 958.

25. Ibid.

26. National Personnel Records Center, Case Reference Number 2001-258-246, National Archives.

27. *Investigation*, Exhibit 45, 1–2; Exhibit 49, 1–2.

CHAPTER 7

1. Morison, *History of United States Naval Operations*, 14:25, 28, 44.

2. Finding of Facts, *Investigation*, 964; Maikawa Testimony, ibid., 193A–95; Soya Testimony, ibid., 230–31.

3. Kanmuri Testimony, ibid., 261–62; Sato Testimony, ibid., 282; Finding of Facts, ibid., 964.

4. Horie Testimony, ibid., 136–38; Sato Testimony, ibid., 281–82; Finding of facts, ibid., 964.

5. Horie Statement, ibid., Exhibit 3A.

6. Kanmuri Testimony, ibid., 260.

7. Matoba Testimony, ibid., 682–84.

8. Matoba Order, *Trial*, Exhibit 2: 1, 4.

9. Suyeyoshi Testimony, *Investigation*, 848.

10. Ibid., 847–48; Uzaki Testimony, *Investigation*, 616.

11. Iwakawa Testimony, ibid., 584–85, 587.

12. Ibid., 586, 588.

13. Uzaki Testimony, *Investigation*, 616–17; Iwakawa Testimony, ibid., 588; Yoshida Testimony, ibid., 591–92.

14. Matoba Testimony, ibid., 676–77; Ikawa's Testimony, ibid., 300.

15. Kanemori Testimony, ibid., 710–11.

16. Sugiyama Testimony, ibid., 702–5.

17. Ikawa Testimony, ibid., 301–2.

18. Ibid., 302.

19. Matoba Testimony, *Investigation*, 679–81.

20. Ibid.

21. Memorandum, 8 March, 20 May 1946, *Investigation*, Exhibits 46, 48; Frazer Testimony, ibid., 519; Finding of Facts, ibid., 965–66; National Personnel Records Center, Case No. 2001-258-240, Military Personnel Records, NA.

22. Takeda Statement, *Investigation*, Exhibit 43.

CHAPTER 8

1. Horie Testimony, *Investigation*, 127; Nishiyotsutsuji Testimony, ibid., 161, 183; Kanmuri Testimomy, ibid., 265; Finding of Facts, ibid., 965.

2. Kanmuri Testimony, ibid., 265–66; Matoba Testimony, ibid., 689.

3. Matoba Order, *Trial*, Exhibit 2: 2, 4.

4. Ibid., 3.

5. Soya Testimony, *Investigation*, 239.

6. Sato Testimony, ibid., 732; Wada Testimony, ibid., 733–34.

7. Soya Testimony, ibid., 239; Sato Testimony, ibid., 605–9; Iso Testimony, ibid., 625–30; Mori Testimony, ibid., 739–42; Nakamura Testimony, ibid., 208–10, and *Trial*, Exhibit 3: 1–2.

8. Investigation Notes, Poutasse Papers, 102; Matoba Testimony, *Investigation*, 692; Konishi Testimony, ibid., 718–20.

9. Matoba Testimony, *Investigation*, 692–93; Konishi Testimony, ibid., 721; Kurosawa Testimony, ibid., 748; Isogai Testimony, ibid., 830–31.

10. Konishi Testimony, ibid., 721; Isogai Testimony, ibid., 830.

11. Matoba Testimony, ibid., 693.

12. Isogai Testimony, ibid., 830; Shinoda Testimony, ibid., 430; Matoba Testimony, ibid., 693–94.

13. Kanmuri Testimony, ibid., 267.

14. National Personnel Records Center, Case File: 2001-258-238, Military Personnel Records, NA.

CHAPTER 9

1. Horie Statement, *Investigation*, Exhibit 3A.

2. Takenaka Testimony, ibid., 495–96; Takeda Testimony, ibid., 498–99.

3. Takeda Testimony, ibid., 500; Investigation Notes, Poutasse Papers, 68.

4. Kosuga Testimony, *Investigation*, 323–26; Horie Testimony, ibid., 135–41; Finding of Facts, ibid., 964–65.

5. Hidano Testimony, ibid., 485; Kosuga Testimony, ibid., 487.

6. Kosuga Testimony, ibid., 325–26; Kato Testimony, ibid., 802; Ikawa Testimony, ibid., 298.

7. Ikawa Testimony, ibid., 299; Nakano Testimony, ibid., 862.

8. Nakano Testimony, ibid., 862–64; Oshida Testimony, ibid., 874.

9. Oshida Testimony, ibid., 874–75; Taniyama Testimony, ibid., Exhibit 26; Investigation Notes, Poutasse Papers, 4.

10. Oshida Testimony, *Investigation*, 875; Taniyama Testimony, ibid., 865; Kishimoto Testimony, ibid., 942.

11. Taniyama Testimony, ibid., Exhibit 27.

12. Oshida Testimony, ibid., 877–78; Finding of Facts, ibid., 966.

13. Investigation Notes, Poutasse Papers, 5.

14. Kosuga Testimony, *Investigation*, 326–27.

15. Tamamura Testimony, ibid., 530–31.

16. Ibid., 530–33; Aruga Testimony, *Investigation*, 563.

17. Tamamura Testimony, ibid., 533–36; Hayashi Testimony, ibid., 751–54; Arai Testimony, ibid., 94–96; Sakamoto Testimony, ibid., 552–56; Aruga Testimony, ibid., 564–66.

18. Tamamura Testimony, ibid., 536–37; Arai Testimony, ibid., 96.

19. Suzuki Testimony, ibid., 816–17; Sakamoto Testimony, ibid., 556.

20. Sakamoto Testimony, ibid., 557–58; Tamamura Testimony, ibid., 537–38.

21. Kuriki Testimony, ibid., 577–78; Arai Testimony, ibid., 96; Shiina Testimony, ibid., 581.

22. Tamamura Testimony, ibid., 550.

23. Kuriki Testimony, ibid., 578; Shiina Testimony, ibid., 582.

24. Shiina Testimony, ibid., 583; Frazer Testimony, ibid., 520; Finding of Facts, ibid., 967.

25. National Personnel Records Center, SSN 245 22 93, Military Personnel Records, NA.

26. Rixey to Shaffer, 21 December 1945, *Investigation*, A; Hiroo Yoshine Testimonial, *Trial*, 38c.

27. Yoshii Testimony, *Investigation*, 842.

CHAPTER 10

1. Ishiwata Testimony, *Investigation*, 478; Tanaka Testimony, ibid., 502–3.

2. Horie Testimony, ibid., 139; Kosuga Testimony, ibid., 329.

3. Oyama Testimony, ibid., 512–15; Horie Testimony, ibid., 139–40.

4. Horie Testimony, ibid., 140; Oyama Testimony, ibid., 330.

5. Horie Testimony, ibid., 147.

6. Ibid.; Yamamura Testimony, *Investigation*, 544; Edwin C. Clarke Statement, ibid., Exhibit 47.

7. Tamamura Testimony, ibid., 544.

8. William Monks Papers, "Warren Earl Vaughn's Story."

9. Ibid., 546.

10. Ibid., 545–46.

11. Ibid., 546; Horie Testimony, *Investigation*, 148.

12. Tamamura Testimony, ibid., 547; William Monks Papers, "Warren Earl Vaughn's Story."

13. Tamamura Testimony, *Investigation*, 547; Okubo Testimony, ibid., 596.

14. Okubo Testimony, ibid., 595–96; Tamamura Testimony, ibid., 549.

15. Gilley Testimony, ibid., 108–9.

16. Okubo Testimony, ibid., 595–96.

17. Kanaumi Testimony, ibid., 84–85.

18. Ibid., 85–87; Gilley Testimony, *Investigation*, 109–10; Okubo Testimony, ibid., 597–99.

19. Okubo Testimony, ibid., 598.

20. Gilley Testimony, ibid., 102; Kanaumi Testimony, ibid., 86.

21. Kanaumi Testimony, ibid., 86; Gilley Testimony, ibid., 110.

22. Kanemura Testimony, ibid., 79.

23. Ibid., 78; Kanaumi Testimony, *Investigation*, 87; Finding of Facts, ibid., 968.

24. Okubo Testimony, ibid., 602.

25. Tamamura Testimony, ibid., 549; Yoshii Testimony, ibid., 843–44; Leroy H. Barnard Letter, ibid., Exhibit 34.

26. Okubo Testimony, ibid., 600; Lt. Edward L. Field Argument, *Trial*, II-15.

27. Charles H. Wilson Letter with Koyama Suicide Note, *Investigation*, Exhibit 35.

28. Warren E. Vaughn Service Record, Naval Personnel Records Group, Military Personnel Records, Case Reference Number 2001-258-243, NA.

CHAPTER 11

1. Shigeyasu Testimony, *Investigation*, 512.

2. Frazer Testimony, ibid., 518; Exhibit 6, ibid.

3. Maikawa Testimony, ibid., 199–203; Soya Testimony, ibid., 239–40; Investigation Notes, Poutasse Papers, 20, 21.

4. Soya Testimony, *Investigation*, 241; Kanmuri Testimony, ibid., 274–75; Isono Testimony, ibid., 857–88, Exhibit 18; Nakajima Testimony, ibid., 249–50.

5. Matoba Testimony, ibid., 696–97; Maikawa Testimony, ibid., 201–2; Kanemori Testimony, ibid., 712.

6. Isono Testimony, ibid., 858; Nakajima Testimony, ibid., 250–52, Exhibit 5.

7. Matoba Testimony, ibid., 697; Nakajima Testimony, ibid., 253.

8. Nakajima Testimony, ibid., Exhibit 5; Frazer Testimony, ibid., 518.

9. National Personnel Records Center, SSN 629 81 32, Military Personnel Records, NA.

10. Wakabayashi Testimony, *Investigation*, 569–72; Investigation Notes, Poutasse Papers, 78.

11. Ishino Testimony, *Investigation*, 743.

12. Hayakawa Testimony, ibid., 505–6; McGinnes Report, ibid., Exhibit 39; Rixey Letter, ibid., Exhibit 48.

13. Kudo Testimony, ibid., 507.

14. McGinnes Report, ibid., Exhibit 38.

15. Kosuga Testimony, ibid., 314, 319–20; Hiroishi Testimony, ibid., 417–18; Takeoka Testimony, ibid., Exhibit 25, 2–3.

16. Cox Telegrams, *Investigation*, Exhibits 49, 51; Oyama Testimony, ibid., 512; Takeda Testimony, ibid., 498–99.

17. Cox Telegram, ibid., Exhibit 49; Tsunoda Testimony, ibid., 345; Kanemura Testimony, ibid., 79–82.

18. Frazer Reports, ibid., Exhibits 36, 37; McGinnes Report, ibid., Exhibit 40; Rixey Report, ibid., Exhibit 42; Tamamura Testimony, ibid., 550.

CHAPTER 12

1. Rixey Letter, *Investigation*, 980; Savory Testimony, ibid., 1.

2. Tachibana Testimony, ibid., 886.

3. Ibid., 886–87.

4. Ibid., 887–88; Horie Testimony, *Investigation*, 919–21.

5. Tachibana Testimony, ibid., 889–90.

6. Nakamura Confession, ibid., Exhibit 4.

7. Tachibana Testimony, ibid., 890–92; Investigation Notes, Poutasse Papers, 140.

8. Mori Testimony, *Investigation*, 893–95.

9. Ibid., 895–98; Mori Statement, *Investigation*, Exhibit 31; Investigation Notes, Poutasse Papers, 141–42.

10. Mori Testimony, *Investigation*, 899–900; Investigation Notes, Poutasse Papers, 141, 142.

11. Finding of Facts, *Investigation*, 969, 972.

12. Ibid., 970, 973.

13. Kato Testimony, *Investigation*, 801–10; Recommendations, ibid., 973.

14. Yoshii Testimony, ibid., 842; Finding of Facts, ibid., 966.

15. Yoshii Statement, ibid., Exhibit 33.

16. Recommendations of Board, ibid., 976.

17. Nakamura Testimony, ibid., Exhibit 4; Recommendations of Board, ibid., 974.

18. Matoba Testimomy, ibid., 286–90, 693–94; Recommendations of Board, ibid., 974; Investigation Notes, Poutasse Papers, 100–103.

19. Ito Testimony, *Investigation*, 786–87; Higashigi Testimony, ibid., 870; Ikawa Testimony, ibid., 309; Recommendations of Board, ibid., 974; Investigation Notes, Poutasse Papers, 120–21.

20. Higashigi Testimony, *Investigation*, 867–72; Recommendations of Board, ibid., 975; Investigation Notes, Poutasse Papers, 137.

21. Nakajima Testimony, *Investigation*, 249–53; Recommendations of Board, ibid., 974.

22. Sato Testimony, ibid., 731–33, 735; Recommendations of Board, ibid., 974.

23. Ikawa Testimony, ibid., 297–301; Yamashita Testimony, ibid., 793–94; Recommendations of Board, ibid., 974.

24. Yamashita Testimony, ibid., 793–95; Recommendations of Board, ibid., 975.

25. Suyeyoshi Testimony, ibid., 847–49; Finding of Facts, ibid., 970; Recommendations of Board, ibid., 974.

26. Rixey Recommendation, 6 June 1946, ibid., 980.

CHAPTER 13

1. John L. Ginn, *Sugamo Prison, Tokyo: An Account of the Trial and Sentencing of Japanese War Criminals in 1948, by a U.S. Participant* (Jefferson, N.C.: McFarland Publishing Company, 1992), 15, 24, 30–31, 33; List of War Criminals, Poutasse Papers; ComMarianas to JAG (War Crimes Division) CINPAC, *Trial*, Exhibit 8.

2. Arguments for the Prosecution, *Trial*, II-1, JJ-1, TT-1.

3. Argument for the Accused, ibid., LL-1, NN-1, PP-2, RR-1, SS-1.

4. Tachibana Statement, ibid., H.

5. For Tachibana's trial, see *Transcripts of Case No. 33, the Trial of Lt. General Yoshio Tachibana et al., Aug. 15–Oct. 4, 1946, JAG Docket No. 154578, Commission Records*; hereinafter cited as *Commission Records*.

6. Mori Statement, *Trial*, J; Morikawa Argument, ibid., RR-3.

7. Yoshii Statement, ibid., L.

8. See Tamamura Testimony, *Commission Records*.

9. Matoba Statement, *Trial*, N.

10. Sato Statement, ibid., P.

11. Suyeyoshi Statement, ibid., R; Flynn Argument, ibid., F-3.

12. Sasaki Statement, ibid., T.

13. Matsushita Statement, ibid., V.

14. Isogai Testimony, ibid., X.

15. Hayashi Statement, ibid., Z.

16. Masutani Statement, ibid., BB.

17. Statements of Mori and Nakamura, ibid., DD, FF.

18. Kido Statement, ibid., HH.

19. Horie Petitions, *Trial*, 437–39, 836, 837.

20. Ibid., 803.

21. Yokota Petition, *Trial*, 807.

22. Ginn, *Sugamo Prison*, 92–101, 164–65.

23. List of War Criminals, Poutasse Papers.

24. Tim Maga, *Judgment at Tokyo: The Japanese War Crimes Trials* (Lexington: University of Kentucky Press, 2001), 104–5.

25. *Law Reports of the Trials of War Criminals*, 15 vols., selected and prepared by the United Nations War Crimes Commission (London: HMSO, 1947–1949), 4: 86–87; Department of the Navy, *Final Report of Navy War Crimes Program in the Pacific*, submitted by the Director of War Crimes, U.S. Navy Pacific Fleet to the Secretary of the Navy, 1 December 1949, Navy Historical Center, Washington, D.C., 1: 184–87, vol. 2, case no. 36, app. B, 38–40, 4: 86–87; George E. Erickson, Jr., "United States Navy War Crimes Trials (1945–1949)," *Washburn Law Journal*, 5 (Winter 1965), 107–8.

EPILOGUE

1. Head and Daws, "The Bonins," 73–74; Chris Cook, "Tokyo's Last Paradise," *Japan Times Weekly* (25 August 1990).

2. Savory, "My Recollections of Uncle Fred."

3. Biographical Sketch of General Rixey, Ann Rixey Boyd Papers, Author's files.

4. Rixey, "Japanese Camouflage," 14–15.

5. Stinnett, *George Bush*, 147.

6. Matoba Statement, *Trial*, N, 19.

Bibliography

DOCUMENTS AND RECORDS

Department of State. *Bulletin*, "Trial of Japanese War Criminals," 20 (1 May 1949).
———. "Trial of Japanese War Criminals." Publication 2613. Far Eastern Series 12. Washington, D.C.: Government Printing Office, 1946.
Department of the Navy. *Final Report of Navy War Crimes Program in the Pacific.* Submitted by the Director of War Crimes, U.S. Navy Pacific Fleet to the Secretary of the Navy, 1 December 1949. Navy Historical Center, Washington, D.C.
Documents in the Possession of the Author
  Ann Rixey Boyd Papers
  Robert J. Gath Papers
  James W. Leary Papers
  John H. Monaghan Papers
  William Monks Papers
    "Grandpa Goes to War" (unpublished monograph)
    Jerry Candelaria Letters
    "Once Upon a Time" (unpublished monograph)
    Robert Gath Letters
    Warren Earl Vaughn's Story
  Eugene F. Poutasse Papers
    "How the Combat of the Chichi Jima Garrison Should Be Conducted," by Major Y. Horie (monograph)
    List of War Criminals
    Muster Role of Officers and Enlisted Men of the U.S. Marine Corps Headquarters, 1st Battalion, 3rd Marines, Fleet Marine Force, Pacific
    Personal Notes of Investigation on Chichi Jima
    Personal Photographic Archive

War Crime Records from Chichi Investigation
Jimmy B. Savory, "My Recollections of Uncle Fred." Jimmy Savory Papers
Marine Corps Historical Center, Washington, D.C.
"Japanese Camouflage, We Penetrate a Prepared Story in the Occupation of
    the Bonin Islands." Papers of Brig. Gen. Presley M. Rixey.
National Archives
    *Record of Proceedings of a Military Commission Convened at U.S. Pacific Fleet
        ComMarianas, Guam: Case of Yoshio Tachibana et al.*, No. 154578, RG 125,
        File 370 21/29/02.
    *Transcripts of Case No. 33, the Trial of Lt. General Yoshio Tachibana et al., Aug. 15–
        Oct. 4, 1946, JAG Docket No. 154578, Commission Records*, RG 125, File 371.
    National Personnel Records Center, St. Louis, Mo.
    Military Personnel Records
Records and Proceedings of a Board of Investigation *Convened at Headquarters of the
    Commander, United States Occupation Forces, Bonin Islands, Chichi Jima . . . by
    order of The Commander, United States Occupation Forces, Bonin Islands.* Brig.
    Gen. Presley M. Rixey Papers in the Possession of His Daughter, Ann R.
    Boyd.

NEWSPAPERS

Navy News, Guam edition

PUBLISHED SOURCES

Buchanan, A.R., ed. *The Navy's Air War: A Mission Completed*. New York: Harper
    & Brothers, n.d.
The Campaigns of the Pacific War: United States Strategic Bombing Survey (Pacific).
    Washington, D.C.: Naval Analysis Division, 1946.
Cant, Gilbert. "Home to Chichi Jima: Yankee Trader's Descendant Welcomes U.S.
    Flag." *Life* (24 June 1946), 17–19.
Carson, Andrew D. *My Time in Hell: Memoir of an American Soldier Imprisoned by
    the Japanese in World War II*. Jefferson, N.C.: McFarland Publishing Com-
    pany, 1997.
Cook, Chris. "Tokyo's Last Paradise." *Japan Times Weekly* (25 August 1990).
Erickson, George E., Jr. "United States Navy War Crimes Trials (1945–1949)."
    Washburn Law Journal, 5 (Winter 1965), 93–108.
Frank, Denis M., and Henry I. Shaw, Jr. *Victory and Occupation: History of the U.S.
    Marine Corps Operations in World War II*. Vol. 5. Washington, D.C.:
    Historical Branch, G-3 Division, Headquarters, U.S. Marine Corps, 1968.
Ginn, John L. *Sugamo Prison, Tokyo: An Account of the Trial and Sentencing of
    Japanese War Criminals in 1948, by a U.S. Participant*. Jefferson, N.C.: Mc-
    Farland Publishing Company, 1992.
Hammel, Eric. *Aces against Japan: The American Aces Speak*. Vol. 1. Novato, Calif.:
    Presidio Press, 1992.
Hayashi, Saburo. *Kōgan: The Japanese Army in the Pacific War*. Quantico, Va.: Ma-
    rine Corps Association, 1959.

Head, Timothy E., and Gavan Daws. "The Bonins—Isles of Contention." *American Heritage* (February 1968), 58–74.

Ito, Masashi. *The Emperor's Last Soldiers*. New York: Coward McCann, 1967.

Johnston, Richard W. *Follow Me: The Story of the Second Marine Division in World War II*. New York: Random House, 1948.

Kato, Masuo. *The Lost War*. New York: Alfred P. Knopf, 1946.

Keenan, Joseph B., and Brendan F. Brown. *Crimes against International Law*. Washington, D.C.: Public Affairs Press, 1950.

Kerr, E. Bartlett. *Surrender and Survival: The Experience of American POWs in the Pacific, 1941–1945*. New York: William Morrow and Company, 1985.

Law Reports of the Trials of War Criminals. 15 vols. Selected and prepared by the United Nations War Crimes Commission. London: HMSO, 1947–1949.

Lewis, John R. *Uncertain Judgment: A Bibliography of War Crimes Trials*. Santa Barbara, Calif.: Clio Books, 1979.

Maga, Tim. *Judgment at Tokyo: The Japanese War Crimes Trials*. Lexington: University of Kentucky Press, 2001.

Miller, Francis T. *The Complete History of World War II*. Chicago: Progress Research Corporation, 1948.

Morison, Samuel Eliot. *History of United States Naval Operations in World War II*. 15 vols. Boston: Little, Brown, 1947–1962.

———. *"Old Bruin": Commodore Matthew Calbraith Perry, 1794–1858*. Boston: Little, Brown, 1967.

Piccagallo, Philip R. *The Japanese on Trial*. Austin: University of Texas Press, 1979.

Ross, Bill D. *Iwo Jima: Legacy of Valor*. New York: Vanguard Press, 1985.

Russell, E.F.L. *The Knights of Bushido*. New York: E.P. Dutton, 1958.

Russell, Michael. *Iwo Jima*. New York: Random House, 1974.

Sherrod, Robert. *History of Marine Corps Aviation in World War II*. Washington, D.C.: Combat Forces Press, 1952.

Smith, S.E., ed. *The United States Navy in World War II*. New York: William Morrow & Company, 1966.

Standish, Robert. *Bonin*. New York: Macmillan Company, 1944.

Stinnett, Robert B. *George Bush: His World War II Years*. Washington, D.C.: Brassey's, 1992.

Sweetman, Jack. *American Naval History: An Illustrated Chronology of the U.S. Navy and Marine Corps, 1775–Present*. Annapolis, Md.: Naval Institute Press, 1984.

Taylor, Theodore. *The Magnificent Mitscher*. New York: W.W. Norton, 1954.

Toland, John. *The Rising Sun*. Vol. 2. New York: Random House, 1970.

Wheeler, Keith. *The Road to Tokyo*. Alexandria, Va.: Time-Life Books, 1979.

Index

About the Author

CHESTER HEARN is the author of numerous books, including *The American Soldier in World War II.*